Osceola

⇒ *and the* ⇐

Great Seminole War

Also by Thom Hatch

꙰ ꙰

Encyclopedia of the Alamo and the Texas Revolution

Black Kettle: The Cheyenne Chief Who Sought Peace but Found War

The Blue, the Gray, and the Red: Indian Campaigns of the Civil War

The Custer Companion: A Comprehensive Guide to the Life of George Armstrong Custer and the Plains Indian Wars

Clashes of Cavalry: The Civil War Careers of George Armstrong Custer and Jeb Stuart

Custer and the Battle of the Little Bighorn: An Encyclopedia of the People, Places, Events, Indian Culture and Customs, Information Sources, Art and Films

Seminole Chief Osceola (1804–1838)
by George Catlin, Smithsonian American Art Museum

Osceola

❧ *and the* ❧

Great Seminole War

A Struggle for
Justice and Freedom

❧ ❖ ❧

Thom Hatch

ST. MARTIN'S PRESS
New York

www.stmartins.com

Design by Kathryn Parise

Map by Paul J. Pugliese

ISBN 978-0-312-35591-3 (hardcover)
ISBN 978-1-4668-0454-8 (e-book)

First Edition: July 2012

10   9   8   7   6   5   4   3   2   1

For my lovely wife, Lynn,
and precious daughter, Cimarron

Contents

✥ ✥ ✥

x ❦ *Contents*

Acknowledgments

There are numerous special people who provide assistance to an author on the wonderful journey from concept to manuscript. I would like to single out only one person to acknowledge by name, however—Edward W. Knappman, my former literary agent. Ed was a warm, intelligent, personable man who freely shared his immense knowledge and talents. His belief that *Osceola and the Great Seminole War* would be not just another history book but a work of historical significance served as a great inspiration to me. I hope I have met his expectations. Ed Knappman passed away on March 10, 2011. He will be truly missed.

Osceola

⚜ *and the* ⚛

Great Seminole War

The Great Seminole War

Introduction

The story of Osceola and the Great Seminole War seems so fantastic at times that it is hard to believe it is all true. One common warrior with courage, cunning, and audacity unequaled by any Native American leader before or after would mastermind battle tactics that would frustrate and embarrass the best officers in the United States Army—including five generals. Osceola, by sheer willpower, initiated and orchestrated the longest, most expensive, and deadliest war ever fought by Americans against Native Americans. And he initiated this quixotic struggle not to gain glory or riches or out of hatred for the white man but simply because he believed in justice and freedom for his people. The story of Osceola and the Great Seminole War is the stuff that legends are made of.

Osceola is never mentioned in the same breath as Geronimo, or Sitting Bull, or Crazy Horse, or Cochise, but his accomplishments overshadow those of these great Native American leaders who challenged the might of the U.S. Army. One can only wonder why these other notable chiefs have enjoyed the attention of historians throughout the years, yet Osceola has fallen into an undeserved obscurity. But this book provides evidence that Osceola's rightful place is at the top of the list of great Native American war leaders.

By the time of his death in 1838, this Seminole warrior was the most famous and respected Native American in the world. When his obituary was splashed across the front pages of newspapers worldwide, he was mourned by Native Americans and whites alike, and ascended into legendary status. For years to come, children would bear his name, and cities, counties, schools, parks, businesses, and landmarks would be named after him.

It all began when the most powerful country on earth ordered the Seminole tribe to relocate from lush, tropical Florida Territory to the relatively barren and frigid West. The indignity of departing a beloved homeland was bad enough, but, at the same time, Southern slave owners petitioned the government to reclaim runaway slaves who had taken refuge with the Seminoles and return them to bondage. These Black Seminoles, many of whom were married to Seminoles or had never been slaves, would be seized and returned to slavery when the tribe assembled for its migration west.

The Seminole chiefs protested this outrageous move but were told that if they resisted, their people would face all the might and power of the U.S. military and possible extermination. There would be no negotiations.

By this time, Osceola had established a cordial relationship with the white authorities with whom he came in contact in his position of policing his tribe. But when removal of his people from their homeland to the West became imminent, virtually overnight he turned against the government. Then, when Seminole chiefs failed to respond immediately to the threat, this common warrior declared war for his people on the United States of America.

What could be more honorable than a race of people fighting for justice and freedom as they tried to protect their homeland, their culture, their sovereignty, their families, and their dignity against the threat of extermination? And fight they did, led by Osceola, the warrior turned war leader.

In one brilliantly executed and daring attack after another, Osceola and his outnumbered warriors assailed army positions or ambushed their columns in the field. When too large a force advanced against his warriors, Osceola would resort to harassing the soldiers with ingenious hit-and-run guerrilla tactics before vanishing into the swamps. Casualties quickly mounted among the ranks of the military within Florida, which would include regular army troops, militias from several Southern states, and even warriors from enemy tribes.

As the Seminoles scored victory after victory, the exploits of Osceola captured the imaginations of people far and wide. During this time of war, oddly enough, many whites throughout the country applauded Osceola's gallant effort and cheered for the Seminoles to prevail. Although unknown to him, he became the subject of public conversation and accolades. His image was used in advertising illustrations, often notably costumed in a Roman toga, and he was regularly toasted in taverns in the North.

As the war raged on, Osceola, who was ill with fever, came to negotiate a peace treaty with army officials under a white flag of truce—a symbol that had always been honored by both sides. In this instance, however, the white flag was ignored and Osceola was captured and imprisoned.

The shameful nature of his capture sparked nationwide protests against the conduct of this Great Seminole War—more than a century before such public outrage became commonplace. His incarceration, the possible loss of his homeland, and the frustration of not being able to lead his people in their ongoing conflict greatly affected Osceola's already declining health. Within months of his capture, he died in prison at the age of thirty-four. His death, however, served to inspire his battle-weary followers to carry on with the war for years to come with his name as a rallying cry.

The journey through Osceola's short but memorable life illuminates the social, political, cultural, and historical events of the era, including treaties, race relations, and tribal histories and customs, and presents a cast of fascinating larger-than-life characters, both famous and unknown, who are vital to understanding this time of turmoil.

Above all, however, this is the story of Osceola, who should now be recognized for his remarkable skills and personal traits and should be elevated to a legendary status not just as a Native American leader but also as a man who sought to do what was right. Justice and freedom have had no greater champion throughout history than Osceola, who paid the ultimate price to defend his beliefs.

» *One* «

The Creek Refugees

» ❖ «

Nine-year-old Billy Powell, the boy who would grow up to become the
warrior Osceola, watched as his whole world went up in flames.

Billy was in the company of his mother and dozens of other members
of the Creek tribe—mostly women, children, and old men—who crouched in
the dense underbrush where they had fled from their homes. One by one
they cautiously raised their heads to view great plumes of charcoal smoke
furiously billowing upward into the distant sky. This fear-inspiring sight indicated that countless fires were raging in the direction of their homes. It was
apparent that every residence and building in the town of Tallassee along
the Tallapoosa River in the region of present-day Macon County, Alabama,
had been set on fire and was burning out of control. Soon nothing would remain but ashes and debris.

These displaced people had been on the move for two days, abandoning
their town when word was received that the soldiers were on their way. They
had been hiding in various places within the thick underbrush between the
Tallapoosa and Coosa rivers, waiting for the time when they could return to
their homes. They had survived thus far by scavenging whatever they could
find in fields or abandoned villages that still stood, or resorting to stealing

when the opportunity arose. It was likely that Billy Powell and the other boys helped provide meat by hunting squirrel, rabbit, or other small game with their bows and arrows.

These desperate Creeks, however, now were struck with the gravity of their situation—it could be assumed that all their homes and the town community buildings had been consumed by the fire and they were homeless and in the hands of fate.

There were no tears or wailing or shouts of anger and revenge. It was imperative that they remain quiet, secreted, and focused. The U.S. Army invaders who had perpetrated this tragedy upon them would be combing the area to search for the missing inhabitants of this town. The purpose of those soldiers raiding any Creek town was not only to destroy homes and possessions but also to take lives, and this enemy had proved itself extraordinarily brutal and heartless. Even young Billy Powell understood that if any of the Tallassee Creeks were found, they surely would be killed.

The faces of the Creek refugees were grave. No one dared speak the words, but each stunned member of this band was aware that they would be compelled to flee without delay from their homeland—perhaps permanently. They had no home to go back to now that their town had vanished into smoldering ruins, and the soldiers would make certain that Tallassee and any other Upper Creek town they destroyed would never be rebuilt or reoccupied. Billy Powell and his Creek neighbors must try to forget about the loss of their town and possessions and focus all their efforts on escaping from this dangerous place.

Such a desperate assessment was not easy to make, nor would flight to a new place be a simple undertaking. The town of Tallassee had been their traditional home for generations. Where could they go, under duress and on a moment's notice, without any possessions other than those they carried on their backs? This question was not spoken aloud but was foremost on everyone's minds. These Creek people were not by any means prepared for an extended journey. The country beyond was rife with danger from extreme elements, from vicious wild animals, from their enemies, from an unforgiving tangled and soggy terrain of swamps and forests, and most of all from the unknown.

Billy Powell watched the final visible vestiges of smoke rise against the blackening sky. It was difficult for him to imagine that everything he knew in life had been destroyed. His mind might have drifted back to relive the memories of his well-ordered childhood in that pastoral place along the Tallapoosa River. He likely could not fathom the fact that he would never again lay eyes on that town and its environs that had become so familiar to him and offered him a sense of security.

Billy's people had lived in that place for as long as anyone could remember. The written history of the Creeks had its foundations in narratives of de Soto's expedition in 1540, but they were much older than that. The Creeks were descendants of the Mississippian culture, the first great civilization in North America, which arose some four thousand years before the Spanish arrived. These prehistoric Muskogees or Muscokees and affiliated tribes were known to build earthwork mounds at regional chiefdoms that spread across two-thirds of the United States.

By the time of de Soto's landing on the islands of coastal Georgia, however, the Muskogean people, who would become known as Creeks, no longer built mounds and had established a confederacy that occupied the greater portion of Alabama and Georgia. This Creek Confederacy had grown to great numbers and was powerful enough to fight off any invasion or threat to their territory from the strong northern tribes—the Catawba, Cherokee, Iroquois, and Shawnee, to name a few. They spoke a typical Muskogean language that was closely related to the Choctaw language, with many words identical in pronunciation. This rather common language was quickly learned by early white frontiersmen with whom the tribe traded.

During the American Revolution, the Creek Nation made an effort to maintain its neutrality, although the tribe had earlier allied with the English. In 1786, the Creek Nation declared war on the state of Georgia, and several attempts at negotiating a treaty had failed. At the time of Billy Powell's birth in the early 1800s, there was no peace between the Creeks and the white people to the north. Incidences of violence between the two enemies were relatively minor, but tensions remained high and those border whites closest to the Creek Nation were in constant fear of an attack. This was the state of the world into which Billy would be born and reared.[1]

The birth and lineage of Billy Powell has been a source of question and controversy over the years. Most historians agree that he was born in or near the town of Tallassee, Alabama—northeast of modern-day Montgomery—in the year 1804. The identities of both his parents and his ancestors, however, are a less settled matter.[2]

The most credible and widely accepted account of Billy's ancestry relies mainly on the reminiscences of Thomas S. Woodward, a contemporary white soldier and distinguished Creek historian. Woodward claimed that Billy's lineage could be traced back to James McQueen, a Scottish sailor who had jumped ship in Charleston in the late 1690s and in 1716 became the first white man to trade with the Creeks. McQueen remained with the Creeks as a trader from that day forth until, according to Woodward, he died at the remarkable age of 128 in the year 1811.

James McQueen, who was known among the Creek people as the Soft-Shelled Turtle, fathered many children during his lifetime. At some point, McQueen married a young Creek woman from Tallassee, who bore him a son, Peter McQueen, and a daughter named Ann. James McQueen's daughter Ann grew up to marry a white man or a man of mixed race named Jose Copinger. Ann Copinger then gave birth to a daughter named Polly, who married a white trader named William Powell. Billy Powell was said to have been born from this union between Polly and William Powell, thereby making him of mixed blood, with Scottish and Creek, or Muskogee, being the most prevalent that flowed through his veins.[3]

There are those interested parties and historians who dispute this accepted theory that Billy was of mixed blood—including Billy himself. He was quoted by George Catlin, who painted his portrait in 1838, shortly before his death, as saying, "No foreign blood runs in my veins; I am pure-blood Muskogee."[4]

This adamant denial has created a major contradiction, because this youngster who grew up to become Osceola has been called "Billy Powell" in countless references. There has been speculation ranging from the idea that Billy Powell was merely a nickname or that William Powell was not his real father but his stepfather to the idea that he could not have had white blood because the man Osceola did not speak English. Lieutenant L. L. Cohen, a contemporary and historian, wrote in 1836 that he believed that Billy's father was a full-blooded Creek who died after Billy was born—Polly then married the trader William Powell. No evidence exists to confirm any of these theories.[5]

Cohen, however, must have known that the Creek family structure was matrilineal, with each person belonging to his or her mother's clan and with descent and inheritance evolving from that side. Young Billy, and later the man Osceola, would have accepted the fact that his mother was full-blooded Creek because her mother had been full-blooded Creek, which, to his way of thinking, would have made him a full-blooded Creek—regardless of whether or not William Powell had been his biological father. Dr. John K. Mahon, a respected historian of Southeastern Native American traditions, wrote that "among both the Creeks and the Seminoles a man was a member of his mother's clan, and home to him was where the mother of his clan lived."[6]

William Powell disappeared from Billy's life by about 1808, as best as can be determined, although he might have remained as late as 1814. In keeping with Creek tradition, however, William Powell would have had little or no influence through the years on his son. His mother and her male relatives—in this case his well-known warrior grand-uncle, Peter McQueen—would have been responsible for rearing the boy. Billy's upbringing by his mother's side of the family would also explain why he did not speak English. Peter McQueen, incidentally, although proved to be of mixed-blood ancestry, always claimed, perhaps on the basis of his own maternal lineage, that he, too, was a pure-blooded Creek.[7]

Billy's people lived in clans, the basic family and social unit, with the oldest and most revered man or woman of the group charged with judging the behavior of each member. This elder would praise, condemn, or punish as he or she saw fit. He or she was by tribal custom responsible for organizing hunting parties, arranging and approving marriages, and distributing land. In fact, many marriages were arranged by the clan without consulting the bride or groom to be. People had little control over their hearts or lusts, which was perhaps why polygamy was commonplace, with the other wife or wives usually living apart from their husband. In addition to marriages, it was the responsibility of the clan and its leaders to ascertain that members adhered to all the Creek traditions and values that had been in place for generations.[8]

Tallassee, the place where Billy Powell was born and reared, was a typical Creek town when it came to its political and social structure. The most important town leader was the *micco* (or *mico*), the town chief or king, who was normally elected. This man led the people in battle, if necessary, and represented the town at tribal meetings, but had no other power than that which persuasion could garner. He did, however, preside over the town council and had great influence over their decisions due to the respect the tribe members had for him.

This council met daily to discuss various topics important to the well-being of the town—war and peace; hunting, fishing, and planting; maintenance of public buildings and grounds; ceremonies—and to settle disputes and punish wrongdoers. The micco would be advised by an assortment of respected townspeople—a second in charge, called the *heniha*; the *micalgi,* or lesser chiefs; the *yahola,* a medicine man who cared for sacred objects; and a *tustenugge,* the ranking warrior who was appointed by the micco. In wartime, a fighting man could earn the title *hadjo,* which meant "great warrior." The authority of the micco was held in check by the clan leaders, who were often the true leaders within the Creek Nation.[9]

Billy Powell had resided in a typical Creek dwelling, which was situated on a street within a complex of streets that ran adjacent to public buildings and grounds. His house likely consisted of four separate buildings, with one room serving as a cookroom and lodgings during winter, another designed for summer living, and another utilized as a granary. Houses in this town were rectangular in shape, with poles for a frame, walls plastered with mud mixed with straw, and roofs that had been shingled with cypress bark. The men of the town could construct one of these structures from start to finish in just one day. A private garden plot was situated beside each house, where a small amount of beans, corn, and tobacco was tended by the family. One morbidly interesting aspect of Creek dwellings is that traditionally, the dead of the family were buried under the earthen floor at the spot where they had died inside the house.[10]

The primary supply of food for all the Creek families was grown in large fields that belonged to the town but were broken down into smaller plots that were cared for by each family. These tracts of land were the richest soil available in the area, usually located at a bend in the river and as close to town as possible. Planting was a community event that was held on the first of May each year. A conch shell was blown early in the morning, which brought out the entire village with farm implements in hand to the town square. Their primitive tools were made of wood, bone, or stone, and they had a number of manufactured axes or hoes procured from traders. They walked to the town-owned field as a group and worked from one end of the field to the other until the planting was completed.

The Creeks raised crops of corn, beans, pumpkins, squash, melons, sweet potatoes, tobacco, and occasionally rice, and supplemented their diets with wild fruits and nuts. One popular delicacy was hickory nuts or acorns pounded in a mortar, stirred in boiling water with the oil skimmed off, and mixed in hominy and corn cakes.

The May planting was a time of great joy and celebration, with songs and jokes, and the chiefs working alongside the common people. Everyone, without exception, was expected to participate. Anyone caught shirking or failing to pull his or her weight would be fined or denied his or her share of the food. If the transgression was serious enough, the offending person could be banned from the town.

Cultivation was once again a community event. This time, however, each family would harvest the crops on its particular assigned plot within the town field. They would carry the produce to their own storehouse—with a portion of the bounty being contributed to public storage. The community town warehouse, a spacious building situated near the field, was held under strict supervision. The doors were opened only to accommodate travelers in need, provision military expeditions, or assist those townspeople whose own supplies had run out.[11]

Billy Powell and his friends, along with the women and the old men, had the responsibility of working in the fields and watching over them closely to drive off birds and other scavengers that might destroy the crops. Every child was expected to toil in the fields to weed and hoe at the bidding of the women. At night, the grown men took over the watch to scare away the deer, raccoons, and bears that might be seeking a meal. No doubt Billy and his friends would watch the men with envy, wishing they were old enough to leave behind the daily toils that they chided as "women's work" and keep company with the men.[12]

Division of labor within the family was not unlike that of white people of the time. The women were responsible for all the household tasks. They would prepare the food; clean the house; make pottery, baskets, and mats; and care for the children. The women also were expected to sew and produce all the family clothing. During the late seventeenth century, the Creek had shed their buckskins and taken to wearing European fashions made of comfortable and colorful cloth. They would trade for bolts of cloth in a variety of colors and textures, and accessorize the styles with bells, ribbons, metal, beads, and pieces of mirror.

The men built the houses, provided the material for clothing, made garden implements, presided over the government, protected the town, and fought the wars. They also hunted for meat, mainly deer, but bear was also sought for its fat, which was stored in deerskins.

The Creek towns along the Tallapoosa each had their own wooded preserve and rights along the river where their townspeople hunted and fished exclusively. Inhabitants of each town were mindful not to trespass onto another town's territory. The people were attentive to ways of conserving nature. Game management was the responsibility of the town council, which would set open and closed seasons on the various species in order to preserve game for the future. In addition to fresh game and fish, the men raised cattle and hogs, and had a corral with horses for both work and pleasure.[13]

Billy Powell and his young companions were not always obliged to work in the fields with the women and old men. He and his friends spent much time roaming the fields and forests with their bows and arrows at the ready in search of game. The men killed big game, whereas the boys learned how to hunt by stalking squirrels, raccoons, opossum, and rabbits. The youngsters were taught how to hunt and clean their kill mainly by watching the men and imitating their actions. This act of hunting was also a lesson for war. Hunting small game with a bow and arrow required much stealth to sneak in close and the skill to remain hidden from the prey until firing one's weapon. Frequent target shooting was also encouraged to further hone their skills.

Creek children played many games, as well as wrestling and running races, both of which were highly competitive. One popular game was similar to our modern-day lacrosse. In this game, played by both boys and girls, teams took positions on either side of a pole. The object was to strike that pole with a thrown deerskin ball. Girls could use their hands, but boys were required to use a pair of rackets. The game commenced when someone threw at the pole. If the ball missed its mark, a player from the opposite team would field the ball and attempt to hit the target or pass the ball to another player. The ball hitting the pole would score a point for that team. These games often resulted in physical contact as the boys and girls jostled each other for control of the ball.[14]

The men would play this same lacrosse game, and it would occasionally become quite violent and lead to the shedding of blood. Perhaps that was why it appealed so much to Creek youngsters, who were attracted to this sport as much as today's children are obsessed with football, basketball, hockey, soccer, and baseball. Unlike the sports of today, however, this early lacrosse game—and other games as well—was a substitute for war in the eyes of the participants. There was no sport to their games. Every time they took to the field, it could be equated to a life-or-death situation. For this reason, oftentimes rules were ignored and arguments escalated into fistfights. Games without competitors on both sides sustaining injuries were rare.[15]

Evidence supports the fact that Billy Powell excelled at these traditional games and was notable as an all-around athlete. Charles H. Coe, a nineteenth-century historian, writes, "As a youth, many testify to the fact that [Billy Powell] was a great favorite with his tribe, being uncommonly bright, accomplished and energetic. 'Cudjoe,' who was interpreter to our army for several years, and who had known [Billy Powell] from his childhood, said he was a very active youth, excelling in the chase, in running, leaping, ball-playing, and other Indian exercises."[16]

These physical accomplishments explain in part why he later emerged as a significant leader. The sporting attributes demonstrated by Billy Powell— courage, skill, mental toughness, and superior strength and conditioning— were the same traits necessary to assume leadership roles in society or as an exceptional warrior.

Now, Billy Powell lamented, the town of Tallassee and its athletic fields with stands built for spectators had burned to the ground. The memories of sports triumphs and defeats were blackened and obscured by the soot and smoke that drifted away at the whim of the wind.

Billy Powell and his neighbors who had resided in the destroyed town could be considered innocent victims, but that would not be entirely correct. The inhabitants of Tallassee certainly had been victims—victims of long-simmering politics that had been escalated by their own people into a full-scale war. And in war, the noncombatants often suffered as much as or more than the fighting men.

This particular conflict that had displaced Billy Powell and his neighbors might have had its roots in, or at least been helped along by, of all things, a comet and an earthquake. The comet was the first to affect the Creek, streaming across the starry sky in March 1811. The story was told that soon after the comet was observed, the Shawnee leader Tecumseh, whose name meant "Shooting Star," visited the town of Tuckabatchee. Tecumseh, whose mother was Creek, which made him Creek in the eyes of the tribe, preached that the Creek must resist the cultural changes that were occurring within the tribe. At that time, he also told the people there that the comet had signaled his coming. This statement was met with great skepticism. Tecumseh informed these doubters that he would provide another sign to prove that the Great Spirit had sent him. On December 11, 1811, the New Madrid fault erupted violently to shake the land—and the nerves—of the Creek, as well as everyone throughout much of eastern North America. This massive earthquake—the most devastating to strike North America in historic times—originated in Missouri but could be felt as far away as Boston, Massachusetts, and Charleston, South Carolina.

Unusual natural occurrences always carried a special meaning to the tribes affected by them, and this comet and powerful earthquake were no exception. The interpretation of their meaning varied from tribe to tribe, but there was no doubt that these frightening natural occurrences—the mysterious streak across the sky and the shaking of the earth—had great supernatural significance. Many Creek people embraced the warning from Tecumseh and believed that his prophetic words about change should be taken seriously.[17]

Change was already taking place within the Creek tribe at an alarming pace, however. It was likely that a faction of the Creek people who lived in central Alabama, who were known as the Upper Creeks due to the location of their towns—led by William Weatherford (aka Red Eagle), Billy Powell's grand-uncle Peter McQueen, and Chief Menawa—did view the comet and earthquake as solemn warnings that the people should return their society to a traditional way of life. It was widely accepted that the residents of too many Creek towns had strayed from their traditional culture and values. These leaders had made an effort to maintain their sovereignty as a tribe in spite of white encroachment for centuries, but they were now engaged in a losing battle for the hearts and minds of great numbers of their tribal members.

The Upper Creek townspeople were also called Red Sticks, from the Creek practice of using bundles of red sticks as a measurement of time before the commencement of war. The conflict would begin in the number of days corresponding with the number of red sticks in a bundle delivered to an enemy. Also, Creek warriors would occasionally leave behind a red war club at the scene of a battle. People in the Lower Towns, who rarely participated in this practice, became known as White Sticks.[18]

William Weatherford and the traditional Red Stick Creeks blamed the radical changes in their lifestyle on Benjamin Hawkins, the U.S. agent to the Creek Indians. Hawkins was a well-educated man who came from a socially prominent family in North Carolina. He had developed a fascination with southeastern Indians at a young age, and in 1796 he received the appointment as Indian agent from President George Washington. Although his family regarded the appointment as a sort of banishment, Hawkins, who could have enjoyed the genteel lifestyle of a privileged gentleman, was personally thrilled. He immediately set out to acculturate the primitive Creek in the white man's culture. Benjamin Hawkins, as had so many whites before and after, vowed to bring civilization to these savages who, in his mind at least, would welcome the improvements to their lifestyle. Incidentally, Hawkins has been credited with coining the phrase "God willing and the Creek don't rise." He allegedly wrote those words in response to a request from President Washington to return to the capital. If the Creek Nation "rose," Hawkins would need to be present to help quell the rebellion.[19]

At the time of Hawkins's arrival, the Creeks had already established their own civilization with effective governmental and economic practices—the Creek Confederation—that predated the earliest European contacts. The tribe had maintained its culture and traditions even though many Europeans had entered their society, as evidenced by the abundance of mixed-blood descendants with names like Weatherford, McQueen, McIntosh, and McGillivray. Their government and economy had flourished for generations. They wondered why anyone would wish to alter a system that had worked so well for centuries.[20]

Hawkins soon commenced tearing down traditional Creek culture and traditions and replacing them with his personal vision of acculturation. Instead of raising food just for their own use, Hawkins promoted the planting of cotton and other cash crops to sell for profit. He also encouraged the abandonment of certain sacred ceremonies, aided and abetted the distribution of communal lands among individual Creeks, and approved of the purchase of African slaves for trade or labor. In other words, Hawkins brought the white man's Southern civilization, a "cotton culture," to the Creeks.

A Creek Council was appointed to oversee a police force that enforced the laws—as determined by the council—which, in a controversial move, had been exempted from the Creek tradition of clan blood vengeance. This move did not sit well with those traditionalists who had difficulty conceiving that the council was betraying everything for which they, the Upper Creeks, stood. Everyone was aware that the council had for all intents and purposes delegated its authority. The real power behind the Creek Council that delved into every aspect of daily life was none other than Benjamin Hawkins.[21]

The Hawkins policy appealed to many Creeks of mixed white–Native American ancestry, especially those who lived in the Lower Creek towns, but was vehemently opposed by the Upper Creeks. It was pointed out by the Upper Creeks that the adoption of these new policies was contrary to tribal tradition, such as gender roles. Only women engaged in horticulture, not men. Any attempt to transform the men—the warriors—into working in agriculture was an attempt by Hawkins to emasculate them and was therefore wrong.

The Lower Town Creeks lived mostly along the Chattahoochee River, which was much closer geographically to whites than to the Upper Towns. Therefore, it was easier for the Lower Creeks to embrace this change to white culture, whereas people in the Upper Towns saw it as too radical and it served to harden their attitude toward the whites. The insistence by Benjamin Hawkins that his plan be adopted by the entire tribe—both Red Sticks and White Sticks—caused the breach that already existed between the towns to widen.[22]

In early 1813, the Upper Creeks were paid another visit by revered Shawnee chief Tecumseh. His mother was Creek, which, because of the matrilineal culture, was why he was regarded as Creek when he was among these people. This charismatic warrior eloquently preached traditional Indian values, anti-Americanism, and resistance by any means to the white encroachment on Creek land. Tecumseh had arrived fresh from his alliance with the British and the capture of Fort Detroit in August 1812. Although Benjamin Hawkins—and even many of the Creek people, both Upper and Lower—regarded Tecumseh's behavior as duplicitous, there was no doubting his influence on the common people. His visit had served to strengthen Creek resolve against these radical cultural changes that were taking place.[23]

The Red Stick leaders—Weatherford (Red Eagle), McQueen, and Menawa—were not as enamored with Tecumseh as their people were, but they were inspired by their own religious leaders and the encouragement of British traders. Although the Creek deerskin trade with the Europeans had nearly depleted the deer population, this decline, as well as the demise of Creek tribal traditions, was blamed on the acculturation schemes of Benjamin Hawkins and his white ways. Following Tecumseh's visit, these Red Stick leaders urged a spiritual cleansing, which included killing domestic livestock and discarding white man's farm implements. They easily won the support of the Upper Creeks to engage in a spiritual rebirth.[24]

This decision by the Upper Towns did not sit well with many leading chiefs of the Creek Nation, most notably the Lower Creek micco and Hawkins's most powerful ally, William McIntosh. The Lower Creek White Sticks had adopted white customs, welcomed white settlers, and embraced the policies of Indian agent Hawkins. They vowed not to reverse this trend anytime soon.

It was inevitable that this smoldering distrust and dislike between the Upper Creek towns and the Lower Creek towns, not to mention betrayal of their Creek roots in the eyes of the Red Sticks, would burst into a full-scale conflagration with encouragement from even the smallest of sparks.

In February 1813, that spark was supplied by a small party of Red Sticks, led by Little Warrior, which was on its way home from Detroit, where it had accompanied the Shawnee in raids. These warriors had just participated in several bloody fights and their own blood was up when they inexplicably butchered two white settler families along the Duck River near Nashville. Little Warrior and his companions were summarily executed under the authority of the Creek Council of old chiefs.

This blatant act of betrayal was viewed by the Upper Creek Red Sticks as nothing more than the Lower Town White Sticks kowtowing to the whites for fear of retribution. This decision by the council could be likened to an earthquake ripping a deeper and wider abyss separating the Upper and Lower towns. Perhaps this was the omen foretold by the comet and the earthquake that had rattled Creek lands in 1811. Regardless, in retaliation for what they deemed was bowing down and pandering to the white man—Hawkins in particular—the furious Upper Creek Red Sticks declared war on the Lower Creek White Sticks and their white allies. Their initial target was Big Warrior, whose Upper Creek town of Tuckabatchee was laid siege to with intentions of destroying the town. The dissidents also wanted to destroy this man who had been a respected leader in his earlier days but now was regarded by the Red Sticks as a coward who had sided with the enemy.[25]

Thus, the Creek Civil War of 1813–1814 commenced.

The first clash of the war occurred on July 27, 1813, when a war party of Red Sticks under Peter McQueen, who was returning from Spanish Florida, was accosted by a group of American soldiers. Those Red Sticks had been visiting the Spanish governor at Pensacola, where they had received arms and ammunition. The Red Sticks fled from the Americans, who then looted the munitions. McQueen's warriors carried out a surprise counterattack, which chased the whites from the field. This affair became known as the Battle of Burnt Corn and broadened what began as a solely Creek civil war to include American forces.

On August 30, the Upper Creek Red Sticks executed their initial major attack when William Weatherford led about three hundred followers to Fort Mims, which stood a few miles north of Mobile on the Alabama River. This fort was occupied by hundreds of mixed-blood people from area plantations who had sought safety and protection from the marauding Red Sticks. The fort commander, however, had neglected to takes steps for protection, and the assault by the Red Sticks became a bloody massacre. Weatherford's warriors burst inside through an open gate and killed 107 soldiers, 160 civilians, and 100 blacks before burning the stockade.

A handful of people managed to escape and spread the alarm. Panic spread throughout the countryside. Settlers armed themselves, with many of them leaving their homes and heading toward the fort with revenge on their minds. This tragedy brought American volunteer militias into the fight as well, with forces assembling in Tennessee, Georgia, and Mississippi. Secretary of War John Armstrong notified commanders in the field that if Spain was found to be involved, there would be a strike on Pensacola. Georgia commenced building forts along the Chattahoochee River, which forms much of the modern-day border between Alabama and Georgia, in order to hold off any offensive from the frontier and allow militias to prepare for war.

The initial counterattack by Lower Town Creeks and American forces took to the field during the winter of 1813–1814. This column was led by future president Andrew Jackson and his Tennessee militiamen and supported by friendly Cherokees and Creek White Sticks. Jackson and his men were relentless in their pursuit of justice for the Fort Mims massacre. His troops defeated a Red Stick force on November 9 at Talladega. Twenty days later, General John Floyd attacked the Upper Creek town of Auttosee on the Tallapoosa River and killed more than two hundred people before burning the town. Less than a month later, the hometown of Red Stick leader William Weatherford was burned to the ground. To say the least, the war was not going well for the Upper Creek Red Sticks.[26]

This was a particularly brutal war, with atrocities committed by both sides. One example of this savage action was related by former congressman and future Alamo defender Davy Crockett, who had enlisted in the Second Regiment of the Tennessee Volunteer Mountain Riflemen. Crockett was assigned to scouting duty due to his reputation as a tracker, woodsman, and hunter. He had led his unit to the large town of Tallussahatchee, Alabama, on November 3, whereupon they received enemy fire. A full-scale battle ensued, with casualties suffered on both sides. Finally, the Tennessee volunteers trapped forty-six Red Stick warriors in a log house in the center of town.

At one point, a Creek woman appeared in the doorway of this cabin and fired an arrow from a bow held by her feet, which killed one of the volunteers. That woman was immediately struck by dozens of musket balls as the unit aggressively returned fire. The enraged soldiers then refused to allow any of the Indians inside to surrender, although entreaties had been made. A massacre ensued. The log cabin was set on fire, and every one of the Creeks who was trapped inside burned to death.

The following day, the soldiers were scavenging for food when they located a potato cellar beneath the burned-out cabin. The famished men hungrily ate the potatoes. Crockett related, "Hunger compelled us to eat them, though I had a little rather not, if I could have helped it, for the oil of the Indians we had burned up on the day before had run down on them, and they looked like they had been stewed with fat meat." In all, a total of 186 men, women, and children were killed and 80 captured at Tallussahatchee that day. The Americans lost 5 men in the "battle."[27]

Fortunately, Billy Powell and his mother's clan had escaped Tallassee and the fate that had befallen Tallussahatchee. In another stroke of fortune, they were advised that Billy's mother's uncle, Peter McQueen, intended to head south with other Red Stick Creek survivors of this tragedy. Billy, along with his mother, Polly, and grandmother Ann, joined this migration of small bands that totaled perhaps one thousand people that would travel toward the Spanish-held land called Florida. At least they now had a trusted leader to guide them. McQueen hoped to seek assistance from the British, who were fighting against the United States in the War of 1812.[28]

This impromptu trip that had been forced upon them would not be without struggle and sacrifice. Billy Powell and his fellow refugees might have been heading south toward relative freedom from military pursuit, but they would endure grim circumstances along the way that would threaten safe arrival at their destination. They feared that the army was chasing them, and they could suffer the same fate as so many of their brethren. In addition, it would be a most difficult task to feed the groups of people who were accustomed to growing their own food and having it available at mealtime. Once again, they would be compelled to rely on hunting, fishing, foraging for berries and roots, theft, and the kindness of strangers they might encounter along the way.

Perhaps worse than the lack of provisions was the spiritual privation they must have experienced. These Creeks regarded their traditional land as sacred—a temporary gift that the Great Spirit had given them for their survival. And now this land that none of them would have ever consider selling or trading because it was not theirs to own but had been shared for the common good had fallen into the hands of the enemy, likely forever. This loss no doubt lay heavy on their hearts.

At the same time that these desperate refugees marched south, the Red Stick warriors, armed primarily with bows and arrows, fought bravely for what they believed was a noble cause. But their resistance would be futile. The enemy was simply too powerful and in numbers that gave them the advantage in any battle.

On March 27, 1814, Andrew Jackson and his volunteers with their Native American allies attacked Horseshoe Bend on the Tallapoosa River. More than one thousand Red Stick warriors led by Chief Menawa had built a defensive position out of logs across the narrow peninsula. Their women and children had been secreted in a swamp downstream for safety.

This was not a battle but rather a wholesale slaughter of the Upper Creek faction of the tribe. Artillery shelled the position for two hours, allowing Creeks friendly to the whites to steal away with the Red Stick canoes at water's edge near the defensive position. Jackson ordered a charge—a frontal assault—which forced about three hundred of Menawa's warriors into the water. Without canoes in which to escape, the Creek men were systematically killed by troops on the opposite banks. At battle's end, Jackson counted the bodies of 557 dead Red Stick warriors, but estimated that only 10 of the original 1,000 had escaped.[29]

The war was lost, and the only way any Upper Creek Red Sticks—men, women, or children—could save their life was to run so far away that Andrew Jackson could never find them.

Billy Powell, the boy who would become the warrior Osceola—born a Creek but forced to leave behind his homeland and tribe—would now have no choice but to make his way in life as a refugee in Spanish Florida.

» *Two* «

Black Drink Singer

»◆«

Commander of the American forces and Creek allies Andrew Jackson—now known as Sharp Knife among the Creeks—had dealt the rebellious Red Sticks a fatal blow at Horseshoe Bend. The Creek Confederation, mainly the surviving White Sticks, would now be faced with negotiating a treaty drawn up by Jackson to formalize the end of the Creek War. Actually, the chiefs would be presented with a treaty and were expected to sign it without protest. The terms of this ready-made treaty would be considered by most observers—including Indian agent Benjamin Hawkins—as excessively harsh. This opinion was based on the fact that the friendly Creek allies who fought on the side of the United States were as severely punished as the enemy. But Jackson intended to do whatever was necessary to finalize and enforce this treaty.

The Treaty of Fort Jackson was read to the confederation chiefs on August 9, 1814. The United States would annex some twenty-three million acres of valuable land—a full one-fifth of confederation landholdings in Georgia and three-fifths of their property in present-day Alabama. This parcel extended from Georgia to Mississippi Territory and constituted nearly a staggering one-half of all the land owned by the Creek Nation. Annexation of this land would mean that the entire nation, not merely the dissident Red Sticks who had not fled, would be reduced to the brink of poverty and starvation. It was also evident that the annexed land would be opened for settlement and thereby change forever the character of the territory—from red to white.

The Creek chiefs were predictably shocked and appalled—not to mention angered—by the severity of the terms. After all, they had been loyal to Jackson and the United States. They had assumed all along that they would be rewarded if they helped put down the rebellion by the Upper Creek Red Sticks. They had fought bravely alongside Jackson and his army, suffering losses without complaint. This affront with the unfavorable treaty was undeserved and outrageous. These chiefs also understood, however, that Andrew Jackson was not a man to antagonize and they must petition him with great care.

The chiefs designated Big Warrior, a loyal Jackson ally from the start, as their spokesman. He pointed out that the Lower Town Creeks had not followed Tecumseh's entreaties to wage war against the white man, and that should count for something. Jackson refuted this argument by stating that the Creeks should have cut the throat of Tecumseh the moment he entered their town, but they had not. Sharp Knife then accused the chiefs of believing that the United States would be easily defeated by the British in the War of 1812 and that they had not respected the power of its military might. Now they knew better, but it was too late to repudiate initial notions. According to Jackson, the entire Creek Nation, not only the Red Sticks, was guilty of disloyalty in one respect or another and must now pay the price for their transgressions.

Big Warrior's impassioned pleas for justice were ignored. Sharp Knife would not entertain any of his protests or those from other chiefs. Jackson then gave them an ultimatum. The chiefs could either sign the treaty right now or renew the war, which both sides knew would mean more slaughters like that at Horseshoe Bend, and the tribe would disappear as a people from the face of the earth.

Ultimately, the chiefs could not chance losing more lives at the hands of Jackson and his troops. The coercion and threats by Andrew Jackson convinced thirty-five friendly Creek chiefs to grudgingly sign the treaty. Only one Red Stick chief complied—most others had already fled for their lives.[1]

The chiefs, who certainly felt betrayed by Jackson, might not have regarded the treaty as being binding, rather believing it was merely a piece of the white man's paper and the Creek world would continue as usual. Jackson had anticipated future resistance under the guise of their claiming not to understand the treaty provisions or later ignoring them or forgetting about them. He told the chiefs in no uncertain terms that if they did not obey the treaty to the letter or if they sought out the British for relief, he would "pursue and drive them and the British into the sea." They understood that the man with the icy-blue eyes was not to be trifled with. They had witnessed his brutality toward their brethren, the Red Sticks, and wanted no part of his wrath.[2]

The unreasonable treaty terms and refusal to compromise or even debate the issue were direct reflections of Andrew Jackson's personal antipathy toward Native Americans. In his own mind, he was representing those white people living on the frontier with long-standing prejudices, fears, and hostility when it came to the Creeks—and all other Native American tribes, for that matter. Jackson himself was a product of the frontier and shared a kinship with others of his kind who were not to the manor born and had raised themselves up by their own bootstraps.

Andrew Jackson was born in a log cabin on March 15, 1767, on the border between North and South Carolina—in Waxhaw, North Carolina, or Lancaster, South Carolina (the borderline between the two Carolinas had not been determined at the time of his birth). Jackson claimed South Carolina as his birth state, which has been disputed by some historians as having been chosen solely for political reasons. Jackson was the third child and third son of Andrew Jackson Sr. and Elizabeth "Betty" Hutchinson, who had emigrated two years earlier from Carrickfergus, County Antrim, Ireland. Andrew Sr. died as the result of a logging accident a few weeks before Andrew Jr. was born, and the children were raised by their mother at the residence of her sister in South Carolina.

At the age of thirteen, along with older brother Robert, Andrew joined a militia of the Continental Army during the American Revolution and served as a courier, or orderly. Their other brother, Hugh, had also enlisted, but he died of heat exhaustion during the Battle of Stono Ferry in June 1779. Two years after that, both Andrew and Robert were captured and soon found themselves gradually starving to death in a British prison camp. While in captivity, Andrew refused to clean the boots of a British officer. The angered man slashed Andrew with his sword, wounding the boy on the head and cutting his hand almost to the bone—scars that he would carry for the rest of his life.

Betty Jackson managed to secure the release of her sons in April 1781, but both brothers had contracted smallpox during captivity and Robert died within days of his release. Betty then volunteered to nurse prisoners of war in Charleston, but shortly thereafter she fell ill—likely from cholera—and died in November 1781. She was buried in an unmarked grave.

Andrew Jackson Jr. had lost his entire family during the Revolutionary War and was an orphan at age fourteen. These tragic childhood circumstances fostered within him an intense lifelong hatred of the British.

Following his war adventures, Jackson lived with relatives and briefly apprenticed as a saddle maker. That profession was not to his liking, however. His formal education had been sporadic thus far in his life, but he decided that academic learning was more appealing than learning a trade. In 1784, at age seventeen, Jackson began studying law in North Carolina. He was admitted to the bar in that state three years later and soon was appointed prosecuting officer for the Superior Court in Nashville, Tennessee, which at the time was part of the Western District of North Carolina. Jackson embraced the rough-and-tumble, unpredictable life adjudicating frontier law and had an affinity for these people who were living a hardscrabble life.

While in Nashville, he engaged in a love affair with Rachel Donelson Robards, a married woman and member of a first family in the Cumberland Basin. Rachel's husband eventually moved away and divorced her, accusing her of desertion and adultery. In 1793, Andrew Jackson and Rachel Robards were wed. The couple would have no children of their own but would eventually adopt one son.

The fact that Jackson had broken up a family failed to affect his popularity or his profession. After Tennessee split from North Carolina in 1796 and became the sixteenth state, Jackson, who had acquired a wide network of friends, relatives, and admirers, was elected that state's first congressman. The following year, he was elected Tennessee's only senator, but he served only one session before returning home to settle in the mansion built on his 640-acre plantation called the Hermitage and to accept an appointment as a judge on the Tennessee Supreme Court.

In 1802, Jackson resumed the military career he had begun during the American Revolution when he was elected major general of the Tennessee militia. He did not immediately see action in that capacity against foreign enemies but did become infamous as a "duelist." It was written that "he fought three affairs of honor, in two of which he was wounded. In a duel in 1806 he stoically received an almost mortal wound, then coolly killed his opponent."[3]

At the outbreak of the War of 1812, Major General Andrew Jackson and his Tennessee militia were ordered to put down the Creek Indian uprising in Alabama. And—as evidenced by his victory at Horseshoe Bend and the subsequent Treaty of Fort Jackson—that was exactly what this loyal soldier had accomplished. He would now be free to pursue his mortal enemy, the British.[4]

While Jackson abandoned the Creek War to chase the British, Billy Powell and his fellow Creek refugees moved steadily southward. The arduous journey had taken its toll on these displaced people. They had departed a land of plenty and were now impoverished and desperate, surviving by whatever means possible, not knowing from one day to the next what would happen to them. These people were not accustomed to migrating like their Great Plains brethren, who would follow great buffalo herds for sustenance. The Creeks were unable to provide adequately for their basic needs. They could not come close to feeding their large band of people simply by hunting, fishing, and scavenging native plants. No record exists, but there can be little doubt that a number of them died and were buried along the way. With no earthly support to sustain them, these hungry and weary people would have sought out a higher authority in which to trust to direct their actions through their uncertain future.

For this, the Creek people turned to the Great Spirit—*Sa-kee tom-mas-see*—also known as the "Master of Breath" or "Breathmaker," from whom all creations and all reasons for being alive were attributed. If there ever was a time to ask for intervention from the Great Spirit, it was now. They needed deliverance from this tragic predicament before starvation and disease overcame them all.[5]

No itinerary can be found for the movements of Peter McQueen and his ragtag band of followers as they fled southward from Tallassee to escape certain death at the hands of Jackson and his army. It was believed that they arrived at the Yellow Water River, a Spanish town near Pensacola, in late 1814 or early 1815. McQueen hoped to receive help from the British garrisoned at Pensacola, but his efforts were in vain—Jackson's troops had already taken the town on November 8, 1814.

McQueen moved on and resumed attempts to make contact with the British but was eventually forced to abandon that notion when entreaties became futile. He then journeyed with his people to the Wakulla River, near the Spanish town of St. Marks, south of modern-day Tallahassee. It was there that they encountered the Seminole tribe at nearby Fowl Town and Mikasuki, located near the Georgia border, which were led by Chief Neamathla.

Much to the delight—and relief—of Billy Powell and the rest of the beleaguered people, Neamathla welcomed McQueen's band into the Seminole fold. Was the arduous odyssey of the Creek refugees finally over? Could they actually cease wandering and settle into a normal life with a sense of safety and security within this tribe living in the wilderness of Florida? Who were these Seminoles, and why would they so readily accept strangers who had drifted into their midst?[6]

Evidence suggests that the Seminole tribe of Florida that McQueen happened upon could have been the descendants of Native Americans who had lived in the southeastern United States some twelve thousand years ago. In more modern times, however, the Seminole tribes for the most part were composed of descendants of Creek people and other tribes, which for unknown reasons had migrated southward beginning in the mid-eighteenth century. One theory for the Creek migration was that the Spanish had attempted to set up missions in Creek country in Alabama and Georgia, but those efforts failed. Some Creeks, however, had embraced the teachings of those missions and were drawn to the south, into Florida, where Spanish missions flourished. This may or may not have played a role, but it was more likely that the Creeks migrated due to the plentiful game and fertile land available in Florida. And another factor that cannot be overlooked is that they might have moved to distance themselves from the expanding white settlements that were steadily encroaching on their traditional homeland.

The first wave of immigrant Creeks likely settled at Coacoochee, near present-day Brooksville, Florida, around 1760 and spread out from that point as additional people arrived and explored this intriguing territory. Therefore, the Seminole Nation of the early 1800s was not a distinct tribe with a long heritage but had been formed from a mixture of Native Americans from various tribes that had wandered down from the north and banded together.[7]

The meeting between Billy Powell and his fellow refugees with the Seminole of the Florida wilderness was assuredly not as awkward as they might have feared. Traveling to a new land under such circumstances as they had endured was stressful enough. Meeting strangers who might or might not accept them was downright terrifying. But they were in for a pleasant surprise. These people were not aggressive toward them and had more in common with the migrating Creeks than they had differences.

The Seminole tribe, due to its rich Creek origin and influence, had predictably adopted many aspects of Creek culture and tradition, including the clan relationship and matrilineal family descent. There were certain differences, however, including the language—or rather, languages—spoken among tribal bands. The earliest Native language in Florida was Mikasuki, which was derived from the Lower Creek Hitchiti. Before long, at least a dozen other variations and dialects were introduced by newcomers, such as Natchez, Yuchi, Alabama, Koasati, Shawnee, and Muskogee.

By the 1800s, towns throughout Florida were known to speak different dialects of a language or different languages entirely. They did conduct trade with one another, but each town was a self-governing oasis carved from the wilderness, where the inhabitants hunted, fished, and raised their crops and livestock to scratch out a living, and they prided themselves on their individuality. The

Seminole also traded with the Spanish, and occasionally engaged in minor skirmishes with the Europeans as these Native Americans strived to maintain their independence from all outsiders.[8]

The origin of the name Seminole cannot be adequately documented. One theory suggests that the word means "those who live apart," which describes the tradition of separating, or isolating, themselves from the Spanish and even from bands of fellow Seminoles. Another respected source states that the name may be derived from the Spanish word *cimarrón,* meaning "wild and untamed" or "runaway." Regardless of name origins, these people for unknown reasons found it necessary to shed their Creek designation and adopt a new name for themselves. Perhaps this was a way of demonstrating that their move south to Spanish Florida had been permanent and they had no intention of ever returning to their traditional Creek homeland.[9]

The group led by Peter McQueen was in a sense merely an extension of the migration to Spanish Florida that had been occurring for the better part of a century, albeit this particular migration had been taken out of necessity rather than choice. Language barriers could be overcome, but culture and traditions were another matter. Thankfully, it would not be necessary for these newcomers to shed their core beliefs and long-held rituals in order to adapt to the Seminole lifestyle. The daily life there was nearly identical to the way Billy Powell and his neighbors had lived in Tallassee. The refugees could not have asked for a better situation. There was one element of Seminole life, however, that was glaringly contrary to the practices of the Creek Confederation—the relationship of the Seminole tribe with black slaves.

The Seminoles had for years welcomed runaway slaves from Southern states into their fold. These black people usually lived apart from the Seminoles in so-called Maroon communities, but they enjoyed a unique relationship as members of the tribe. Although living in virtual freedom, the blacks regarded themselves as obligated to the Seminoles. They would work their fields and raise animals, and hand over a portion of their crop or slaughtered livestock as a tribute for this communal affiliation, which could be likened to the European feudal system. The tribe also owned slaves in the traditional manner, but these blacks were usually treated more like members of the household than property and did not have to fear cruelty or having their families broken up. Seminoles and blacks would occasionally intermarry, and over time any inequality between the two races within the tribe vanished.

The black population was quite an asset to the Seminoles. Most of them spoke English and other languages, and could serve as interpreters with traders. They also understood the ways of the white man and could advise the Seminole what behavior to expect from those individuals. The blacks were excellent farmers and builders, skills they had learned during their enslavement. White observers would write that the Black Seminoles were on the whole more "intelligent" than their fellow Native American tribesmen. This observation was based solely on judging the "white" abilities of the black people compared to the native Seminoles who were loyal to their own culture. Over the years, more and more slaves in the South fled their masters to find refuge in Spanish territory as word spread that a life of relative freedom awaited them among the Seminoles.

This arrangement between the Seminoles and the runaway slaves predictably angered white slaveholders to the north. Citizen militias from Alabama, Georgia, and Tennessee would seek retribution against the Seminoles for harboring former slaves by marching into north-central Florida and destroying the tribe's farms and villages. These militias were not greeted with apathy, however. The Seminoles put up a stiff resistance to any foreign invader, whether Southerner or Spanish patrols.[10]

By 1815, both the Creek War and the War of 1812 had drawn to a close, and Billy Powell and his fellow Tallassee refugees looked forward to a period of peace and prosperity. Billy and his mother and grandmother—and probably Peter McQueen—put down roots in the vicinity of Chief Neamathla's Fowl Town and set to work establishing themselves as Seminoles. The Seminole people owned sizable herds of livestock, the luxuriant Florida climate produced food in abundance, and they traded for other goods with British and Spanish settlers. The Powell family could not have asked for a better circumstance with which to reestablish their lives. This comfortable and secure lifestyle enjoyed by Billy Powell and the Seminoles would be short-lived, however.

The Seminoles for years had been raiding white American settlements along the Georgia and Alabama borders. The whites had retaliated with raids of their own, both to search for slaves and to try to regain stolen goods—as well as simply to keep the Seminoles on their heels. Relations along the border had deteriorated into a series of small but spirited firefights resulting in only minor casualties or property loss, but they fostered hatred nonetheless.

More alarming to the Americans than the threat of these raids, however, was the growing relationship between the Seminoles and the escaped slaves. The outcry for a way to return this human property to the slave owners became louder and louder. Given the volatile social environment of the time, it was inevitable that this contentious situation would escalate into serious violence and bloodshed.

During the latter stages of the War of 1812, the British had built a fort—named British Post but commonly referred to as Negro Fort—on Prospect Bluff some fifteen miles up the Apalachicola River inside Spanish Florida. Negro Fort received its common nickname from the fact that, in addition to Seminoles who would congregate there, the fort became a refuge for hundreds of runaway slaves from the North seeking protection. This fort was intended to serve as a supply depot for the Seminoles, who had been British allies during the War of 1812. Members of that tribe, however, were not particularly inclined to garrison the fort due to its proximity to the whites, choosing instead to build towns farther away.

Negro Fort was a mere sixty miles from the U.S. border, and the Spanish, who in truth had little control over the territory, ignored its existence. This closeness of a black fortress to American settlements was recognized as not only a slap in the face of slave owners but also a dire threat to safety. It was known that the fort was armed with at least four pieces of heavy artillery, six light cannons, thousands of small arms, and large quantities of ammunition.[11]

As time went by, the British abandoned the fort, leaving behind the arms and ammunition. Most of the Seminoles had departed to establish towns some distance away. Consequently, the fort was left in the hands of hundreds of runaway slaves who worked the land and raised livestock for fifty miles along the Apalachicola River. Whites argued that the fort was a base of operations for what could amount to an invasion of Alabama or Georgia by armed blacks. The weapons and manpower at the fort could certainly support a group of agitators who wanted to incite a black rebellion—or even an all-out war against the slave owners.[12]

In time, this situation at Negro Fort came to the attention of the newly appointed U.S. Army southern division commander—Major General Andrew Jackson, the man the Seminole called "Sharp Knife." The general had become a national hero after the War of 1812 for his smashing victory over the British at the Battle of New Orleans. "Old Hickory," as Jackson was now known to his adoring public, told the governor of the colony in Pensacola that the conduct of the slaves at the fort "will not be tolerated by our government, and if not put down by Spanish authority will compel us in self Defence to destroy them." The governor was sympathetic, but admitted that he could not do anything about this haven for runaway slaves.[13]

Jackson, in his typical cavalier fashion, did not want to waste any time dealing with this threat. West Florida governor William Crawford advised Jackson that any decision regarding Negro Fort should rest with President James Monroe. Jackson completely disregarded the pleadings of Crawford, which was typical behavior for him. President Thomas Jefferson perhaps best described the often reckless Jackson when he said, "His passions are terrible." Jefferson went on to say, "When I was President of the Senate, he was Senator, and he could never speak on account of the rashness of his feelings. I have seen him attempt it repeatedly, and as often choke with rage. . . . He is a dangerous man."[14]

True to form, Sharp Knife did not wait for the president's advice or approval. He gave General Edmund P. Gaines discretionary power to attack Negro Fort and return the slaves to their rightful owners.[15]

General Gaines established a base in Georgia at the confluence of the Flint and Chattahoochee rivers called Fort Scott, just upriver from the Apalachicola River where Negro Fort was located. From this fort on July 10, 1816, Gaines dispatched regular troops and naval vessels commanded by Lieutenant Colonel Duncan Clinch toward Negro Fort. Clinch had orders that if fired upon he was authorized to destroy the fort.

On the way, Clinch encountered a slave-chasing party of about 150 White Stick Lower Creeks led by Captain William McIntosh. Clinch recruited the help of these slave chasers, offering them the booty seized at the fort in addition to $50 for each captured slave. This played into Jackson's hands as well. He had wanted the Creeks to join in the fight so it would not appear as if the Americans had taken the initiative on their own without the involvement of concerned Native American allies.

Clinch had been pleased when he was informed that a rowboat of sailors that earlier had been sent out to seek drinking water had been attacked by the blacks from the fort. This unprovoked aggression by the fort's inhabitants would now justify an assault by his troops.

Clinch pushed on with his 116 regular troops and Creek allies, and by July 27 he had surrounded Negro Fort. He demanded that the fort be surrendered, which was met by the estimated 320 people inside with taunts and ridicule, the hoisting of the Union Jack and a red battle flag of death, and finally the firing of one of their cannons.

Clinch answered with a barrage of cannon fire from the naval vessels. One of the shells fired from Gunboat 154 had been heated cherry-red in the cook's galley. This shell struck the fort's powder magazine, where more than seven hundred barrels of powder had been stored.

The resultant explosion struck awe in the hearts of even the most experienced and jaded artillery observers. This spectacular burst of smoke and flame caused Negro Fort to disintegrate into ruin almost instantly. Splintered logs, random debris, and charred and mangled bodies were blasted skyward by the impact of this colossal explosion. The discharge was so powerful that it was said to have been heard by people one hundred miles away in Pensacola.

As a result of this direct hit, just about every person inside the fort was instantly killed—at least 270 men, women, and children, most of them blacks. There were perhaps fifty who remained alive, writhing in pain on the ground, more than half of who would die later. Those runaway slaves who had witnessed this catastrophe from nearby now fled into the forest to find refuge as far away as possible.[16]

Several of the black and Native American leaders found alive inside the fort were handed over to McIntosh's Creeks and suffered slow, painful deaths. McIntosh's men then set out to round up blacks who had been living in nearby cabins who could not escape or hide. These unfortunates were trussed up and, in the company of the twenty or so shaken blacks from within the fort who had survived the explosion, were marched off to Alabama and Georgia to be returned to their white masters. For his efforts, McIntosh received booty of three thousand muskets and carbines, four hundred pistols, five hundred swords in steel scabbards, more than one thousand kegs of powder, bars of lead, clothing and uniforms, and stores of food.[17]

From that day forth, the American flag would fly over Prospect Bluff in Spanish Florida—the former site of Negro Fort—almost continuously until the United States finally acquired the territory permanently in 1821.

This act of brutality infuriated the Seminoles, the blacks, and the Spanish. The Seminoles immediately formed a war party and set out for the site of the former fort with intentions of exacting revenge. Colonel Duncan Clinch welcomed this enemy deployment and marched out to confront the war party. By that time, however, the Seminole had learned of the enormous cache of arms and ammunition that had fallen into the hands of McIntosh and his Creeks. The Seminole decided that there had been enough slaughter for the time being and slipped away from the soldiers and their allies. Clinch called the Seminole "cowardly wretches" for not standing and fighting.[18]

As the months passed, however, the Seminole stepped up their attacks just inside the Florida border, especially on those settlers living near the mouth of the Apalachicola River. They were also accused of several murders in Georgia, which they justified by stating that they were merely seeking satisfaction for all the killings the Americans had been committing.

Billy Powell and his family were not immune to this escalating conflict. White people, including soldiers, had been intruding in the vicinity of Fowl Town, where Billy and his family resided, about fourteen miles east of Fort Scott. Chief Neamathla, the man who had so warmly welcomed the homeless Creek refugees two years earlier, warned the military to stay away from his town or his warriors would attack. He claimed that the Flint River was the dividing line under the Treaty of Fort Jackson, and whites had violated that boundary.

Neamathla's message to Fort Scott in November 1817 basically read, "I warn you not to cross, nor to cut a stick of wood on the east side of the Flint. That land is mine. I am directed by the powers above and the powers below to protect and defend it. I shall do so."[19]

It was evident that the chief felt so fervently about his responsibility to protect the land that he had implied that the Great Spirit was directing his actions. Just as it was with the Creeks, the land was mystical—sacred—to the Seminole. There was no sense of personal ownership; rather, when Neamathla claimed that "That land is mine," he actually meant that he and his tribe had been permitted to use that land for their own benefit by none other than the Great Spirit. The land could not be ceded, sold, or given away, or abused in any manner. Any threat to their land, such as whites or soldiers tramping around on it, would be viewed as a spiritual threat. The land was their life and breath, and to part with it was to part with the blood that flowed through their veins.

General Edmund Gaines, commanding officer of Fort Scott, had no understanding or knowledge of the attachment of the Seminole to their land— not that it would have mattered. The insolent tone of the message from Neamathla infuriated the general. He was not accustomed to being threatened or given ultimatums by defiant savages. On November 21, Clinch dispatched Major David E. Twiggs and 250 soldiers to Fowl Town with orders to arrest Chief Neamathla.

The army promptly marched on the town but did not specifically seek out the chief. Instead, they simply opened fire. Four warriors and a woman were killed, a number of others were wounded, and the soldiers burned every structure to the ground.

It can be taken for granted that not only had Peter McQueen initially tried to defend the town but also he was forced to flee from the scene to avoid capture. Other inhabitants who would have escaped with him were the teenaged Billy Powell and his mother and grandmother. Once again the extended family had managed to evade an attack by Jackson's soldiers and was on the run with nothing but the clothing on their backs.[20]

This destruction of Fowl Town by the soldiers started a sequence of bloody clashes that would become known in history as the First Seminole War.

Peter McQueen took an active role in the retaliation for the unprovoked attack on Fowl Town. Nine days after that incident, McQueen and a band of Seminoles located a boat on the Apalachicola heading toward Fort Scott that contained forty soldiers, seven soldiers' wives, and four children, which was under the command of Lieutenant R. W. Scott. The historian James Parton described what happened next:

> A heavy volley of musketry, from the thickets within a few yards of the boat, was fired into the closely-compacted company. Lieutenant Scott and nearly every man in the boat were killed, or badly wounded at the first fire. Other volleys succeeded. The Indians soon rose from their ambush and rushed upon the boat with a fearful yell. Men, women and children were involved in one horrible massacre, or spared for more horrible torture. The children were taken by the heels and their brains dashed out against the sides of the boat. The men and women were scalped. . . . Four men escaped. . . . Laden with plunder, the savages reentered the wilderness, taking with them the women whom they had spared.

One of the women, identified as a "Mrs. Stewart, or Stuart" was "treated with great kindness" as a prisoner in Suwannee Town. It might also be noted that the presence of the children has been disputed but is probable. Six injured survivors were able to make it safely back to Fort Scott.[21]

This brutality demonstrated by McQueen's Seminole warriors compelled Secretary of War John C. Calhoun to order Andrew Jackson, who had aggressively urged that he be appointed, to take personal charge of the army in Spanish Florida and invade. President Monroe, however, instructed Jackson "not to attack any post occupied by Spanish troops, from the possibility, that it might bring the allied powers on us." It was no secret that Monroe wanted possession of Florida, but he did not trust a hothead like Jackson who could easily make a rash mistake that might ruin his plans.[22]

On March 9, 1818, Jackson arrived at Fort Scott and amassed an army of fifteen hundred soldiers—composed mainly of Tennessee volunteers and Georgia militiamen—and two thousand Creek warriors. Jackson immediately constructed a new fort, named Fort Gadsden, at the former site of Negro Fort. He then marched into the Seminole homeland. His initial attacks took place on March 31, when he scoured the countryside for supplies and at the same time burned down a number of towns. Jackson estimated that more than three hundred Seminole homes were destroyed and an abundance of corn and cattle was confiscated that day.

Jackson then turned southward and arrived at the Spanish fort at Bay of St. Marks on April 6. The general, contrary to the spirit of his orders not to attack a Spanish post, dispatched a message to the commander at the fort stating that "the occupation of St. Marks is essential to the accomplishment of my campaign." Jackson's warning was ignored. The following day, after determining that the Spanish were stalling with their answer, Jackson decided to take the fort by force. He formed his troops for an assault and moved them forward. The Americans and their allies passed through the gate and entered the fort without resistance. The Spanish colors were quickly lowered and replaced with the Stars and Stripes. Andrew Jackson was now in possession of a Spanish fort in Spanish territory. Instead of inciting an international incident, however, Spain apparently had no desire to protect its interests with force. President Monroe was probably horrified when he heard about the act, but privately breathed a sigh of relief and was pleased with the results.[23]

Billy Powell's great-uncle Peter McQueen had been taking an active part in the attacks along the Florida border. On the morning of April 12, 1818, General Jackson and his army of soldiers and McIntosh's Creeks surprised McQueen's small band at Natural Bridge on the Ecofina River. McQueen escaped into the swamps, much to the chagrin of Jackson, but thirty-seven Creeks were killed and six men and ninety-seven women and children were captured—including the Mrs. Stewart or Stuart who had been taken by the Seminole months earlier and whose husband and father were said to have been accompanying Jackson.

It was during this conflict that fourteen-year-old Billy Powell had a first-hand taste of American military power and his first personal encounter with the enemy. The leader of the offensive later mentioned the presence of Billy Powell—still "but a lad"—among the captives, as well as his mother. Billy and the other prisoners became a nuisance to Jackson, who wanted to move without delay to Suwannee Town and did not wish to waste the manpower to guard them.

According to the popular account, while the boy was in the hands of the enemy, an old woman, thought to have been Billy's Creek grandmother, Ann Copinger, approached Jackson with a proposal. She promised to deliver Peter McQueen if the general would release the captured women and children. Jackson must have known that this woman would not betray her own brother. The idea of a swap, however, would satisfy Jackson's desire to rid his army of the burdensome prisoners. The general agreed to the release. Billy Powell, his mother, and the others were set free. Ann Copinger predictably did not make good on her promise to hand Peter McQueen over to the army. McQueen had long since escaped into the swamps to the south and managed to hide from Jackson.[24]

Billy Powell had survived the terrifying experience of captivity but once again found himself homeless by the destruction of his town. The tactic employed by Jackson that subjected the civilian populace, not just the enemy fighting force, to a reign of terror would later be termed "total war." Credit has been given to various generals—Haney, Sherman, Sheridan, and Custer among them—for perfecting this tactic. But perhaps no one in this country's history was as proficient at invading the enemy's homeland and mercilessly destroying property and terrorizing the noncombatants as Andrew Jackson.[25]

Jackson's invasion, which eventually concluded on May 28 with the surrender of the Spanish garrison at Pensacola, ended the prosperity of the northern Seminoles, and a general panic set in. Many Seminoles abandoned their farms and retreated southward to the marshlands, where, half starved, they survived as best they could.

During this time of hardship, Billy and his mother also fled south to the area around Tampa Bay, where Peter McQueen had set up a new town. In that place, they were removed from hostilities and had a home in which to live and enough food to eat. They could start rebuilding their lives—again.

It was there, in the wake of two wars, captivity, and that rigorous retreat from certain death, that Billy Powell would officially pass into manhood. Although no direct record of this event has been discovered, it is likely that it was in 1822, when Billy had turned eighteen years of age, that he participated in the ceremony that would welcome him into adulthood and bestow upon him his permanent, or adult, name. According to Creek and Seminole tradition, a boy's initiation took place at the Green Corn Dance, an annual ceremony of purification, forgiveness, and thanksgiving held every summer in honor of the corn festival.

The season from April to October was filled with ceremonies, but the Green Corn Dance was—and remains—the most significant Seminole tribal ritual. This festival, also known as the Ceremonial Fast, has been described as being as sacred and significant to the Seminoles and other Southeastern tribes as Easter is to Christians and Yom Kippur is to the Jewish faith. It was held for a period of four or five days toward the end of July or in early August when the green corn is ripe—at a time chosen by the micco and his council—to celebrate the corn harvest and express gratitude to the Creator for providing the tribe with food. One way to demonstrate obedience was by fasting. Everyone was strictly forbidden to partake of any fresh corn until completion of the religious rites of this great festival that ushered in the New Year.

An interesting aspect of the advent of the Green Corn Dance is that a general amnesty would be declared. All crimes except murder and rape, which were executable or banishable offenses, were forgiven. The transgressions of thieves, adulterers, and those guilty of other minor misdeeds, including feuds and disputes that had developed between individuals or clans throughout the year, were forgotten. Everyone started the Seminole New Year without the fear of reprisal or punishment hanging over them or enemies seeking to harm them.

Each member of the town would participate in preparations for the important occasion. The women would fashion new garments and make new pottery and other necessary household items for the entire family. They would also thoroughly scrub and clean their homes and environs, much like modern-day spring cleaning, with repairs being made, broken or worn-out items being replaced, and even, if necessary, tearing down and rebuilding.

The men would tidy up the town square by removing the old dirt, carting it away, and applying new dirt or sand. They would then gather all the trash, the stored food from the last harvest, and the old clothing. This refuse would be tossed into a huge pile and burned. They would then lay four logs in the shape of a cross at the center of the refurbished square, which would be used to build a "new fire."

The first ceremonial act of the Green Corn festival would be for every fire in the town to be extinguished and the hearths cleaned by the women and sprinkled with fresh dirt. Five chiefs would then start a fire with the logs that had been laid by the men using the archaic method of rubbing sticks together to spark the flame. Sticks from this fire would then be lighted and distributed to every house in the community so that each family could start the year with a new fire.[26]

As one of the honorees on the verge of manhood, Billy Powell would have had responsibilities to perform leading up to his special moment. The Green Corn festivities were held in a remote place away from any village. He would have been expected to help the medicine man and his adult assistants at the dance site with whatever was necessary to prepare the several-acre clearing carved from the forest where the Green Corn Dance would be held, such as by clearing away grass, brush, and weeds. Inside this clearing would be the dance circle, a smooth area about forty feet in diameter, with the dance—or "Grandfather"—fire at the center. This fire was considered to be a sacred living being, and it was said that the prayers of the people would be communicated to the Breathmaker through the fire. Arbors would need to be constructed at the four points of the compass around the square in which the men would sit, and clan houses would be situated around the clearing. Another important task for the boys being honored would be readying the nearby building known as the *tchoc-ko thloc-go,* or "warriors' clubhouse."[27]

At the direction of the medicine man, Billy and the other young men would have been charged with gathering the herbs used in making the cere-monial "black drink." This was usually yaupon tea, made from the leaves of a bushy evergreen shrub from the holly family. It was called the "black drink" by outsiders on account of its color, but the Creeks and Seminoles called it "white drink" and believed that it held sacred properties. Other ingredients—such as button snakeroot, Saint-John's-wort, and the inner bark of the willow tree—might have been used along with or in place of the yaupon.

No one, save members of the Seminole present at the time, can be certain about the actual ceremony in which Billy Powell participated the night of his acceptance into manhood—few white people have ever witnessed the Green Corn Dance or its rituals. Caleb Swan, who claimed to have been present at one of these early ceremonies, however, wrote about the Creek and Seminole spiritual attachment to the black drink: "They have a reli-gious belief that it purifies them from all sin, and leaves them in a state of perfect innocence; that it inspires them with an invincible prowess in war; and that it is the only solid cement of friendship, benevolence, and hospi-tality. Most of them really seem to believe that the Great Spirit or Master of breath has communicated the virtues of the black-drink to them, and them only . . . , and that it is a particular blessing bestowed on them, his chosen people."[28]

The men would remain at the sacred square throughout the days of the Green Corn Dance to guard against intruders. Women would at times be permitted to participate in the dances, but children were strictly forbidden to attend. Every aspect of the ceremony held deep religious significance and rituals were carefully followed. The dances themselves would symbolize and celebrate the community's social and spiritual life—everything from war to the mystical relationship of the people with the nature around them on which they depended for their existence. During these days, the leaders would lecture their tribe about moral and ethical issues, which were received with great interest and solemnity. These serious talks were punctuated by joyous celebrations as the entire tribe looked with anticipation toward another year of prosperity.

This ceremony was called, after all, the Green Corn Dance, and dancing was the featured attraction. For hour after hour, the people would perform the stomp dance, a single-file, methodical, weaving style of dancing that has become traditional with the Seminole. A medicine man or another dance leader would chant, and the men who were dancing would loudly answer, while the women remained silent but made noise with shakers that were tied to their legs. These dances would continue nightly under the stars and illuminated by the dance fire at the center of the clearing until at least midnight and often later. One of the dances would include sacred objects, the most revered of which were the seven mysterious copper and brass plates of the Tuckabatchees. These hallowed plates were said to have been given to the people by the Master of Breath, and the well-being of the town was dependent upon their protection and preservation. The objects were carried by the priests in a single procession at the Green Corn Dance and then locked up and guarded for the remainder of the year.

At dawn on the final day of the festivities, the women would depart the dance ground and return home to prepare a feast of meat and corn. While the women were away, many of the men and boys would participate in a scratching, or bloodletting, ceremony. This ritual of ripping open the flesh was performed in the belief that it would purify the blood, prevent illness, and ensure a long life. Thorns or other sharp objects would be used to tear the skin on the arms, legs, or chests deep enough to cause bloody gashes. A number of the men who finished the blood baptism or did not participate would enter the hut near the medicine man's fire for a sweat bath. All of the men, who had been fasting for several days, would then cleanse themselves in a stream or creek before returning to the ceremonial square. Once there, they would perform one brief dance and then depart for their homes to share a feast with their families. The fasting was over for another year.[29]

It was the nightly drinking of the black drink, however, that elevated Billy Powell to a higher status. He would become an adult who would now leave behind the games and frivolity of youth and take on responsibilities within the tribe. Caleb Swan described the ritual of drinking the black drink that might have been performed by Billy Powell as he passed into manhood on that warm evening in 1822:

> The warriors and chiefs being assembled and seated, three young men acting as masters of ceremony on the occasion, each having a gourd or calabash full of the liquor, place themselves on front of the three greatest chiefs or warriors, and announce that they are ready by the word choh! After a short pause, stooping forward, they run up to the warriors and hold the cup or shell parallel to their mouths; the warriors receive it from them, and wait until the young men fall back and adjust themselves to give what they term the *yohullah,* or black-drink note. As the young men begin to aspirate the note, the great men place the cups to their mouths, and are obliged to drink during the aspirated note of the young men, which, after exhausting their breath, is repeated on a finer key, until the lungs are no longer inflated. This long aspiration is continued near half a minute, and the cup is taken from the mouth of the warrior who is drinking at the instant the note is finished. The young men then receive the cups from the chiefs or head warriors, and pass it to the others of inferior rank, giving them the word choh! but not the yohullah note. . . . It is generally served round in this manner three times at every meeting; during the recess of serving it up, they all sit quietly in their several cabins, and amuse themselves by smoking, conversing, exchanging tobacco, &c., and in disgorging what black-drink they have previously swallowed.[30]

The consumption of this black drink was not a pleasant experience by any stretch of the imagination. The ingredients acted as both an emetic that produced vomiting and a cathartic, a purgative medicine. The men believed that if they did not partake of this drink, however, they would suffer sickness during the upcoming year and that they could not even safely consume the green corn of the feast. In other words, this drink acted as a way to both spiritually and physically purge bad spirits from the body and thereby cleanse the soul.

At some point during this event, when the men were drinking their herbal tea, their black drink, Billy Powell was invited to join them. It was evident by the name bestowed upon him that he was much revered as a singer while accompanying the men in partaking of this drink—and the resultant vomiting. He shed his childhood name and apparently was given his adult name based on his talents and enthusiasm as a singer of the song that accompanied the serving and consuming of this distasteful drink. His new name would be derived from the word *asi,* which meant "black drink," and *yaholo,* which meant "singer." Some sources mention that *yaholo* was the cry made by the drinker of the black drink. Regardless, Billy Powell would now and forever be known as Asi Yaholo—"Black Drink Singer."

Historians have provided countless variations of his name, some of which are As-see-a-hala, As-se-se-he-ho-lar, Asseola, As-sin Yahola, Assiola, Assyn-ya-hola, Hassee Ola, Ocela, Os-cin-ye-hola, Oseola, Ossen Yaholah, Usso Yahola, and Yose-ya-hola. This venerable name, however, would eventually be anglicized by whites to Osceola.[31]

Osceola, the Seminole warrior. His name in the future would be revered or despised depending on which side of justice he was viewed from. There would always be those who would know him as "Powell," but from that day forth he preferred this new name that allowed him to sever ties with the Creek and establish himself as Osceola, a member of the Seminole tribe of Florida Territory.

Three

Treachery at Moultrie Creek

»◈«

S cant material exists to accurately chronicle the daily life of Osceola for the next several years, but that does not mean that there were not significant and suspenseful events occurring during that period that would shape his worldview for the remainder of his days. The time in which he now lived was one of conflict and expansion, with ever-changing boundaries of the country as well as vacillating political and social sentiments.

Nothing of substance can be found about Osceola's mother or grandmother, either, but it can be assumed that Osceola lived with them and would have been the family provider of wild game as the primary hunter. The whereabouts of Peter McQueen have been shrouded in mystery. He would likely have been quite old by this time and might have simply removed himself from active participation in tribal affairs, if he was even alive. Regardless, this man who had bedeviled Jackson and the enemies of his tribe disappeared from the pages of history at some point after arriving at the village near Tampa Bay.

Osceola, as an apprentice or warrior-in-training, would have sat on the fringes of town councils, paying close attention as the leaders discussed, debated, and made important decisions that affected the lives of their people.

Osceola might have had an opinion about various issues, but he would not have spoken. As a young man, he was present to observe and learn and prepare. The time would come someday in the future when he would be called upon to assume a leadership role within his town and for his tribe. He would need to be well versed in every aspect of Seminole culture, tradition, and policies in order to gain the respect necessary for a position of trust. For now, he would strive to please his family clan and the tribal leaders by excelling at whatever task was assigned him.

It can be concluded, however, that Osceola no longer regarded himself as a member of the Creek Nation. He was now a Seminole. Neither Osceola nor his fellow refugees entertained any thoughts of returning to their former homeland. They held bitter memories and a deep-seated resentment of the brethren they had left behind—both the Red and White Sticks—and wanted nothing more to do with them. The refugees had turned a page in their lives and were not about to leaf back through folded-away chapters of tragedies and lament about what might have been. They would make their way as Seminoles in Florida—or perish trying.

From all indications, Osceola would have been considered the epitome of a young Seminole warrior as described by Clay MacCauley, an early visitor to the Seminole Nation:

Physically both men and women are remarkable. The men, as a rule, attract attention by their height, fullness and symmetry of development, and the regularity and agreeableness of their features. In muscular power and constitutional ability to endure they excel. . . . I noticed that under a large forehead are deep set, bright, black eyes, small, but expressive of inquiry and vigilance; the nose is slightly aquiline and sensitively formed about the nostrils; the lips are mobile, sensuous, and not very full, disclosing, when they smile, beautiful regular teeth; and the whole face is expressive of the man's sense of having extraordinary ability to endure and to achieve. . . . We may pronounce the Seminole men handsome and exceptionally powerful.[1]

Osceola would have worn the traditional dress of the day—a cotton shirt, long leather stockings, a belt, moccasins, and a cloth turban that might have been adorned with ostrich feathers obtained from traders. On hunting trips he would carry his bow and three-foot-long arrows with fire-hardened tips, along with a knife in a sheath and a hatchet. He probably would have dreamed of owning a muzzle-loading musket, but as a young man without livestock or other trade goods, he would have to wait. Perhaps he could collect enough skins from deer, raccoons, panthers, otters, and other furbearers to one day trade for a firearm with an American or Cuban trader. His bow and arrows were effective for hunting, but a Seminole man should have a weapon with which to defend himself and his people against any enemy.[2]

Although not every movement made by Osceola is available, it is possible to reconstruct his life through the state of affairs that affected his tribe. This was a period of great adversity and uncertainty for the Seminole, and Osceola would have been directly affected by it all. The United States was debating the fate of Native Americans in Florida. Decisions made and actions undertaken now would have a major effect on the Seminole for years to come—and the fate of Osceola was tied to the fate of the Seminoles.

In the United States, Major General Andrew Jackson was both praised and vilified for his conquest of Florida, which brought an end to the First Seminole War. Many in Congress, including Speaker of the House Henry Clay, believed that Jackson should be censured for his campaigns. But Jackson was too prominent a hero in the eyes of the public. It would not be politically expedient to rebuke or punish him for what could be perceived as a disobedience of direct orders from the president by engaging the Spanish. In the end, Clay and his allies gained nothing but the enmity of Andrew Jackson, who never forgot or forgave an enemy.[3]

In truth, Jackson had fulfilled the private wishes of President James Monroe. Jackson's successful invasion had convinced Spain that she should dispose of the territory while still in a position to gain consideration for it. In February 1819, Spain turned over Florida to the United States, but it was not until two years later that a treaty was ratified. Those Native Americans who had fled into Florida to get away from the United States were now once again living in U.S. territory. To make matters even worse, Andrew Jackson—Sharp Knife—was appointed governor.

Actually, Jackson's appointment was a political payoff that could have been worse for the United States. When the military was downsized and Jackson was legislated out of the army, President Monroe was obliged to find a new position for the former major general. The president asked Thomas Jefferson about making Jackson minister to the court of the Russian czar. Jefferson replied that there was no question in his mind that Jackson, if appointed, would provoke an international crisis with the Russians within days or weeks. Monroe, who concurred with this assessment, had a quandary on his hands. The problem was solved, however, when Jackson was offered and accepted the governorship of Florida.[4]

White business speculators took advantage of the precarious situation of the vanquished Seminoles. They lied to the various bands, telling them that General Jackson was on the march with his army with intentions of either wiping out the Seminoles or driving them down to the balmy swampland at the southern tip of Florida. Many frightened people believed these lies and panicked. They sold their livestock and other goods to the speculators at absurdly low prices before disappearing into the interior to hide.

At the same time, white slave owners from Georgia and Alabama petitioned the U.S. government to make the Seminoles return all former slaves who were living with them, as well as call for the Seminoles to be moved out of Florida. They reasoned that once the Seminoles were gone, the slaves would no longer have a safe haven and therefore would not run away. The threat of removal—above any other rumor or demand—struck fear into the hearts of the Seminoles.[5]

Jackson indeed had already expressed his opinion that the Seminole—the Red Sticks who had fled during the Creek War of 1813–1814 in particular—should return to their Creek homeland to the north. "These Indians," Jackson wrote, "can have no claim to lands in Florida, humanity and justice is sufficiently extended to them by permission to return, and live in peace with their own nation." The general genuinely—and naïvely—believed that the displaced Creek Seminoles longed to return to their homeland and would gladly reunite with their northern brethren.[6]

There were others with knowledge of the Seminole people who differed with Jackson. Acting East Florida governor William Worthington, for one, voiced his opposition to Jackson's recommendation of removal of the Seminoles back to the Creek Nation. He wrote to Secretary of War John C. Calhoun that "if they are ordered up amongst the Creeks, they will take to the bushes."[7]

This was a wise assessment. Osceola and the young warriors would certainly resist any attempt by the army to herd their people north. It was the hot-blooded youth of every nation throughout history who would inevitably comprise the bulk of the military force and fight the wars on the front lines. The opportunity to become a soldier in battle was high on the list of manly endeavors for young men, especially Native American warriors who sought the glory and tribal honors that only war could provide. Osceola had been kicked around by the white man and White Stick Creeks throughout his childhood and had witnessed so much bloodshed and misery, it is likely that he would have welcomed a chance to test his skills as a warrior against his enemy, especially when the fate of his adopted tribe would be at stake.

Micanopy, the most prominent Seminole chief, however, decided to be proactive with the dilemma in an attempt to save his people from further destruction. He worried that any decision about their future would be made without their input if they simply ignored the situation and waited for the government to act. The chief made entreaties through two trusted white men to Jackson to meet and discuss a treaty. But the victor of Horseshoe Bend disregarded the "self made" Indian agents and passed the word that there would be no treaties during his tenure as governor. With no one to take up their cause, the Seminoles waited apprehensively for Jackson to take up arms against them. To their surprise, he didn't.[8]

The reason was that Jackson—this man of swift and ferocious action—had resigned his position in October 1821, only eleven weeks after he had assumed authority. Sharp Knife, who was greatly bothered by the heat and humidity, declared that his mission in Florida had been accomplished and that his health and that of his wife required that he return home to the Hermitage in Nashville. The Seminole could breathe a sigh of relief. Their tribal issues were by no means solved and their fate remained up in the air, but at least their nemesis, this man who had caused so much grief for them in the past decade, would not be coming after them to do more harm.[9]

There was a puzzling and interesting aspect to the treaty signed by the United States and Spain in 1821. One area that needed to be addressed by the U.S. government was contained in Article VI: "The inhabitants of the territories which his Catholic Majesty cedes to the United States, by this treaty, shall be incorporated in the Union of the United States as soon as may be consistent with the principles of the Federal Constitution, and admitted to the enjoyment of all privileges, rights, and immunities of the citizens of the United States."[10]

This provision would appear to mean that anyone living in Florida—red, black, or white—had been granted all the rights of citizens of the United States of America.

It was a given that blacks living with the Seminoles would never be invited to share in this citizenship. Southern whites would never tolerate freedom and citizenship for blacks living in Florida. After all, most of them were runaway slaves who had entered Florida illegally and could not even be considered legal residents of that territory. The blacks, however, had assimilated for the most part into the scattered Seminole bands—and in some cases were said to wield great power over those Seminoles—which offered them a tribal bond that engendered a sense of freedom.

The lifestyle of these Black Seminoles was not much different from that of their red hosts. Their Floridian culture typically combined white, Native American, and African influences, with African being the weakest. Surnames, if they chose to adopt one, were those of their Seminole masters or former owners—McGillivray, Micanopy, or McIntosh. First names were often English—Abraham, Sally, or Jack—with an occasional West African name, such as Cudjo or Juba. They would live in towns, raise crops, tend horses and cattle, hunt, fish, and often spin cotton. In fact, one theory suggests that the blacks were superior farmers, having come from coastal plantations in West

Africa or in the American South, and in some cases worked the crops while the Seminoles hunted, fished, and provided security. Most blacks also were quick to embrace Seminole spiritual beliefs—the Master of Breath, the corn dance, and other rituals—which were not that much different from various West African religious practices. There were those blacks who remained aloof and refused to accept the ceremonies and traditions of the Seminole Nation. These independent blacks, however, would assuredly ally with the Seminoles and the former slaves should it become necessary for survival.[11]

One anonymous eyewitness of the period described these Black Seminoles thus: "The Negroes, who dwell among these people as their slaves, are intelligent, speak the English language, and have great influence over the Indians. They fear being again made slaves, under the American government, and will omit nothing to increase or keep alive mistrust among the Indians, whom they in fact govern. If it should be necessary to use force with them, it is to be feared the Indians would take their part. It will, however, be necessary to remove from the Floridas this group of lawless freebooters, among whom runaway Negroes will always find refuge."[12]

This opinion indicated that the former slaves would, if necessary, fight for the right to remain in Florida, and more than likely the Seminole people would be incited to fight alongside them. This was a disconcerting scenario to those who were charged with breaking apart this red-black alliance. How were they to separate the blacks from the Native Americans when in truth about the only thing that separated them as tribal members was the color of their skin? And, with the inevitability of intermarriage, the reds and blacks would have blood ties of clan and family in addition to that of tribal allegiance.

The fate of Native American citizenship in Florida was addressed by President Monroe in his annual message in December 1822. He was of the opinion that Article VI of the treaty with Spain assuredly did not intend to make Native Americans citizens of this country. In fact, he declared, the Seminole tribe should be removed from Florida entirely or at least confined to a specific and much smaller area. Congress should open an investigation to study the matter and render a recommendation as soon as possible.[13]

The House of Representatives immediately established a committee, chaired by Thomas Metcalf of Kentucky, to make a determination with respect to Seminole citizenship. This committee evidently interpreted Article VI literally. It was the opinion of the committee that in accordance with the treaty, the Native Americans must be regarded as citizens of the United States. Further, the committee recommended that each Seminole family should be awarded a piece of land, which would serve to sever their tribal communal bond and introduce them to private ownership and enterprise. The Seminole would then be on the way to attaining the basics necessary for assimilation into white society.

This recommendation was perhaps meant to be fair and humane, but it did not take into consideration the bond of tradition and culture of the Seminole people. They would not easily betray who they were and where they had come from. These were descendants of an ancient race of people who took pride in their tribal identity and viewed their ceremonies and culture as sacred. And with respect to those newcomers who wanted to join the tribe? They deserved to share in this way of life if they so chose.

In the end, that was not the recommendation that the president, Congress, or the public wanted to hear. The committee's decision was summarily dismissed. There would be no blanket citizenship forthcoming for the Seminole Nation and other Native Americans in Florida Territory.[14]

Eventually, the consensus within government was that the best course of action would be to confine the Seminoles to a reservation. At the urging of Joseph M. Hernández, the territorial delegate to Congress from Florida—who in the future would play a major role in Osceola's life—Secretary of War Calhoun appointed a commission to hold talks with the Seminole for the purpose of concentrating them on a reservation of the government's choosing. The commission did have the authority from the beginning of negotiations to amend the treaty should the initial land grant be unsuitable for cultivation.[15]

At the same time, William Pope DuVal was chosen to succeed Andrew Jackson as governor of the Florida Territory. As a young man, DuVal, a Virginian of French descent, had left home to become a hunter in Kentucky. Like Jackson before him, he had abandoned a trade for the study of law, toiling long and hard to become a licensed lawyer. Perhaps his main claim to fame—other than his dealings with the Seminole—was that at some point he had come to the attention of Washington Irving. DuVal, who stood "five-foot-seven, with light brown hair and a round, humorous face had a gnomish look about him." He was an excellent teller of tall tales and loved to sing. Irving was fascinated by the man and wrote several stories in which DuVal—as the character Ralph Ringwood—was the protagonist.[16]

DuVal recognized that the Native Americans in Florida had been so wary of Jackson's army marching on them that many had not planted crops and were compelled to live on an insufficient diet of wild game and roots and berries. These people were starving and agitated—a dangerous combination, indeed. DuVal was aware that this discontent could lead to dire circumstances for everyone concerned if some sort of relief was not on the horizon.

The new governor also realized that the Native Americans were being preyed upon by unscrupulous whites seeking high profits at the expense of these downtrodden people. DuVal issued a proclamation that made it illegal for whites to purchase livestock or slaves from Native Americans without a special permit. Whites were also forbidden to reside or loiter near towns populated with Native Americans. As might be imagined, this edict made William DuVal extremely unpopular in Florida with a certain segment of society. Although the proclamation could not be enforced and violations were numerous, it sent a clear and welcome message to the Seminole that Governor DuVal was nothing like his predecessor. Perhaps there was hope that one day the Seminole could once again establish towns and plant crops and raise their families in peace, without white intervention.[17]

DuVal's next order of business was to arrange a meeting between representatives of the government and all Native Americans in Florida. This council was scheduled for November 20, 1822, at St. Marks. Unfortunately, through a series of miscalculations and departures—DuVal abruptly returned to Kentucky; another person fell ill; one man failed to arrive in Florida—the government was forced to cancel this meeting. Word of the cancellation was passed to the chiefs. None other than Chief Neamathla, who five years earlier had threatened General Gaines at Fort Scott, cordially assured the commission that the Seminoles would wait patiently and peacefully until the government could accommodate them. The chief's response demonstrated how desperate the Seminole people were for a new beginning.[18]

In the meantime, the powerful James Gadsden of South Carolina had joined the commission. Gadsden was a Jackson man, having served as an aide to the general on his invasion of Florida in 1818. He had attained the rank of colonel in 1820 and soon after gained an appointment to adjutant general. He had resigned from the service, however, when his appointment to that post was not confirmed by the Senate. It was glaringly evident that he was a quick-tempered, no-nonsense man cut from the same mold as Jackson.

Colonel Gadsden, for better or worse depending on which side your loyalties lay, became the driving force behind the commission. His first statement after setting a new date and time for the council was a warning that "those tribes who neglect the invitation, or obstinately refuse to attend, will be considered as embraced with the compact formed, and forced to comply with its provisions." This diplomat with the abrasive style of Jackson held a strong opinion that the Native Americans should be removed from Florida altogether, and he had attempted to persuade Secretary of War Calhoun to undertake that course of action. Calhoun agreed with the premise in principle, but for the time being there was nowhere to relocate the Seminole west of the Mississippi. Therefore, a treaty must be negotiated.[19]

The parley—called a "treaty of peace and friendship" by the U.S. government—was finally held in September 1823 on the north bank of Moultrie Creek, about five miles south of St. Augustine. The government estimated that at least fifteen hundred Seminoles would attend and shipped in three tons of rice to feed them. Many families, however, stayed home to tend to crops and livestock—or perhaps out of fear—and only about 425 people, mostly men, attended. Indian agent Gad Humphreys and interpreter Stephen Richards accompanied a party of 350 more than 250 miles to make certain they would not skip the negotiations. Needless to say, due to poor attendance there would be an abundance of rice left over.[20]

One of those present was Osceola. He would have traveled with those members of his band led by Chief Micanopy. The young warrior would not have participated in any formal aspect of the event, however, nor would he have been asked for his counsel. He would have remained with the other young men who lingered on the outskirts of the event to observe and learn and act as moral—and, if necessary, physical—support for the leaders.

A bark conference house had been constructed at the treaty site and was guarded by twenty-five soldiers and four officers from the Fourth Artillery who were on duty acting as infantry. This detachment served as the "show of force" that James Gadsden intended as an intimidation factor. The Seminoles, on the other hand, had not been specifically asked to disarm, but by some accounts might have left their weapons back in camp so as not to bring attention to themselves by the American military. The soldiers were a constant reminder of the brutal attacks that had wiped out towns and taken so many lives.[21]

Perhaps on account of his defiant attitude toward the white man in the past, the Seminoles elected Chief Neamathla as their principal spokesman. The tribe by no means enjoyed a cohesive society, yet this chief was well respected by all—and likely the only leader present who could exert authority over the various bands. Governor DuVal was certainly impressed by the fierce bearing of Neamathla, calling him the most remarkable red man he had ever seen. The chief has been described as having "long, wavy black hair, a broad nose, thin mustache, and a resolute but aggrieved countenance."[22]

The only surviving account of the first day of the treaty negotiations—September 6, 1823—was written by eyewitness Reverend Joshua Nichols Glenn of St. Augustine. Glenn, in the company of other townspeople, was lured to Moultrie Creek by curiosity about the assembled Native Americans, soldiers, and American officials.

Sat 6th, the Treaty with the Floriday Indians commenced to day in the morning Capt. Wm. Levingston his wife and Daughter Mr. and Mrs. Streeter and my Self went up to Moultry the place of holding the Treaty in a very comfortable Boat—accompanied by many other gentlemen and Ladies in other Boats—a little after we landed the Indians came from their Camps to the Commissioners Camp to Salute the Commissioners & hold their first talk this was quite Novel—the Indians came in a body with a White Flag—beating a little thing Similar to a Drum and Singing a kind of a Song and at the end of every apparent verse one of them gave a Shrill hoop—which was succeeded by a loud and universal Scream from them all—in this way they marched up to the Commissioners—when two of them their Birthday Suit and painted all over white with white sticks in their hands and feathers tied on them—came up to them (viz. the Commissioners) and made many marks on them—then their King Nehlemathlas came forward and Shook hands and after him all the chiefs in rotation—after which the King Smoked his pipe and then observed that he considered us gentlemen as fathers and Brethren and the ladies as Mothers and Sisters the Commissioners then conducted the chiefs into the bark house they had [built] to hold their talk in and after they had all Smoked together they held their first Talk—in the evening were returned to Town and the Governor was unwell he came with us.[23]

Commissioner Gadsden opened the conference at eleven A.M. by addressing about seventy chiefs and warriors inside the bark house. Gadsden did not mince words. He reminded the Seminole that General Jackson had defeated them on two occasions, and that the general could have driven all of them into the ocean had he chosen to do so. Nevertheless, the president, their "Great Father," was willing to forget about the transgressions of the past. But in return the Seminole would have to agree to be restricted to assigned territories rather than live anywhere they pleased around Florida.

Gadsden then told the assemblage, "Four years ago, the same Redsticks, with false prophets McQueen and Francis and bad men from across the water, poisoned the minds of some warriors. Friends and brothers: the hatchet is buried; the muskets, the white men's arms, are stacked in peace. Do you wish them to remain so? Listen then, to the talk of your father the President. He wishes the red stick eternally buried; he drinks with you the black drink; he exchanges with you the white feather; he unites with you in the feather dance and eagle tail song. He smokes with you the pipe of eternal peace."[24]

There could be no doubt in the minds of the Seminole chiefs that Gadsden was implying that force would be brought against them again if they did not agree to the demands of the government. And the soldiers drilling outside were ominous evidence of that possibility.

There was a two-day delay in the reply from Chief Neamathla for which official records fail to account. Perhaps this elapsed time was due to the illness suffered by James Gadsden that was alluded to at the end of Reverend Glenn's first-day account, or perhaps the Seminole were embroiled in an eternal rift while debating this threat of violence if they disobeyed the U.S. government. How far were they prepared to go to avoid war and appease their conquerors? What were they willing to relinquish in the name of peace? Where would they draw the line in the sand and refuse to comply? No doubt those two days in the Seminole encampment were highly volatile with many voices wanting to be heard and heeded.

Regardless of reasons for the delay, when the two sides did reassemble, Chief Neamathla let the governor know in no uncertain terms that the Red Stick Creeks that had joined their tribe were now full-fledged members. They could not betray their brethren and simply abandon them to save themselves. These former Creeks were now Seminoles and must be included in any disposition of the tribe.

This defiant statement received a stern warning from Gadsden. In fact, it became apparent that this unyielding answer, and possibly the other events of the day, none of which have been recorded, served to bring about a drastic change in the attitude of the Seminole. It was as if the tribe and its leaders had now resigned themselves to the notion that the United States was in complete control of their fate, and this realization had broken their spirit. At present, they just hoped to leave Moultrie Creek with a treaty that did not mean the end of their people or the expulsion of any of them.

Remarkably, Chief Neamathla, the man who had sternly ordered troops to stay away from his land when he ruled Fowl Town, had an unexpected change of heart. He now reacted with passivity toward his hosts and spoke with a humbleness that heretofore had been missing in his temperament during the proceedings. Neamathla exhibited a vulnerability that for all practical purposes removed any bargaining power he might have held. The chief begged the commissioners not to send his people to a reservation in the South where the soil was poor and where it was too close to the big water where the young men could be corrupted by bad influences.

He said in part, "We are poor and needy; we do not come here to murder or complain. . . . We rely on your justice and humanity; we hope you will not send us south, to a country where neither the hickory nut, the acorn, nor the persimmon grows. . . . For me, I am old and poor; too poor to move from my village to the south. . . . I am attached to the spot improved by my own labor, and cannot believe that my friends will drive me from it." The reference to the hickory and acorn was not merely symbolic. The Seminole derived necessary oils from these nuts.[25]

Whether this submissive posture by Neamathla reflected the wishes of the tribe or was merely a ploy developed by the chief alone—likened to throwing himself on the mercy of the court—cannot be determined. Sincere or not, this was definitely the direction in which the commissioners had hoped negotiations would turn.

It should be noted that Red Sticks were not the only ones residing with the Seminole that concerned the government. Neamathla was asked by the commissioners how many slaves, or Maroon Negroes, or half slaves were living in the Seminole towns. There were at least 800 former slaves—150 men—in Seminole towns according to a rough census the previous year. Neamathla, however, did not directly answer the question. He did list thirty-seven Seminole towns with a total of 4,883 inhabitants for the commissioners, but, curiously, omitted the town of Peliklakaha, which at the time was the main Black Seminole community.[26]

Oddly enough, there are no records of minutes of the talks at Moultrie Creek from September 12, 13, or 14. On September 15, the outline of the treaty was read to the Seminole, but nothing has been recorded about how the provisions were developed or how the Seminole reacted to them. In other words, it cannot be judged whether the treaty was an edict from the government or if an actual give-and-take negotiation took place. This silence, or concealment, continued on September 16 and 17 as well.

On September 18 it was recorded that the chiefs had signed the treaty. It was widely known that the most respected chiefs—Neamathla, Emathlochee, Econchatimico, Blunt, Mulatto King, and Tuski Hajo—adamantly refused to leave their lands and move south. Why then had these chiefs signed the treaty along with twenty-six others? The answer came on September 19 when an additional article was drawn up and signed. This article provided that the aforementioned six powerful and influential chiefs be awarded private reservations, and, wonder of wonders, these reservations of various sizes were located on roughly the same land that these chiefs at present occupied in the valley of the Apalachicola River. They would not be moving far to the south after all.[27]

Only one conclusion can be made from this final provision: the six chiefs had been personally bribed to sign the treaty for their people. In fact, the treaty commissioners informed the secretary of war that these six chiefs would not have signed the treaty without the "equitable provision." Dr. Rembert W. Patrick, former president of the Southern History Association, summed it up best: "In 1823 American commissioners bribed and intimidated the Seminoles into the Treaty of Moultrie Creek."[28]

The Seminole agreed to "relinquish all claim or title . . . to the whole territory of Florida, with the exception of such district of country as shall herein be allotted to them." The tribe would cede roughly 28,253,820 acres of land, and "be concentrated and confined" to a reservation, which covered 4,032,940 acres. The southern boundary ranged from the latitude of Tampa Bay toward Vero Beach on the east, with the northern boundary resting just above modern-day Ocala. The western boundary was to be no closer than fifteen miles from the Gulf of Mexico and twenty miles from the Atlantic Ocean. The location of this reservation away from the coasts was intentionally designed to prevent them or at least make it more difficult for them to trade with Cubans and others for arms, ammunition, slaves, and livestock. It was believed that they would be forced to concentrate on agriculture, which would eventually "civilize" them.

In return for ceding this land and settling on the reservation, the government promised to reward the Seminole with financial assistance, equipment, implements, livestock, and protection. They would receive $6,000 worth of livestock and agricultural equipment. They would be paid an annuity of $5,000 a year for twenty years. The government would make certain that unauthorized whites were kept off the reservation. Those Seminoles who would be required to move to the reservation would be provided with meat, corn, and salt for twelve months. The government would pay $4,500 for those who had to abandon improvements outside the reservation. A sum of $2,000 would be allotted for transportation to the reservation. An Indian agent, subagent, and interpreter would be appointed for the reservation. For twenty years, the Seminole would receive $1,000 a year to maintain a school on the reservation, along with $1,000 a year to pay for a blacksmith and a gunsmith. The treaty also provided that the Seminole agreed to prevent runaway slaves from taking refuge on the reservation, and they promised to capture any slave who tried to gain entry.

The total monetary consideration of the treaty can be calculated at about $221,000. This amount, when translated in payment per acre of the ceded land, comes to about 78/100 of a cent per acre—a steal even back 1823.[29]

With the signing of this treaty—whether they understood it or not—the Seminoles had given up any independence they might have had and were now entirely dependent on the United States. It was likely that the government viewed the treaty as a prelude to removing the Native Americans from Florida. If the Seminole or other tribes violated the terms of the treaty in even the slightest way, there would be sufficient justification to take away their land and ship them out west. Commissioner James Gadsden could puff out his chest and soak in the praise of Andrew Jackson for taking the hard line with these savages and putting them in their place.

Worst of all for the Seminoles, beyond the provisions of the treaty, was the betrayal by Chief Neamathla, who had accepted a bribe to sign the treaty. He would be permitted to remain on his land while other Seminoles not only would have to move but also were forbidden to ever again freely roam around Florida Territory. This act had not gone unnoticed by Osceola and other tribal members. The one man who could have united the Seminoles was now tarnished forever in the eyes of his tribe.[30]

Micanopy encouraged his people to abide by this treaty, but many Seminoles refused to leave the land they believed was theirs by birthright and tradition. To the government's dismay, only a little more than one thousand Seminoles actually moved to the reservation in central Florida.

It was no wonder that the Seminoles balked at leaving their homes. This reservation, set in the marshy Florida interior, consisted of land on which an experienced farmer would have difficulty raising a crop, and there were few animals to hunt. Even Governor William DuVal admitted that the land was "by far the poorest and most miserable region I have ever beheld." The tribe was on the brink of starvation. Desperate for food, they began to steal from neighboring white settlements. Cattle and other livestock that belonged to whites were regularly killed and butchered for food.[31]

Meanwhile, the Seminoles were outraged that white slave catchers were permitted to come onto the reservation to seize blacks, many of whom were married to Seminoles or had been born free and had never been slaves. In certain instances, whites would sell a black to a Seminole and then turn around and reclaim him or her as a runaway. Conversely, there were Seminoles who were forced to return runaway slaves to authorities or face having their precious rations withheld. Many former slaves were compelled to leave their Seminole towns and establish primitive camps in remote areas where they could not be easily found and captured. In spite of their new advantages in capturing their runaway slaves, white slave owners were still not satisfied with the cooperation of the Seminoles. They stormed the governor's office demanding that he more effectively enforce the terms of the treaty.[32]

Throughout Florida Territory, the entire populace—Seminoles, blacks, white settlers, slave chasers, and government troops—clashed over land, slaves, and food supplies. No one could live in security or conduct business as usual.

Travel by whites without armed protection, whether they were transporting goods or fleeing with their families, was brought to a halt. The Seminoles were hardest hit, however, and were aware that their lives and future existence as a tribe were in jeopardy, no matter how much they asked for justice to prevail. It would be necessary to find a permanent solution to this impasse soon or else risk a general uprising of Seminoles.

» *Four* «

Payne's Landing Betrayal

»◈«

During the 1820s, Osceola established himself as a highly respected warrior with his tribe. He and his band had conformed to government expectations and moved to the reservation, but his wanderings throughout the territory as a hunter brought him in contact with his own people as well as whites. He went out of his way to socialize at forts and settlements, and from all accounts he became known and respected by both races. It would not be out of the question to believe that he even picked up a little of the English language, although most historians express doubts about that possibility.

During this time of socialization, Osceola was known throughout the "white" world as "Powell," his birth surname. There are numerous references over the ensuing years to him as Powell, such as in official government reports and letters, and no evidence to indicate that he objected to its use. It cannot be determined whether this was the way he introduced himself to be more agreeable and in harmony with the whites with whom he was associated, or if people simply knew him by that name from his mother's lineage.[1]

At some point, Osceola was appointed to the position of tustenugge—the police chief or, in the time of war, the military leader—of his small band under the leadership of Chief Micanopy. He would work with the reservation's government agent to maintain order among Seminoles within and around their borders, which at times would require great diplomacy. There was also a possibility that Osceola had assisted the government as a guide when the boundary lines of the reservation were surveyed in accordance with Article 8 of the treaty.

At this time, Osceola came to the attention of Thomas L. McKenney, who had been involved in policing trading posts until being appointed to the head of the Office of Indian Affairs. McKenney wrote that "the mind of Asseola was active rather than strong, and his conduct that of a cunning and ambitious man, who was determined to rise by his own exertions. . . . His habits were active and enterprising."[2]

It might be imagined that the physical presence of Osceola in his prime of life was intimidating—that he was a hulking, muscular brute, with a fearful, scowling countenance and the glaring eyes of a wolf. Nothing could be further from the truth. Osceola has been described as slight, graceful, handsome, dignified, and composed.

Myer M. Cohen wrote, "His eye calm, serious, fixed—his attitude manly, graceful, erect—his rather thin and close pressed lips, indicative of the 'mind made up' of which he speaks—his firm, easy yet restrained tread—free from all stride or swagger—his dignified and composed attitude—his perfect and solemn silence."[3]

John T. Sprague, a contemporary army officer and historian, added, "In stature, he was about five feet eight inches, with a manly, frank, and open countenance."[4]

Paintings bear out this gentlemanly image of Osceola. Perhaps his rather passive appearance accounts for his never having been regarded as a fierce warrior in the same vein as Geronimo, Sitting Bull, or Cochise, whose portraits portray their hatred and militancy. Make no mistake about it, however: a fiery, passionate spirit burned within this Seminole warrior whose strong will and determination were destined to set Florida and the country aflame. One characteristic that has endured over the years is that, although said to be slight, Osceola was a physically powerful man who would try to move mountains if they stood in his way.

In 1824, Brevet Colonel George M. Brooke arrived in Tampa Bay accompanied by four companies of the Fourth Infantry Regiment. At the direction of James Gadsden, the colonel established Fort or Cantonment Brooke. The site chosen was a plot of land developed by Robert J. Hackney, with tall oaks, orange trees, and sprawling plantation buildings. Hackney, incidentally, was on vacation in Pensacola when the fort was built and would later sue the government over the confiscation of his property.

From his fort, Brooke studied the situation of the Seminoles and wrote to his commander in chief in Washington: "The Indians appear to me, to be more & more displeased at the Treaty, and I am not unapprehensive of some difficulty. They have an idea, that the nation, is about to go to war with Great Britain, and was it to be the case, they would most certainly join our enemy. In consequence of its having been reported to me that a large number of Indians were seen near the camp, after tattoo, who appeared to have an intention of taking us by surprise, the Troops were put under arms, and Continued so during the night, but no Indian was discovered."[5]

Brooke might have had good reason to be worried. At the same time, Governor William DuVal was receiving numerous reports that warriors under Chief Neamathla were raiding the countryside, killing cattle and hogs belonging to whites, and threatening to make war. DuVal decided to take immediate action. After hearing that three hundred armed, agitated warriors had assembled at Neamathla's town, he hurried there with only an interpreter. The warriors were there all right, and in a most foul mood. The feisty DuVal, however, faced them down and delivered a stern talk. He then ordered them to meet him for a serious parley at St. Marks on July 26 or face dire consequences.

This episode was written about in dramatic prose by Washington Irving in "The Conspiracy of Neamathla." In the story, DuVal—in an act of incredible or perhaps suicidal bravery—grabbed the chief by the throat and roughed him up in front of the stunned gathering of warriors, and then ordered them all to meet him at St. Marks. Whether Irving's story contains any truth cannot be known, except that the talk or the alleged physical attack worked. Six hundred warriors arrived in St. Marks for the parley.

At this meeting, DuVal claimed he personally replaced Neamathla as chief of the Seminole bands west of the Suwannee River with Tuckose Emathla, who was called John Hicks by the white man. This act—meddling with internal tribal affairs—which was illegal, was rebuked by Secretary of War John Calhoun. But the deed had been done. Former chief Neamathla eventually left Florida in disgrace to join the Creeks in Georgia. And no one in the Seminole tribe, including Osceola, shed tears at his leaving. Although the new chief John Hicks had signed the Treaty of Moultrie Creek, he was not one of the chiefs who had betrayed the tribe by receiving special favors for persuading the rest of the chiefs to sign.[6]

DuVal had pacified the Seminole only for the time being, however. Quite simply, the warriors were restless due to their miserable circumstances, and it was apparent they would not settle down until conditions improved. A severe drought had struck the reservation in 1825. No one could grow enough food or scavenge for edible plants and roots in sufficient quantities to feed their family, and wild game was virtually nonexistent. To make matters worse, the time limit for the issuance of rations promised in the Treaty of Moultrie Creek had ended. Hunger became so prevalent that people were actually dying from starvation. For that reason, there was much movement around the territory by tribal members—mainly men—who were seeking relief from this food shortage by whatever means necessary.

Acting governor George Walton sent a telling letter to Thomas McKenney in Washington while DuVal was temporarily out of the territory:

Many of these Indians, resident in the Reserve East of the Suwannee River, have recently abandoned their country; and I have received information that most, if not all, of those who formerly resided between the Rivers Suwannee & Appalachicola are on their return hither. They state to me as a reason for their return, that they have always been furnished with scanty supply of provisions only & which has sometime since ceased altogether; that they have no means of subsistence within themselves; that there is no game in their country; that it is moreover exceedingly unhealthy, exposing them to sickness and inevitable death; and in fine, that no part of the country allotted to them for a residence is of such a description as to afford them comfortable settlements; or of such a quality as will enable them either to have stocks or raise corn.[7]

The reason for the unrest of the Seminole also came to the attention of Colonel George Brooke at his fort in Tampa Bay. He was certainly sympathetic to the disaster unfolding within the territory, but he also feared for the safety of white settlers if the warriors were not able to feed their families. Brooke pleaded with Washington to allot additional rations to the starving Seminole. To its credit, Congress moved to appropriate more aid to the tribe, but it would never be enough to satisfy the need.[8]

Governor William DuVal conducted a tour of the reservation and was appalled by what he observed. Land that appeared to be fertile was covered by only several inches of topsoil before it gave way to a base of sand, and potable water was not readily available in many places. Although he regarded an area known as Big Swamp as being too wet for cultivation, he recommended that it be given to the Seminoles. In truth, Big Swamp had already been granted to the tribe for temporary use, and people—Osceola and his band included—had moved into this area.[9]

As the year 1826 progressed, the situation in Florida became more desperate and violent. Relations between the Seminoles and their white neighbors had deteriorated considerably. Cattle rustling, runaway slaves, starving people, robbery, and even murder had turned Florida Territory into a most dangerous place. Rum had been introduced to the tribe as a payment or trade item, which only served to exacerbate the original issues. Osceola in his role as a policeman was kept busy, not only apprehending wrongdoers but also attempting to make certain that justice was adjudicated fairly. The Seminoles were victims of a system that often blatantly favored whites.

The army became concerned with these unsettled conditions and acted in typical military manner by establishing another fort. Colonel Duncan Clinch, commander of military forces in Florida, ordered that Fort King be constructed near the reservation and Gad Humphreys's Indian agency, near present-day Ocala.

Set on a grassy knoll overlooking a forest and a lake, the fort featured an impressive twenty-foot-high stockade made of split logs with the flat sides turned inward. This sturdy stockade was rimmed near the top by a three-foot-wide platform, and a blockhouse stood at each corner. Another two-story blockhouse was built at the center of the compound, where a sentry was on duty at all hours and clanged a cowbell when anyone approached. Two companies under the command of Lieutenant James M. Classell were dispatched from Fort Brooke to garrison Fort King.[10]

Late in 1826—a time period chosen by deduction—an encounter of great significance in the life of the twenty-two-year-old Osceola took place. He was visiting a village near the Seminole agency when he spied a "particularly pretty" young girl of Creek ancestry. Her name was Che-cho-ter, or Morning Dew, and she was probably about fifteen years old. Whether it was love at first sight as romantics would design it cannot be determined. There can be no doubt, however, that Osceola was seriously smitten by this comely young lady.

Historians have generously described Morning Dew as being everything from remarkably beautiful to possessing a slim, magnificent figure. Unfortunately, no photo, painting, or drawing, not even a reliable eyewitness account, endures to confirm her beauty. Regardless of what historians might have perceived, Morning Dew was Osceola's choice as a girl with whom he wanted to share his life. He set in motion the procedures that would lead to his marriage to Morning Dew.[11]

The marriage, in the tradition of the Seminoles, would have been initiated with Osceola informing his relatives of his desire to marry the girl. His mother or another female relative would have contacted the women of the girl's family, who then would inform the girl's brothers and maternal uncles. Occasionally, her father might be consulted, but only as a courtesy. If the men had no objection, the prospective husband was given the go-ahead to marry the girl. Morning Dew also had the option of refusing Osceola, but she accepted the proposal. Osceola would then have presents delivered to Morning Dew through the women of his family. The marriage would become

official if she accepted his presents. There could have been a simple ceremony, such as sticking two reeds in the ground and then pulling them out
and exchanging them. Nevertheless, formal ceremony or not, Osceola had
taken Morning Dew as his wife.

The newlyweds, according to tradition, would live with the wife's family
until after the next crop was planted, and then they would establish their
own home. Contrary to popular myth, the Seminole wife was not chattel or a
domestic slave, as was the case in so many other tribes, but could be considered a person of value and worth regardless of her sex. The average white
woman would have worked just as hard and, surprisingly, had fewer rights
than her Seminole counterpart.[12]

One account worth repeating was provided by Joshua Giddings, the former eight-term congressman from Ohio and avowed abolitionist, who alleged that Morning Dew was black. He wrote that Osceola "had recently
married a woman said to have been beautiful. She was the daughter of a chief
who had married one of the Exiles; but as all colored people by slaveholding
laws are said to follow the condition of the mother, she was called an African
slave." There have been other stories characterizing Morning Dew as a former slave or asserting that her mother was a slave. None of these accounts has
been substantiated by historical data, which is not unusual given the time
period, language difference, and lack of record keeping. Accordingly, it cannot be dismissed that Osceola might have married a young lady of color.[13]

As fate would have it, Osceola and Morning Dew were not to live happily
ever after. White settlers, many of whom had lost farms in Georgia, Alabama,
and Tennessee, had been steadily migrating to Florida to make a fresh start.
Nicknamed "crackers" for the sound of the long bullwhips they cracked when
driving cattle, they resented the presence of the Seminoles and called upon
the government to tighten regulations on that tribe.

In January 1827, the Florida territorial legislative council, responding to
citizen demand, passed "An Act to Prevent the Indians from Roaming at
Large through the Territory." This law made it illegal for Native Americans to
leave the reservation for any reason. Any citizen who found a Seminole roaming outside the reservation boundaries could personally take custody of the

offender and drag him or her before a judge for sentencing. The mandatory sentence for disobeying this order was thirty-nine lashes and confiscation of their firearm. Officials at the Indian Office in Washington worried that whites would not take the criminal before a judge but would instead administer the punishment themselves. Nonetheless, this law—for the time being—satisfied a populace that had been victimized by theft from renegade Native Americans.[14]

One advocate for the Seminole tribe was the Indian agent Gad Humphreys. He had always given the Seminole the benefit of the doubt when trouble arose, which did not sit well with many settlers. At one point, the agent had been considered for impeachment by Governor DuVal for allegedly disobeying the provisions of the treaty and not aiding slave chasers enough in the return of their property. No one could say for sure that Humphreys had intentionally shirked his duty in those cases, however, and charges were not pressed.

For years, the sympathetic agent had helped secure additional rations for the reservation Seminoles whose provisions were inadequate to feed them. On various occasions over the years, Humphreys had been accused of condoning the Seminoles leaving the reservation to seek food, which was doubtless true. He was outraged when he heard about the new law punishing Native Americans so severely merely for being caught outside reservation boundaries. In addition, he had been told—whether true or not—that one Native American offender had been whipped to death by a citizen.[15]

Gad Humphreys immediately dashed off a letter to Indian Affairs superintendent Thomas McKenney in Washington: "Carry this law into effect and war in reality may be expected sooner or later to follow as a consequence: indeed, if I may take the word of a member of council, such consequence was calculated upon by that body, when the bill was under consideration. 'For,' said he, . . . 'it is found impossible to bring them to negotiate for a removal from the territory, and the only course, therefore, which remains for us to rid ourselves of them, is to adopt such a mode of treatment towards them, as will induce them to acts that will justify their expulsion by force.'"[16]

On a number of occasions, Osceola was called upon to hunt down and capture Seminoles who had ventured off the reservation and killed livestock owned by settlers. He would take the offenders back to the Indian agency rather than before a judge, where Gad Humphreys would adjudicate punishment. Osceola would reason with Humphreys and ask that the mandatory whipping be suspended and the renegade not be forced to relinquish the weapon he needed for hunting. The man's only crime was that he and his family had been hungry, Osceola would explain, which was why he undertook such drastic action all the while knowing the consequences. The victimized settler would be compensated by the tribe for his livestock, and the chiefs would punish the offender. Gad Humphreys would usually concur with this accurate assessment of the crime and the criminal, and release the offender to the custody of Osceola.

Meyer Cohen wrote, "By his [Osceola's] boldness and energy, he always succeeded in bringing them in to receive punishment, for the offences committed—latterly he would beg them off. The U.S. Officers as well as the Indians, all looked to Osceola to secure offenders—knowing his resolution and prowess. And for this purpose, as well as to restrain the Seminoles within their limits, he has taken more pains, and endured more fatigue, than any four of the Indians put together." Needless to say, these offenders were much better off when Osceola captured them than they would have been had they fallen into the hands of a white settler.[17]

Gad Humphreys—and even Governor DuVal—were willing once in a while to bend the law for humane reasons. They were aware of the suffering endured by the Seminole. People with little more than roots and the core of the cabbage palm to eat had starved to death. It was a time of great misery for these Native Americans who had made an effort to obey the treaty terms. An incensed Humphreys wrote a letter to DuVal that summed up his view of this tragedy unfolding on the Seminole reservation, and added, "Truly, this is the most extraordinary lesson in humanity for a civilized nation to place before a people who barbarism we so loudly and freely condemn."[18]

Over time, Indian agent Gad Humphreys became a polarizing figure in Florida. The Seminoles found in him a trusted ally who stood up for their rights, whereas the white populace despised him. He continued to be accused of failure to properly carry out treaty provisions by not always turning over runaway slaves to the owners or taking too much time in returning this human property. Humphreys denied the charges against him but made the mistake of admitting that he did not care for the policy. This confession brought additional charges that he profited from private transactions for slaves and livestock with the Seminoles, and that he had kept runaway slaves that had been turned in and had them working his own land instead of his seeking the rightful owners. DuVal and Humphreys clashed over these matters, and the governor eventually cut off communication with the Indian agent and requested a War Department investigation.[19]

Hearings were held by the new John Quincy Adams administration in St. Augustine over this issue of Gad Humphreys not returning runaway slaves to their owners in accordance with the Treaty of Moultrie Creek. Few people who had accused Humphreys of malfeasance attended, however. DuVal blustered that the Indian agent had somehow caused his accusers not to appear and testify against him. This assumption could be regarded as absurd. The white settlers wanted nothing more than to be rid of Humphreys. If there truly was an eyewitness who could speak against the Indian agent with testimony that would hold up under cross-examination, he or she would have been brought forth. In the end, the government investigator found no evidence to support the charges. Much to the chagrin of DuVal and the white Floridians, Humphreys had escaped punishment or dismissal.

Gad Humphreys, however, could not avoid controversy for long. Part of the 1828 annuity had been withheld from the Seminole by the government on the grounds that they had not returned all the runaway slaves living with the tribe to the proper owners. Humphreys pled the case for the Seminole, and Judge Joseph L. Smith ruled that the annuities could not be withheld. Humphreys had triumphed for the Seminole in this instance, but he would soon face a formidable challenge from the man who had always prevailed over the Seminoles and their allies—Andrew Jackson.[20]

In 1828, anti–Native American forces gained a friend in the White House when Andrew Jackson, the national war hero, was elected the seventh president of the United States. It would be Jackson who would decide the fate of

Gad Humphreys. Predictably, the president listened to his friend Colonel James Gadsden and finally in 1830 removed Humphreys as Indian agent for cause. The Seminoles' benefactor had been forced out not because of any proven wrongdoing but on account of his opposition to the policy of returning former slaves to their owners. Major John Phagan, who had been a sub-agent for the previous four years, was appointed to replace Humphreys.[21]

President Jackson, who viewed the Native Americans as an obstruction to progress not only in Florida but also throughout the Southeast, resumed the push begun by the Adams administration for the removal of the tribes to the West. In May 1830, Congress passed Jackson's Indian Removal Bill, which permitted the government to trade land in the West for Native American land in the East, and allotted $500,000 for that purpose. The bill passed by a slim 101-to-97 margin in the House and with slightly less opposition in the Senate.[22]

It can only be supposed what the Seminole thought about this Indian Removal Act. They had signed the Treaty of Moultrie Creek, which, according to their calculations, offered them at least twenty years of living on their present reservation—and only seven years had passed since the signing. Would the government break its solemn word and try to send them away to the West? The chiefs could not fathom such a betrayal.

In the subsequent two years, conditions on the reservation not only failed to improve but, in fact, the situation of the average Seminole family became markedly worse due to the migration of additional white settlers into the territory. These newcomers regarded the Indians as the primary hindrance between them and a prosperous life. The unfair competition for land and resources had rendered the Seminole people bitter and bewildered.

The Florida Legislative Council astutely summed up the circumstances faced by the Seminole in a petition to Congress that asked for removal of the tribe:

The Treaty of 1823 deprived them of their cultivated fields and of a region of country fruitful of game, and has placed them in a wilderness where the earth yields no corn, and where even the precarious advantages of the chase are in a great measure denied them. They are thus left the wretched alternative of Starving within their limits, or roaming among the whites, to prey upon their cattle. Many in the Nation, it seems, annually die of starvation; but as might be expected, the much greater proportion of those who are threatened with want, leave their boundaries in pursuit of the means of subsistence, and between these and the white settlers is kept up an unceasing contest.[23]

After two more years of continued crisis and misery, the Seminoles would face another challenge. Congress had finally provided enough funding to relocate eastern tribes to west of the Mississippi River. The government sent Colonel James Gadsden, who had negotiated the Treaty of Moultrie Creek, to meet in council with a delegation of Seminoles to discuss a treaty for their removal from Florida Territory.

Osceola was present when Micanopy and other chiefs arrived at Payne's Landing on the Oklawaha River northeast of Fort King (near modern-day Eureka) during the first week of May 1832.

Osceola attended not as a chief, negotiator, or councillor but rather in his role as a tustenugge, with thirty or forty warriors at his disposal to keep order if necessary. This contingent of Seminoles was said to have been positioned closest of any to Gadsden in the treaty room. The historian Meyer Cohen wrote that Osceola made a remark to the colonel that he, Osceola, was "like the white man," as if referring to his own white blood.

It is doubtful that Osceola would toady up to Gadsden or try to curry favor—and he surely would not admit that white blood flowed through his veins even if it were true. Gadsden was the man who had brought so much misery to the Seminole with the Moultrie Creek treaty. It is more probable that if Osceola made such a statement, it was a reminder to Gadsden that the Seminole warrior had thus far obeyed and helped to enforce the rules and regulations, but there was no guarantee that he would do so in the future. In other words, it might have been an attempt by Osceola at a mild form of intimidation.[24]

In any event, Osceola's veiled threat, if it was indeed intended to be that, would have been meaningless. What actually occurred at Payne's Landing endures as a matter of dispute to this day but stands as a shameless act nonetheless. Oddly enough, no official record of the proceedings was kept, although a secretary was paid $5 a day to record the minutes. The name of the secretary, Douglas Vass, appears on the signed treaty, even though he had not been hired to sign, only to write an account of the day-to-day business, which he obviously did not do. Vass even had three interpreters to assist him—Stephen Richards, who was a veteran of Moultrie Creek, and two blacks from the Seminole tribe, Abraham and Cudjo. Still, there was no written daily chronicle of discussions or events. Erastus Rogers, the agency sutler, also served as a witness, as did Indian agent John Phagan, two other unnamed men, and a citizen, B. Joscan. The names of every chief and subchief in attendance also were never recorded.[25]

Colonel James Gadsden, who would be the lone negotiator, had one mission to accomplish. He had to persuade the Seminole to relinquish their present territory in Florida and move west of the Mississippi, where, he would tell them, they could sustain themselves. There was one huge problem with this notion: the Seminole would be moving onto a part of the Creek Nation and sharing that land with their enemy. This was, of course, a grievous insult to the Seminole. These were the same Creeks who had allied with the Americans in the Creek War and again in 1818 when Jackson had invaded Florida. In addition, the Creeks had been raiding Seminole settlements over the years and stealing former slaves. Now the Seminole people were being asked to renounce their identity and for all intents and purposes become Creeks.

The Seminole chiefs also questioned the need for another treaty when the Treaty of Moultrie Creek, according to them and the words on the paper, was in effect for twenty years, the term for which it said they would be provided. The rationale of Gadsden and Jackson, however, was that the Seminole people were in such desperate circumstances that they would agree to just about anything in the hope of alleviating their suffering.[26]

The preamble to the treaty was the primary stipulation; all other articles went into effect only after this requirement had been fulfilled. The Seminoles would send seven of their "confidential chiefs" west to inspect the lands they would be moving onto, and "should *they* [emphasis mine] be satisfied with the character of that country, and of the favorable disposition of the Creeks to reunite with the Seminoles as one people," then the entire treaty would be binding to all parties. The Seminoles would depart Florida within three years, with one-third of the population going west in each of those years.

Additional articles provided for annuities promised in the Moultrie Creek treaty to be paid plus an additional $3,000 a year, but this amount would be added to Creek annuities and divided between the two members of the Creek Confederation. Also, the government would generously pay the Seminoles about $80,000 to purchase their four-million-acre reservation in Florida— 2 cents an acre.

It seems absurd that even one chief would agree to touch the pen to such a preposterous and outrageous treaty. On May 9, 1832, however, the Treaty of Payne's Landing was signed by the seven chiefs and eight subchiefs present.[27]

How could this signing have happened? Did the Seminole signers actually know to what terms they were agreeing as explained by Abraham, the interpreter? Did the chiefs and subchiefs truly understand the intent of the preamble, the one stipulation that triggered the rest of the treaty articles, or were they desperate to give their tribe a new beginning elsewhere? Move west away from Florida? Join the Creeks? How could a proud people like the Seminole have consented to those provisions under any circumstances?

It becomes quite apparent that the chiefs and subchiefs did *not* know what they were signing. Evidence points to the fact that they had been deceived— perhaps, as some historians have suggested, by one of their own.

The likely culprit who could have betrayed the Seminole was a trusted and strong leader among the tribe—the black interpreter Abraham—and, to a lesser degree, Cudjo. Could it be that Colonel Gadsden had persuaded the interpreters to knowingly alter the meaning so that the chiefs did not know the intent of the preamble?

Major Ethan Allen Hitchcock, who was not present but interviewed those who attended, wrote in his diary that Abraham had purposely misrepresented the preamble to the treaty to the chiefs. The interpreter had changed the wording so that the Seminole had no idea they would be required to leave

Florida anytime soon. The tribe expected to remain on their present reservation at least until the twenty-year limit provided for in the Treaty of Moultrie Creek had expired. Hitchcock had been informed of this governmental treachery by Captain Charles M. Thurston, a West Point graduate, who was present during a conversation about the matter between President Jackson and James Gadsden.[28]

Why would Abraham, a respected and trusted man, betray his own people? Abraham had been born to slave parents in Pensacola around 1790. He had escaped his original master during childhood and at some point became slave to Chief Micanopy. He was emancipated in 1826 after serving as an interpreter for a Seminole delegation that had visited Washington, where he had distinguished himself with his "conspicuously polished manners. Tall and sparely built, he had a courtly manner and a clear, fluent, genteel style of speech. His smiling, intelligent face, however, was marred by a badly crossed right eye." Abraham was said to have married Hagan, the widow of Billy Bowlegs, and moved easily between Seminole and white society, which—along with his close relationship with Micanopy—was the reason he exercised great power within the tribe.[29]

On the surface, it would appear that the reason for this betrayal by Abraham was not a great mystery. It was spelled out in Article 2 of the treaty. Abraham and Cudjo would receive $200 each when the tribe arrived in the West. Few treaties single out individuals for special treatment unless there is quid pro quo involved. The Treaty of Moultrie Creek had provided reservations for certain chiefs, but only if they signed the treaty and encouraged others to do so as well. Had Abraham been bribed as well?[30]

Two hundred dollars was not a huge fortune at the time—certainly not enough for someone of esteem to betray lifelong friends and the tribe responsible for his freedom. This poses the theory that perhaps even Abraham, although he could read and write English, was unaware that his translation was faulty. Surely he did not desire to move west into Creek Territory where his status would change for the worse. There was a good chance that he would be taken by the Creeks or whites as a runaway slave or enslaved merely because of his color.

A close examination of the evidence provides a probable answer to this mystery. Major Hitchcock apparently chose Abraham as the guilty party by a process of elimination. The major simply could not bring himself to believe that either Gadsden or Phagan would participate in such treachery. Given his "Jacksonian" personality, hatred of the Seminole, and the need to remove the tribe from Florida as soon as possible, it stands to reason that Colonel James Gadsden—and not Abraham—should shoulder the blame for any misinterpretation, intentional or otherwise. Further, it should be noted that neither the chiefs nor the tribe members ever accused Abraham of being unfaithful as a result of this treaty. Abraham has been condemned in some quarters throughout history, but he was likely innocent of any intentional wrongdoing.[31]

On the seedy side of the ledger was another dark and deceitful blot—an apparent conspiracy between the government and land speculators. The Treaty of Payne's Landing, according to Major Hitchcock, had already been drawn up with specific land designations before the proceedings began. It had been Gadsden's job simply to get it signed—by any means possible. There was an urgency to removing the Seminoles from the area known as the Big Swamp—Osceola's home—as quickly as possible. This intention was later explained in a letter from John H. Eaton, the territorial governor of Florida to then-Secretary of War Lewis Cass: "The Big Swamp, which in the treaty is declared to be the first of their country to be vacated, . . . is that on which the eyes of the speculators are fixed."[32]

It now becomes evident why minutes of the treaty meetings were not kept or were destroyed. The fact that the government was in concert with private speculators who could not wait to get their hands on that prime real estate was not something any of the involved parties would want made public knowledge.

It was not only the government and the land speculators but also the common people of Florida who were pleased to know that the "savages" would soon be leaving for the West. One person, however, who was not on the side of those who wanted the Seminole to emigrate was former Indian agent Gad Humphreys. He had settled near the reservation, opened a trading post, and maintained his friendly relationship with the people. In the following years, Humphreys, who had made a habit of being a thorn in the side of the government, would be rightfully accused of encouraging the Seminole to resist moving.[33]

The Seminole chiefs who took part in the council—Micanopy in particular—would later assert that their signatures had either been forged or were the result of chicanery. They alleged that they had assuredly *not* signed a treaty calling for the tribe to leave their present land. The paper on which they made their marks and the treaty now explained to them were two different documents entirely. But disagreements and disputes between whites and Native Americans traditionally have always gone the way of the whites.[34]

Regardless of protests from the chiefs, the government had in its possession a signed treaty stating that a delegation of Seminoles would tour a section of the Creek reservation in the West and consider relocating to these lands. According to that treaty, if the new location was acceptable to the delegation members, the tribe would be out of Florida within three years.

In October 1833, seven Seminole chiefs—Jumper, Charley Emathla, Coa Hadjo, Holata Emathla, John Hicks, Nehathoclo, and Yahadjo—in the company of Indian agent John Phagan and their faithful interpreter, Abraham, set out for the land promised them—the promised land—in Creek territory. The entourage traveled by boat to New Orleans, then by steamer up the Mississippi and the Arkansas rivers to a point about two hundred miles below Fort Gibson. They rode by horseback to Fort Gibson, located near the present-day city of Muskogee in the eastern part of Oklahoma. They met with Indian commissioners Monford Stokes, Henry L. Ellsworth, and John F. Schermerhorn, who were waiting there to ensure the warmest of welcomes with gobs of gifts, such as tobacco, blankets, colorful cloth, and beads.[35]

The Seminole chiefs spent five weeks examining the region on horseback. They were more accustomed to the tropical heat and lush vegetation of Florida, and found this winter landscape cold and uninviting. In addition, the Creeks, on whose land they would be settling, had demonstrated an outward hostility toward the visiting Seminoles—as had the Pawnee and Comanche to the southwest. The only reason the Creeks entertained the idea of sharing land with the Seminoles was a treaty between that tribe and the government that stipulated that the Creeks would control the Seminole annuities—in addition to exerting control over the Seminole blacks.[36]

The seven chiefs voiced their displeasure with the land, the weather, and their prospective neighbors to the commissioners at Fort Gibson. The commissioners were unsympathetic with the negative assessment. On March 28, 1833, the seven chiefs were presented with what has been called the Treaty of Fort Gibson. This document stated that the chiefs were "well satisfied" with the land, and the Seminoles "shall commence the removal to their new home, as soon as the Government will make arrangements for their emigration. . . ."

In the preamble to the original Payne's Landing treaty, there was a question about the interpretation of the word "they" when referring to the delegation of chiefs who would be inspecting the western lands. The whites believed that "they"—the signers—had full power to obligate the entire tribe to the treaty. But that was not the Seminole way. The tribe had not designated a leader or leaders for that treaty negotiation, and more than twenty important chiefs had not signed. According to Seminole tradition, the various bands would have to consent to any treaty before it was ratified by the tribe.

In this new Fort Gibson treaty, the wording of that passage had been changed to read: ". . . and should *this delegation* [emphasis mine] be satisfied with the character of the country." No record exists to identify who was responsible for this change in wording. The change might have been promoted by Indian agent John Phagan, who knew more than the commissioners about Seminole culture and also had much to gain personally with the move. In the second-to-last paragraph of the Fort Gibson treaty, Phagan was appointed by the commissioners to facilitate the move of the tribe, which would afford him access to the considerable amount of money involved.

Remarkably, despite their objections to that Western real estate and protestations that they could not sign for the entire tribe, the marks of the seven chiefs appear on the treaty.[37]

How could this have happened—again? It would have been assumed that the chiefs would have learned by now not to sign anything until going into council with the tribe.

The only logical explanation can be found in the diary of Major Ethan Hitchcock. He confirmed that the chiefs had refused to sign because they did not possess the authority to speak for the tribe. It was then that Major Phagan interceded and addressed the Seminole. He warned that either the chiefs signed the statement saying they were well satisfied with the territory and would move their people there—or they would not be allowed to return to Florida. This threat struck fear into the hearts of the seven chiefs. After much deliberation and with great reluctance, the chiefs made their marks on this new document.[38]

The Indian commissioners at Fort Gibson ignored the protests of the Seminole chiefs and traveled to Washington with their signed treaty in hand. The agreement was unanimously ratified by the Senate in April 1834. It was now official: the Florida Seminoles would be removed to Arkansas Territory in the Trans-Mississippi Far West.

The Seminole delegation returned to Florida unable to adequately explain to the tribe why they had signed this new treaty, which brought upon them much ridicule and contempt. Several of the chiefs swore they had never signed, that their marks had been forged. Others claimed they believed that the tribe would not be bound by this treaty because it had not been presented to every chief. Regardless, these chiefs lost respect and authority within the tribe, which, combined with the desperate condition of the people, served to create additional unrest.

In November 1833, John Hicks, the head chief—a man who had lost the respect of his people for his signing of both the Payne's Landing and Fort Gibson treaties—passed away. He was replaced by Micanopy, who became the highest-ranking chief according to heredity. This change brought Osceola closer to the throne of power. He had been the loyal tustenugge of Micanopy's band and no doubt could now exert great influence over the chief when necessary.

Soon after the Fort Gibson fiasco, an investigation into the finances of the tribe was undertaken by the government. The target of the inquiry was none other than Major John Phagan. The agent was accused of altering vouchers from merchants, with the difference going into Phagan's pocket. Acting

Governor James D. Westcott determined that there indeed had been fraud committed and garnished Phagan's paycheck to reimburse the government. Such investigations were usually political in nature, however, and this one was no exception. Phagan had come to the attention of Florida territorial delegate Joseph M. White after the agent allegedly declared that he would not hire anyone who had voted for White. The outraged delegate charged that Phagan was unfit to serve as Indian agent and called upon his political allies to have him removed. Major John Phagan, who never admitted to either transgression, could not withstand the political heat and was dismissed from his post.[39]

Perhaps the real reason for the firing was that Phagan had apparently become a liability to those in power, who then exploited his greed for their own devious purposes. He had allegedly manipulated the signing of the Treaty of Fort Gibson for the opportunity to handle the removal funds. His dismissal meant that there would be one less credible witness who could testify against the government in treaty matters.

The successor to Phagan was Wiley Thompson, who had served with Andrew Jackson during the Creek War. He was often referred to as "General" due to his service between 1817 and 1824 as a major general in the Georgia militia. Before his appointment to Indian agent at $1,500 a year, Thompson had represented Georgia in the House of Representatives for twelve years. Although known as an honest man, right from the start of his tenure he tried to conceal from the Seminole chiefs the fact that the tribe would soon be moving west to live alongside their enemy.

Privately, however, Thompson related his apprehension about the future of the Seminoles to Thomas McKenney, the commissioner of Indian affairs. The agent believed that if the tribe was moved to the West they would become enslaved by the Creeks, and if they remained in Florida they would be enslaved by the whites. Indeed, he wrote, many blacks who had been born and reared among the Seminoles, and who had never been slaves, already had been taken and enslaved by the people of Florida and Georgia.[40]

This dire assessment by the Indian agent was the exact fate that faced the Seminole as they entered the year 1835. Most rank-and-file tribe members continued to believe that they had been betrayed by the government and, further, that the delegation of chiefs had not been authorized to speak for the entire Seminole Nation. As rumors that their removal from Florida was forthcoming, they began to raise their voices in protest within the reservation towns.

Osceola had up until now shown only moderate interest in the events that were so deeply affecting his nation. He had obediently relocated to the reservation in central Florida, settling there among his fellow Creeks to live a quiet life. He was the father of a daughter, the first of his four children with Morning Dew. And, as Chief Miconapy's tustenugge, he had, in essence, been helping the government enforce its policies. But the discussion among his fellow tribe members about what had transpired at Payne's Landing and Fort Gibson had apparently struck the chord of revolt in Osceola. Virtually overnight, he made the decision to turn against the U.S. government. He commenced secretly rallying his fellow Seminoles around the cause of resistance.

Osceola threw himself into his new role with a fury and did his best to persuade Micanopy and the other Seminole leaders that the United States was following a course that would lead to the annihilation of their people. He stressed the fact that the Black Seminoles undoubtedly would be seized and returned to slavery either when the tribe assembled for its migration west or after they had arrived. Micanopy became convinced that Osceola's fears and opinions were well-founded. Although relations with the whites progressed as usual, Micanopy and his allies surreptitiously prepared to wage war rather than abandon their homeland for resettlement among the hostile Creeks.[41]

On April 23, 1835, Indian agent Wiley Thompson summoned all the Seminole chiefs and leaders, including Osceola, to Fort King for a parley. Duncan Clinch, now a brevet brigadier general, a huge, intimidating man weighing 250 pounds, also attended this meeting, while waiting outside were about 130 troops. It was the job of Thompson and Clinch to impress upon the chiefs the necessity of their orderly removal to the West.

Micanopy did not attend this meeting, claiming that he was ill. The absence of this most influential chief raised the ire of Wiley Thompson. He called Micanopy lazy, fat, and old, and accused the chief of shirking his responsibility to his tribe.

Thompson had a statement translated and read aloud by Cudjo that summarized the provisions of the Fort Payne and Fort Gibson treaties. This document stated that the chiefs "voluntarily acknowledge the validity" of those treaties and "freely and fully assent to" all their "provisions and stipulations." For the first time the true purpose of these treaties that had been carefully concealed from the chiefs became shockingly clear. They would be required to move west *now,* not after the term of the Moultrie Creek treaty. The rumors had been true. Certain chiefs had apparently signed two agreements that could doom the Seminole Nation to leave Florida. Chief Jumper, who was Micanopy's brother-in-law and a most respected man among his people, rose and spoke for the tribe. He was an accomplished orator and held the floor for quite some time. His meaning was clear: Jumper declared that the Seminole people had no intention of leaving Florida.[42]

Thompson hinted that an additional annuity might be paid to sweeten the pot for the tribe to move. In his estimation, this dangling carrot was a powerful motivation. The Seminoles had endured another hard winter and many of them were starving. Before they could receive any more money, however, they would be required to sign the contract reaffirming their acceptance of the two treaties. Thompson ordered them to step forward one by one and sign this new document as a show of good faith.

Eventually, eight chiefs reluctantly made their marks on the document, but four—Jumper, Alligator, Fuch-ta-lus-ta-hadjo (Black Dirt), Arpeika (Sam Jones)—would not sign.

General Clinch warned the rebellious chiefs in no uncertain terms that if they did not agree to the treaty, the might of the U.S. military was ready and willing to force them to comply.

The four chiefs still refused to make their marks on the document.

Wiley Thompson, usually the consummate diplomat, was provoked to anger. He rashly declared that the five chiefs who would not sign—he included the absent Micanopy in that number—no longer represented the Seminole Nation. He emphasized his decision to remove these chiefs by grabbing his pen and slashing it across a paper five times as if crossing out their names.

This illegal and outrageous act by Thompson caused an uproar among the assembled Seminole that was eventually quelled by the eight chiefs who had signed the document. These men restored order and then made a request of Thompson. Could the government postpone the departure of the tribe until at least January 15, 1836, so that they could harvest their crops in Florida and arrive out west in time for spring planting? The Indian agent magnanimously agreed, now confident that he had convinced the tribe to accept their fate.

This betrayal of the Seminole people was too much to bear for one observer. Osceola rose to his feet and strode forward. In dramatic fashion, he stunned the onlookers by removing his knife from its sheath and viciously plunging the blade into the treaty paper. Osceola reportedly vowed, "This is the only treaty I will make!"[43]

» *Five* «

Osceola Declares War

»❖«

Great controversy swirls to this day around the question of whether Osceola actually stabbed his knife into the treaty document. This act certainly ignites that romantic vision of bold defiance from which legends are born. But sparse evidence can be found to confirm that he actually did stab that piece of paper. Although numerous historians and authors have repeated the story as fact, there is room for skepticism, not only about whether the act actually happened but also about what document may actually have been damaged by Osceola's knife blade.

There was allegedly only one eyewitness to an incident where Osceola brandished a knife, and this account may be suspect, inasmuch as the author has remained anonymous and identified himself only as "Viator."

I recollect once to have seen him [Osceola] on the piazza of the officers' quarters [at Fort King], whilst Micanope, the ostensible Chief of the nation, was closeted with General Clinch, in his office, which opened upon the stoop. Micanope is . . . ever a stupid fool, when not replenished by his "sense-bearer," (as he calls him) Abraham, who was on the present occasion absent. Osceola knew well this, and therefore, it was, that he betrayed the anxiety he did, to be near Micanope, to give him the proper cue for a non-commitment. He would stand in the door apparently in the attention of an eaves-dropper; then he would be peeping into this and then into that window; ever assuming that peculiar air of curiosity, discernible only in the Indian. Becoming more and more impatient of his exclusion from the conference, he suddenly stalked across the stoop, jerked out his knife, and flourished it around his head with the most savage vehemence. Never have I seen a more striking figure than he presented at that time.[1]

The first mention of Osceola's knife penetrating the treaty document came five years later, in 1841. The British author Andrew Welch wrote a sensationalized story in which Osceola's knife blade not only stabbed the treaty paper but went straight on through the table as well. Several years later, Thomas Storrow wrote in *Knickerbocker Magazine* that Osceola's knife was savagely driven into the "midst" of the paper. This account has similarities to the one recounted by John T. Sprague in 1848, except that this contemporary army officer contended that Osceola thrust his knife into the table, and no mention was made of striking the treaty paper. Perhaps Sprague read the story in the *Army and Navy Chronicle* in 1836, or he could have even personally known and conversed with the mysterious "Viator." [2]

Another military man of the period, John Bemrose, claimed to have seen a report of an incident between Osceola and Wiley Thompson at Fort King that occurred in June 1835. The report stated that Osceola "broke out with ungovernable rage, drawing his knife, which he brandished in a threatening manner." The date of the episode in Bemrose's account was not far from the rumored April stabbing of the treaty document, and it does serve to confirm the other account that Osceola at some point had pulled his knife at the fort and displayed it in a threatening manner.[3]

A more modern researcher, Mark Boyd, claims, "There is a break in the copy of the Treaty of Fort Gibson in the National Archives, and an attached note which describes the 'lateral crack or tear' as the 'mark of Osceola's knife.'"

No such claim has been made about the Treaty of Payne's Landing or the document presented to the chiefs to sign by Wiley Thompson in April at Fort King.[4]

Perhaps the line spoken by a newspaperman in the 1962 motion picture *The Man Who Shot Liberty Valance* applies to this incident. Jimmy Stewart in his role as Ransom Stoddard, the lawyer elected to the U.S. Senate after the public believed that he had shot and killed notorious badman Liberty Valance, explained to the newspaperman that it was Tom Doniphon, the character played by John Wayne, who had actually shot Valance. The newspaperman, although realizing he now had the truth, refused to make public Stoddard's version of events. He burned his notes and said, "When the legend becomes fact . . . print the legend." Stoddard, not Doniphon, would forever be known as the man who shot Liberty Valance.

Accordingly, the printed legend endures—Osceola thrust his knife into the treaty document presented by Indian agent Wiley Thompson and defiantly stated, "This is the only treaty I will make!"—or words to that effect.

This legendary stabbing of the document, if it indeed occurred, could have been the only one or one of a series of personal disputes between Osceola and Wiley Thompson that might have brought their relationship to a breaking point and resulted in Osceola's incarceration.

Joshua Giddings wrote that Osceola was on a trading visit to Fort King with Morning Dew when a white slave chaser allegedly captured the woman, claiming that she was a runaway. Osceola was incensed when he discovered that his wife was missing and had to be restrained. This story for all intents and purposes has been dismissed as fiction by Kenneth Porter.[5]

In another inflammatory situation, the Seminole people had been buying up large quantities of guns and ammunition during the winter and spring, which concerned authorities. Consequently, Thompson banned the sale of these items to Seminoles. Up to that time, it had been illegal to sell ammunition, powder, and shot to slaves. Osceola allegedly confronted Thompson and proclaimed, "Am I a Negro? . . . A slave? My skin is dark, but not black. I am an Indian—a Seminole. . . . I will make the white man red with blood;

and then blacken him in the sun and rain, where the wolf shall smell his bones, and the buzzards live upon his flesh."[6]

Apparently Osceola also had a habit of visiting Wiley Thompson's office and verbally abusing the Indian agent about various grievances. Thompson sent off a letter to the commissioner of Indian affairs that stated, "Powell [Osceola] used such language, that I was constrained to order him into irons."[7]

Regardless of whether there were stab wounds in documents, or a wife who was captured by slavers, or a protest over the prohibition of the sale of ammunition, or simply a pattern of verbal abuse by Osceola, the result was that at some point Thompson ordered his guards to seize the Seminole warrior and place him in irons.

Osceola was dragged out of the agent's office and taken to the fort's guardhouse. Thompson knew that to a Seminole—or any Native American, for that matter—confinement was the worst form of degradation. Being locked up for any offense was virtually nonexistent in Native American culture. An offender might be banished from a camp or suffer some other form of punishment but never incarcerated. But Wiley Thompson believed that his credibility with the tribal leaders would be weakened if he allowed Osceola to challenge him with impunity. The agent informed the outraged warrior that he would remain in confinement until he promised to control his explosive behavior.[8]

Osceola was furious and fought his guards like a wild animal. He shouted curses and threats, and trashed his cell. He was a proud warrior—a tustenugge—and was not accustomed to such disrespectful and scurrilous treatment, especially by a white man.

Over time, however, Osceola became perceptive enough to realize that he could be of no help to his people while locked up in the guardhouse. After two days—with the advice and then intervention of friendly chiefs—he sent for Thompson. He told the agent that he regretted losing his temper and apologized for his bad behavior. He promised that, if released, he would return within five days with his band and sign the treaty agreement to show his good faith. Thompson agreed to grant Osceola his freedom under those terms.

True to his word, Osceola came back to the agent's office, accompanied by seventy-nine followers, and made his mark on the Fort King agreement.

Wiley Thompson was thrilled with the transformation and welcomed this influential warrior back into the ranks of Seminoles to be trusted. He wrote, "I now have no doubt of his sincerity."[9]

Osceola, with sly and cunning intentions, had outwardly done his best to convince Thompson that he would comply with the treaty and accept removal. In a show of contrived friendship, Osceola even invited soldiers to visit his home—called "Powell's Town" by the whites—along the nearby Withlacoochee River (near present-day Lake Tsala Apopka). Thompson was delighted with the perceived change of heart of this influential young leader. As a reward for Osceola's cooperation, Thompson gave the warrior a silver-plated Spanish rifle, a firearm far superior to the muzzle-loading flintlocks that were standard army issue of the day.

Osceola realized that he must play the role of a "good Indian" for the whites at the fort and curry favor with the authorities. His outbursts would only bring punishment and scrutiny that would prevent him from freely coming and going without suspicion. But he would never forget the humiliation that he had endured by the imprisonment at the hands of Wiley Thompson. The Indian agent now became the sworn enemy of Osceola. And during this period of make-believe conciliation, Osceola would be secretly preparing for war.

It would seem that Osceola had a real hatred for the white man, but that was not necessarily the case. He apparently had struck up a close friendship with John Graham, an officer at Fort King. It was reported that Osceola and Graham, a Pennsylvanian who had graduated from West Point, were seen together daily at the fort. Myer Cohen wrote, "It seems that Powell has a little daughter, to whom Lt. G was kind, and presented with frocks, in which the young girl, who grew very fond of him, always insisted on being dressed, whenever she perceived Lieut. G. (for whom she often looked out) coming to visit her." It is not known if this little girl was the basis of the friendship between the army officer and the Seminole warrior. The relationship, however, became much closer than merely conversation about a child and would endure for the rest of Osceola's life.[10]

It was about this time that Osceola married a second wife. Polygamy was commonplace among the Seminoles. The second wife occasionally lived in a separate dwelling, but, in contrast to the Creek wives who would usually live apart, more often than not the two wives lived together in perfect harmony with no bad feelings whatsoever toward each other. Osceola would have had to ask and receive consent from Morning Dew before marrying this other woman. If he failed to receive that permission, the first wife's clan could have both Osceola and his new wife punished for committing adultery. Divorce was an option, but it happened rarely due to the responsibility of raising children. In the case of a divorce, the children and all possessions became the property of the wife.[11]

Little is known about Osceola's second wife—not even her name—although it has been written that she was the sister of Morning Dew. An account by Joshua Giddings published in an antislavery magazine in 1837, which was close to the time period, asserted that she was at least part black, either a former African slave or a descendant of a runaway who had taken up residence with the Seminole. Joshua Giddings, the former schoolteacher, lawyer, and congressman, was a known abolitionist whose concern for the Seminole slaves has caused some respected historians, such as Kenneth Porter, to question his accuracy. Porter does admit, however, that "it should be kept in mind that, whether or not Osceola had a part-Negro wife, Seminole Indians did have wives of Negro blood."[12]

Another reason for confusion over the race of Osceola's wives could be the propensity of Seminole women to avoid whites. They would usually attend events en masse where identities were not readily revealed. Osceola's wives would not have been paraded around socially at forts or trading posts, either, although they would visit upon occasion. It was the man who handled the public business of the family; the woman was a domestic who managed the household. Also, by this time, it should be noted, so many blacks had married into the tribe that it might have been impossible for an outsider to know for sure whether or not a person was of mixed race. The artist George Catlin depicted the two wives and a child of Osceola in the background of a sketch rendered in 1849, but it is impossible to determine the ethnicity of the women.[13]

Once again, however, it would be a romantic notion to attribute the militancy of Osceola solely to his protection of the runaway slaves who had joined his tribe, especially if one or both of his wives were black. There can be no denying that the guardianship of blacks was a part of his purpose, but the roots of his resistance were embedded much deeper.

He had been a refugee—chased, tormented, and even captured by the enemy—during his childhood and teen years. Osceola knew the fear and danger of an odyssey to an unknown land. He had found a home with the Seminole there in Florida and had grown to adulthood and formed a kinship with that tribe. Osceola was a Seminole through and through. He would never be able to erase from his memory the agony of his Creek past, but he now desired to maintain the stable and settled environment he had established there in Florida for his own wives and children. Certainly, Osceola had vowed to spare his family and friends the indignities that had befallen him and his Tallassee neighbors two decades ago. He remembered enough about the enemies in his former tribe—the White Sticks—and their alliance with the United States to know that he could never rejoin them and live in peace.

During this time of great tension and disorder on the reservation, many of the Black Seminoles had moved deep into the swamps and took no part in negotiations. They vowed to remain in Florida and would defy their Seminole masters and the will of the tribe if necessary to do so. They were not naïve enough to believe they could emigrate with the Seminoles and maintain their freedom. If the Creeks did not enslave them, then the whites would—whether or not the Creeks or whites had any claim to them. The blacks would take their chances in the remote wilderness areas of Florida until matters were settled.

These Black Seminoles had found in Osceola a warrior and friend they could rally behind. The young warrior not only shared an affinity with the black race in Florida—and perhaps a kinship through his wife or wives—but they also had a common goal. Osceola and the blacks had chosen to resist moving to the West and would lay down their lives if needed to remain where they were, free from oppression. The blacks would ally with the militant Seminoles in whatever course of action was necessary, including fighting, to ensure that they would not fall into the hands of the enemy slavers.[14]

The old adage "out of sight, out of mind" did not apply to the Seminole Blacks, however. They might have taken to the backwoods swamps to hide, but their future was very much on the minds of various influential people and the government.

Major General Richard Keith Call sent a message to President Andrew Jackson that contained a proposal. The general requested permission for him and his associates to purchase black slaves—at least 150 people—who were residing with the Seminole. He viewed this sale as a way to help in the removal of the Seminoles. "The Negroes have great influence among the Indians. They are better aggriculturists and inferior huntsmen to the Indians, and are violently opposed to leaving the country. If the Indians are permitted to convert them into specie [money], one great obsticle in the way of removal may be overcome."[15]

Wiley Thompson responded to this message by stating that he believed that the Seminole would not sell their slaves any more than they would sell their children. In addition, the Seminoles and the blacks had been assured at the Treaty of Payne's Landing that they would move together, which was important in persuading them to sign. "I have given them a pledge that I will do everything in my power, consistent with the rights of others, to save Blacks from worse bondage . . . and that I will not permit a sale of any slave unless it be clearly dictated by Humanity."[16]

Rumors circulated throughout the Seminole Nation, as well as the government, that Thompson opposed the sale of the blacks only because he had designs on the slaves for himself. While Thompson attempted to refute these falsehoods, a party of citizens with permission from the War Department to purchase Seminole slaves arrived at the Indian agency. Thompson told these men that they were in great danger at the present time and must wait until another day to see about buying slaves. The agent worried that if word leaked out that the War Department had authorized the sale of Seminole Blacks, the territory would be overrun with speculators. The evidence indicates that Thompson found the sale of slaves detestable, but he failed to convince anyone that his opposition was sincere and not simply to protect his own interests.

Thompson made an effort to reason with the War Department over the sale of the Seminole Blacks, but the government was adamant—the president sided with General Call. The acting secretary of war, C. W. Harris, suggested that Thompson could dispel those nasty rumors about him "by your own publication of the views of the department on the subject, and interposing no further obstacles to the purchase of these slaves, than may be necessary to secure their owners a fair equivalent." Thompson understood that this issue would not disappear; at some point he would be required to deal with it again—unless he could accelerate the timetable for removal.[17]

Seminole-white relations deteriorated throughout the summer and fall. In June, a skirmish between a Seminole hunting party that had strayed beyond reservation boundaries and whites resulted in one Seminole killed and one wounded, and three whites wounded. In early October, an express rider was killed on the road from Tampa Bay to Fort King. Plantations were coming under attack more often, and rumors were rampant that the Seminole were amassing weapons to be used in war. Despite the ban on arms and ammunition, Osceola at that time reportedly had accumulated and stored 150 kegs of gunpowder.[18]

Wiley Thompson feared that circumstances could rapidly escalate into widespread violence. Consequently, he saw the need to intensify his efforts to persuade the Seminoles to migrate west and to hurry their departure. Thompson was in charge of the emigration and had completed his plan and submitted it to the Indian office. His proposal called for the Seminoles to gather at Tampa Bay, travel by schooner to New Orleans, and from that point ride in wagons to their new home. They would be fed bread stuffs and fresh beef on the overland journey. He did make it clear that a military force would be required to guard the removal and encourage any stragglers to leave.[19]

On October 23, the Indian agent summoned the chiefs to a conference to explain his emigration plan. Osceola also attended this meeting and would be the voice in the background prompting Micanopy to make certain that the head chief was not misunderstood in his opposition to the move.

Thompson, although aware of the objections of the tribe to moving, conducted this meeting as if the emigration were being taken for granted. He did not ask the chiefs to sign any documents or profess their willingness to move. After laying out his plans, the agent simply asked in a friendly manner if the chiefs preferred to travel to their new home by land or by sea. He also wanted to know how they wanted to be reimbursed for their livestock and land improvements.

At this point the chiefs asked for a recess to allow them to speak in private. Thompson, however, must have planted a spy. The following warning from Osceola appears as part of the official record of the meeting:

My brothers! The white people got some of our chiefs to sign a paper to give our lands to them, but our chiefs did not do as we told them to do; they done wrong; we must do right. The agent tells us we must go away from the lands we live on—our homes, and the graves of our Fathers, and go over the big river among the bad Indians. When the agent tells me to go from my home, I hate him, because I love my home, and will not go from it.

My brothers! When the Great Spirit tells me to go with the white man, I go: but he tells me not to go. The white man says I shall go, and he will send people to make me go; but I have a rifle, and I have some powder and some lead. I say, we must not leave our homes and lands. If any of our people want to go west, we won't let them; and I tell them they are our enemies, and we will treat them so, for the Great Spirit will protect us.[20]

From then on the assembled chiefs, other than Charley Emathla, refused to discuss details of the move and ignored the agent's questions. Several of the chiefs made brief statements, including Jumper, who referred to the Moultrie Creek treaty when he said, "We are not satisfied to go until the end of the twenty years." Holata Micco said, "I never gave my consent to go west; the whites may say so but I never gave my consent." Emathla admitted that he had signed the Payne's Landing treaty, although he added, "The white people forced us into the treaty. I was there. I agreed to go west."[21]

Micanopy was the legal hereditary chief of the Seminole tribe, in spite of

Thompson's angry removal of him months earlier. He ended all discussion with the agent by affirming that he would not move, much to the satisfaction of Osceola.

The undaunted agent told the assembled chiefs that January 8, 1836, would be the date when the tribe must gather at Tampa Bay to board transports. He then offered a chilling ultimatum. If they did not prepare to move now and ignored that date, the army would come after them and force them to comply or kill them all if they chose to fight.[22]

Thompson was discouraged and angered by the opposition that had apparently hardened as the days went by, but he must have experienced a twinge of guilt as well. He understood that whether they moved or stayed, the future of the Seminole tribe—both red and black—was precarious. There would be overwhelming challenges for them to overcome no matter where they lived. All Thompson really cared about now, however, was the arrival of January when the tribe would be gone—one way or another—and he could wash his hands of the matter.

Osceola noticed with scorn that many Seminole chiefs were in compliance with Thompson and were preparing their people for the move west. The deadline for moving was fast approaching. Something dramatic needed to be done to disrupt this disastrous occasion, or all would be lost.

To that end, a secret meeting was held at the Big Swamp, with at least fifteen hundred Seminoles in attendance, including Micanopy, Alligator, Jumper, Abraham, and Osceola—the group of individuals who comprised the leadership of the anti-removal faction of the tribe. These chiefs reaffirmed their refusal to leave Florida and vowed to fight to stay. In addition, it was decided that those Seminoles who voluntarily went along like sheep with the government's removal plans would be dealt with severely—a death sentence was imposed.

Osceola now decided that it was time to reveal his true intentions to everyone in Florida Territory with respect to the impending removal by taking matters into his own hands.

Seminole chief Charley Emathla was agent Thompson's most important ally within the tribe. Emathla had verbally condemned the removal treaties but nonetheless had decided to move as ordered and had been preparing his band for that day. Emathla had rightfully begun to fear tribal reprisals for his close association with Thompson and was eager to leave for his new home in the West. He must have known that his tribe subscribed to a law stating that anyone who abandoned his people to aid the whites would forfeit his life.[23]

On November 26, 1835, Charley Emathla had just sold a herd of cattle in preparation for his departure, and had gone to the agency to collect his payment in gold and silver coins. He was returning home with his two daughters and an unidentified black man when he was confronted by Osceola, Holata Micco, Abraham, and a contingent of warriors.

Confusion exists with respect to the details of the incident. Some sources report that Osceola and his warriors opened fire without warning and killed Charley Emathla outright with a barrage of bullets. In a more popular and likely the accurate version, Osceola confronted Charley Emathla and the two men exchanged bitter words about the removal. Osceola would have wanted the chief to know who was about to kill him and the reason for it. All at once, Osceola shot dead this man whom he considered a traitor.

In either case, Emathla was killed by Osceola. As further humiliation, Osceola contemptuously threw the gold and silver pieces from Emathla's sale of the cattle herd into the air, where they scattered in every direction. Charley Emathla's daughters and the black man were not harmed. Incidentally, Abraham had initially been opposed to this murder, but there was little he could do to stop it.[24]

Alarm seized the territory—among both whites and Seminoles—as word of this vicious murder spread. White settlers by the hundreds sought refuge in the forts, which placed a burden on available supplies. Food and drink became precious commodities, and prices escalated to boomtown levels. The army was now faced with what they would deem a dangerous uprising that had to be dealt with promptly and severely before it spun out of control.

Wiley Thompson wrote to General George Gibson that Charley Emathla had been assassinated "through the treachery of Powell [Osceola], who professed to be and was considered friendly. The consequences resulting from this murder leave no doubt that actual force must be resorted to for the purpose of effecting removal, as it has produced a general defection."[25]

The cold-blooded murder of Charley Emathla also served as an ominous warning to the other chiefs who favored removal that they, too, could suffer the same fate should they carry through with plans to move. At least eight chiefs along with five hundred of their people fled in panic to Fort Brooke to seek protection from the wrath of Osceola and his followers. These people had departed their homes so quickly that they had not brought along anything on which to subsist. The post commander, Captain Francis S. Belton, however, managed to secure government rations that would feed them until they could be transported to Tampa Bay for removal. It was feared that if the government did not feed these people, they would join Osceola and the hostiles. In fact, most of Charley Emathla's band later deserted the fort, choosing to join forces with Osceola and fight rather than go west.[26]

Sensing the power that this new leader named Osceola held with his people, civilians and soldiers alike prepared for an insurrection. Five hundred horsemen were signed up for a period of four weeks under the command of Major General Richard K. Call. There was no appropriation for these new men, but General Clinch persuaded President Jackson to allot funds from the federal government to pay for their duty. Jackson understood the volatility of the situation but was confident due to his own past successes that the army would quickly and easily prevail over the savages. In addition to the new enlistees, Clinch ordered Major Francis L. Dade to march a company of regulars from Key West to Fort Brooke to bolster the garrison.[27]

Back in the swamps, a council of chiefs was held, and Osceola was overwhelmingly endorsed as the tribal tustenugge thlocklo—the commander in charge of defending the life and lands of the people in the Seminole Nation. This was quite a promotion, from common warrior to commanding general. His appointment was a testament to the fairness and professionalism in which he had gone about his duties as Micanopy's police chief, as well as the respect everyone had for his leadership abilities. His trusted chiefs Alligator and Jumper would serve as his top lieutenants, while head chief Micanopy, who was past his prime, would act as an adviser. Osceola immediately set to work teaching military discipline and drilling his warrior troops, which was a difficult task given that Native Americans were notorious for fighting as individuals in battle. All the men, and even the older boys, were required to take daily rifle practice. Most of all, Osceola stressed that every warrior must obey his commands and those of the other tustenugges. Failure to do so would result in the death of that warrior.[28]

It was also decided that the rebellious Seminoles would move southwest of Fort King to the Cove of the Withlacoochee River. This almost impenetrable area of wild swamps and tangled undergrowth was an ideal location to elude and discourage an enemy from invading while still remaining within striking distance of the road connecting Fort King, Fort Drane, and Fort Brooke. The women and children of the tribe relocated to this safe place and commenced establishing a camp with as much hominess as was possible in the wilderness.[29]

The reinforced U.S. military presence that had been called up on account of the panic over the killing of Charley Emathla was a signal to Osceola that war was at hand. The new head war chief did not want to disappoint the army by not responding to this threat. He would throw down the gauntlet by striking a violent blow against a white objective.

The first real battle of the Great Seminole War occurred on December 18, 1835. Colonel John Warren of Jacksonville had brought his baggage wagon train to Kanapaha with plans to travel to Wetumpka. In the so-called Battle of Black Rock, Osceola and about eighty warriors attacked and captured Colonel Warren's wagon train. While the Seminoles were ransacking the contents, thirty militiamen under the leadership of Dr. John McLemore, who had escorted the train, were poised to ride to the rescue. But when McLemore called for his militiamen to charge into the group of Seminole warriors and save the wagon train, only twelve of the men obeyed. Osceola's warriors then proceeded to kill six and wound eight of both the brave and the hesitant horsemen, while the others were forced to retreat.

Several days later, Osceola's band was discovered by a force of six companies of cavalrymen. The horsemen quietly dismounted and charged into the surprised Seminole camp. This engagement was fought at close quarters, with hand-to-hand combat and small arms, but produced few casualties. Osceola and his men escaped into the forested swamp beyond, leaving behind possessions and papers taken in the wagon train attack as evidence of their guilt. No doubt Osceola made a mental note to post sentries in the future to prevent another attack.[30]

These two skirmishes were only the first of a long series of bloody fights between the Seminole and the U.S. Army. Osceola would continue his violent protest of the Treaty of Payne's Landing by leading his band on raids on white settlements, which resulted in a few small clashes but only a handful of casualties on either side. It was his intention to teach the whites a lesson while encouraging the government to leave the Seminole alone on their Florida homeland, and an excellent opportunity was about to present itself.

Osceola possessed a wide network of intelligence-gathering sources. His scouts learned that on December, 23, 1835, a column that included five line officers, a surgeon, and one hundred men of the Third United States Artillery, under the command of Major Francis Langhorne Dade, had marched out of Fort Brooke on a hundred-mile trip to Fort King. These were artillerymen trained to fight as infantry, called "red-legged infantry" for the red artillery stockings they wore. The two-company column, accompanied by only one small six-pounder cannon, moved slowly without flank guards or scouts as it followed a trail that only seven years earlier had been hacked out of the dense scrub forests of central Florida. Thick wilderness lined this primitive pathway in an area where there were no other roads and only a handful of intersecting, barely passable trails. It was truly a no-man's-land for the army.

Dade had practiced caution as he led his men down this narrow trail. At night, he would have the men cut logs and put up a temporary stockade around their perimeter. Sentries were posted outside the walls to alert the troops to any movement. Little did the soldiers know, however, that Osceola's scouts were never more than listening distance away from the column or its bivouac.

By Christmas morning, Dade had reached the Hillsborough River and discovered that the bridge had been burned. The troops were compelled to wade through the icy water. The cannon was going to be transported across on a makeshift raft, but the wood platform capsized, which caused more work than planned to move it across.

Osceola intended to attack Dade's column and outlined specific plans to his lieutenants. But at the same time, Osceola had unfinished business waiting for him elsewhere. He assigned a group of Seminoles led by Alligator to watch and follow Dade's army column as it moved northward. Osceola gave Alligator orders that if he must attack—or was attacked—before the war leader returned, they were not to take anything personal from the soldiers other than confiscating weapons and ammunition. Some accounts state that he also forbade them from abusing the bodies by taking scalps, a practice in which some but not all Seminole participated.

Osceola was preparing to strike a double blow. He had split his force, leaving at least two-thirds of them with Alligator along the road to Fort King, while he hurried away with another detachment of perhaps sixty warriors toward that fort.

At about the time Major Dade and his men were approaching the southern forks of the Withlacoochee River, Osceola and his war party had slipped stealthily into the underbrush about six hundred yards from the main gate of Fort King. He was aware that Colonel Alexander Fanning had departed the fort with four companies of troops to rendezvous with Colonel Clinch at Fort Drane. Only a small detachment of soldiers remained behind. The fort, however, was not the target of the Seminole war leader.

From his concealed position, Osceola commanded a clear view of both Fort King and the Indian agency office. For two days Osceola and his men patiently lay in the chilly air hidden within the palmetto trees and tall grasses. He had waited all summer and fall for an opportunity to settle accounts with agent Wiley Thompson, who had humiliated him by locking him up and parading him around as an example of a "good Indian." The decision to eliminate the agent had been brought up in council and approved. Osceola would now carry out the sentence as executioner.

Finally, on the early evening of December 28, the moment that Osceola had waited for arrived. He moved his men stealthily forward. Thompson and his lieutenant, Constantine Smith, had finished their supper at the officers' mess and had gone for an evening stroll. The two men walked through the fort's main gates, passed the agency office, and were headed toward the sutler's store when a shot rang out. This lone bullet struck Wiley Thompson.

That first shot had come from the Spanish silver-plated rifle given to Osceola as a goodwill gesture by the Indian agent. Immediately following Osceola's shot, a fusillade of bullets poured from the ambuscade. Within a matter of moments, both Thompson and Smith lay dead. Thompson had been shot fourteen times, Smith twice. Osceola and his warriors swarmed around the dead men. The agent's scalp was removed and cut into pieces so that everyone who had participated could have a personal trophy. Osceola and his band then surrounded the store and killed Erastus Rogers, the sutler, and his two clerks with rifle shots through the windows as they ate their dinner. The black servants present inside the house were spared.

This surprise attack at Fort King had been so effective that not one of the forty-six defenders inside had fired a shot. The confused fort commander, not knowing that anyone had stepped outside the fort, closed the gates and waited some time before sending out a reconnaissance party. Osceola was later identified as the leader of this attack by friendly Native Americans inside the fort who had recognized his shrill, piercing war whoop.[31]

The murder of Wiley Thompson was a personal vendetta by Osceola rather than an assassination to produce political change. Thompson, a man with a conscience, had been a relatively good friend to the Seminole, especially when compared to previous agents such as John Phagan, who had viewed the tribe as a vehicle for lining his pockets with riches.

It is unlikely that it would have mattered to Osceola that Thompson had understood and sympathized with the Seminole plight and that it was the government in Washington that had dictated the agent's policies and actions. The threats made by Thompson to the Seminoles had been passed down from the War Department and the president and were not necessarily the views of the Indian agent. Thompson's only recourse would have been to resign, but perhaps he regarded that act as deserting the Seminole people. He had intended to make this difficult removal as painless as possible for the tribe. But his degrading treatment of Osceola—the most important Seminole of his time—had cost him his life. Although the murder was personal, Thompson could also be viewed as a symbol of the government's mistreatment of the Seminoles, and his death sent a clear message that the tribe would no longer be passive.

Osceola and his warriors immediately galloped away from the fort on their ponies. They intended to join Alligator and the group of Seminoles who were poised to attack the army column that was at present on the move about thirty miles away. Osceola had not only avenged the humiliation he had suffered at the hands of agent Thompson, but, if it had not been apparent before, he had also in effect declared war on the white man in a loud and clear voice.

Alligator's approximately 180 Seminole warriors—including a number of blacks—had hidden themselves at daybreak among the tall grass and palmetto scrub of an islandlike pine barren opposite a pond on the west side of the road to Fort King. Alligator was becoming impatient, and not because of the chilly, rainy weather they endured. He was afraid that their ambush would fail if he did not act without delay. He told everyone that they could wait no longer for the arrival of Osceola. Their location along the tree-lined road was perfect. Farther north, the forest thinned out and concealment and the element of surprise would be more difficult, if not impossible. Chief Micanopy, who had just arrived, was reluctant to attack without Osceola present, but Jumper and the others convinced him that they must attack now or their opportunity would be lost. Micanopy grudgingly agreed, and the warriors deployed into position.

Eventually, Major Francis Dade, riding in the advance of his hundred or so men, drew even with the nearest concealed Seminoles, moved along their line, and then was beyond it. The troops followed, marching in two columns, looking straight ahead, blue overcoats buttoned over their muskets to protect them from the cold drizzle. Behind them came the cannon and carriage that was being dragged by four horses.

With a blood-curdling war whoop, Alligator sprang the trap. The horde of warriors, screaming wildly, rose from their hiding places among the palmettos and began firing into the troops at point-blank range. The entire left side of the column—one-half of the total force, including Major Dade—fell dead in the initial volley. The remaining men frantically tore at their overcoats to reach their weapons and return fire. The ambush had worked to perfection.

Captain George Washington Gardiner, a West Pointer, took command and rallied the survivors, who now numbered perhaps only thirty men. The soldiers fell back into the trees, and the cannon was brought into action. The devastation wrought by this artillery piece, although mainly to the vegetation, caused Alligator and his men to lay low for almost an hour. During this lull in the action, the soldiers managed to erect a triangular, knee-high log breastwork that they could hide behind and fire at their attackers.

Gardiner ordered that those killed and wounded in that initial volley be retrieved from where they lay and be brought inside the log breastwork. He did not wish to see any of his men—dead or alive—tortured, although the Seminole rarely participated in such practices. Gardiner, a stout man barely five feet in height, gained the admiration of the Seminole, especially Alligator, who later noted the man's bravery as he constantly exposed himself to their fire and dodged bullets while directing his troops.

Eventually, Alligator ordered that his warriors maintain a steady fire into the enemy position. A spirited defense by the soldiers kept the warriors at bay, but soon the firing from the fortification became less frequent and the cannon ran out of ammunition. The Seminoles, with tomahawks, knives, and war clubs, attempted a frontal assault of the entrenched soldiers, but they were repulsed. Gradually, Alligator's sharpshooters picked off the soldiers one by one, mostly with shots to the head. The trees and breastwork around the soldiers were riddled with a multitude of bullets, and the men fought while wading in pools of blood.

At about four P.M., the coup de grâce was administered by about fifty mounted black warriors who rushed the breastwork from the rear and overwhelmed the remaining defenders. Major Francis Dade, feisty Captain George Gardiner, and more than one hundred soldiers were now dead. There were only four survivors: one man was later killed on the road, one died of his wounds, and one reached the fort but died several months later.

The fourth person from the army side was found hidden behind a tree and was spared. This man was Louis Pacheco, who escaped on account of his race. Pacheco was a slave from Sarasota who had been hired from his master at $25 a day to guide Dade's column. The black guide gladly joined the Seminoles and attached himself to Jumper for the remainder of the war. Another survivor was Captain Gardiner's dog, which also defected to the enemy.

Seminole losses were said to have been only three killed and five wounded.[32]

Alligator and his Seminoles did not take anything of value from the dead—in accordance with Osceola's orders. They confiscated only food, ammunition, and clothing, mainly greatcoats, but left personal items and valuables alone. *Niles' Weekly Register* reported that "Major Dade's uniform coat was not found. With this exception, not one of these brave but unfortunate men, had been plundered. Silver, gold, jewelry and watches were untouched—nothing seems to have been taken but arms and ammunition." The article went on to praise Osceola for having such control over his warriors, calling him a "master spirit."[33]

This report may or may not have been completely accurate. True, the Seminole warriors did not loot the bodies of the dead. Later, however, it was claimed that a group of blacks arrived on the battlefield and reportedly stole everything they could find of value. These looters also have been accused of taking scalps.[34]

The Seminole and black participants of the Dade Massacre returned to Wahoo Swamp to celebrate their victory. They had slaughtered a considerable number of troops from the mighty U.S. Army and had suffered only a handful of casualties. This was reason enough for a victory dance. The scalps that had been collected were handed over to the medicine men, who attached them to a tall pole that was raised in the middle of a clearing. Osceola and his war party arrived and announced that the agent was dead, which evoked great jubilation. He tossed a piece of Wiley Thompson's bloody scalp to the medicine man for display on the pole.

It was around this sacred pole that the victory dance took place. The Seminoles, many dressed in army overcoats and hats, danced, feasted, sang, bragged, drank liquor, and even went as far as to mimic the murdered Wiley

Thompson, much to the delight of everyone present. It can be assumed that the blacks, who spoke better English, led this mockery of the dead agent. The celebration continued throughout the night until the warriors collapsed from exhaustion or simply passed out from consuming too much alcohol.[35]

The quiet camp in Wahoo Swamp was visited the next morning by reconnaissance scouts that Osceola had dispatched to monitor movements of the army. These scouts related the news that a large column of soldiers—numbering at least 250 men—was marching from Fort Drane toward the Withlacoochee River. There was no haste in their march, the scouts reported, which signified to Osceola that these troops were unaware of the massacre of the Dade column.

Osceola was pleased to hear about this new troop movement. His people had already killed more than one hundred soldiers, and now another opportunity to strike a serious blow was marching directly toward them. The young Seminole leader must have envisioned making another fear-inspiring statement of defiance that would further shatter the nerves—and hopefully the willpower—of the military and civilian populace of Florida Territory. He immediately set to work gathering and preparing his men for a war party and formulating a strategy to go out and meet these soldiers in battle.

Six

Battle of the Withlacoochee

»✦«

The U.S. Army never fully realized the genius of the tactics employed and executed by Osceola that had served as his declaration of war. The Seminole chiefs and warriors had wholeheartedly endorsed Osceola as their tustenugge thlacko, and he had responded by spreading panic among the settlers across the entire northern half of Florida Territory.

In an act of personal revenge, he had killed Indian agent Wiley Thompson. He had also planned the ambush of Major Dade's party at a location ideal for a surprise attack followed by a strategic withdrawal to the safety of the Withlacoochee swamps. Now he intended to lead his people to further victory.

It was not necessary for the United States to make a formal declaration of war against Osceola and his Seminoles in response to these attacks. President Andrew Jackson and Congress merely recognized a dangerous situation and appropriated the money and designated the troops necessary to conduct military operations. Even though this Seminole conflict was taking place in one of the least known parts of the country, it received coverage in most American newspapers. Nevertheless, it did not loom very large in the realm of the nation's affairs. The public's attention was focused on the greedy exploitation of the riches of the continent under the patronage of Jacksonian Democracy, which was in full bloom.

During 1835, the government had paid off its bonded indebtedness for the first time in history. Consequently, the disposition of the surplus that was accruing each year in the national treasury became a subject of great political debate. This surplus also had been increased by purchases of public lands. The speculation in public lands was only one factor in what appeared to be an unprecedented boom. Business was thriving in all sectors, with the cotton market in the South especially prosperous. New enterprise was expanding impressively and reaping remarkable profits. Most Americans were pleased with the direction of their country.[1]

The public was captivated by the fight for liberty against Mexico taking place in Texas. Jackson's friend Sam Houston, who commanded the Texan troops, had captured the attention of the country. The impending birth of the Republic of Texas would likely bring to the forefront the issue of slavery. The Missouri Compromise of 1820 had established the boundaries of slavery, but the possibility of annexing Texas had once again opened up this divisive subject for discussion and debate.

The fifteen million people in the United States, however, were busy making money and worrying about matters close to home. The actions of Osceola and the advent of war—with its undertones of slavery—were certainly topics of casual conversation, but the preoccupation with profits reduced the importance of this conflict in faraway Florida.

What would come to be called the Great Seminole War would be directed by Secretary of War Lewis Cass, who would benefit from the advice of the old Indian fighter in the White House. Cass was fifty-three years old and had served his country in one capacity or another for thirty years. He had been an officer in the War of 1812 and had advanced to the rank of major general in the Ohio militia and brigadier general in the regular army. Cass had also served as governor of the Michigan Territory for eighteen years. By 1835, he was suffering from ill health and was at times less than effective in carrying out his duties, but nonetheless he believed it his obligation to share his experience and continue to serve his country. In the controversy over slavery,

Cass demonstrated sympathy for the slave owners and therefore paid attention to the Southerners who were clamoring for the removal of the Seminoles from Florida to the West.[2]

When Osceola had declared war on the United States, Cass was occupied with planning and establishing an adequate defense against possible European aggression. This had been necessitated by the recent brinkmanship exercised by Andrew Jackson. The president had rashly threatened that if France did not pay its debt to compensate for damages done to American property during the Napoleonic Wars more than twenty years ago—a settlement they had promised but never delivered—he would be obliged to use military force against them. This saber rattling by a president who was widely known to prefer violent confrontation over compromise in foreign and domestic policy had brought the country to the precipice of war with France. Consequently, the uprising of Osceola and the Seminoles seemed small in comparison to the risk posed by a powerful country like France.

The prevailing opinion was that the proper response to such a trifling threat as the Seminoles was to expedite their departure to that portion of the West allotted them according to treaty provisions. The U.S. Army consisted of more than eleven thousand officers and well-trained enlisted men, and if sent in force to Florida, they could easily overwhelm a few thousand primitive savages. And once the removal had been completed, a string of forts could be erected along the border to keep runaway slaves from entering Florida. This would greatly appease the white settlers in that territory, not to mention the slave owners in Georgia and Alabama who had protested having their human property run away to find refuge with the Seminoles. When it was announced that the army would answer Osceola's challenge, *Niles' Register* predicted that "the miserable creatures will be speedily swept from the face of the earth."[3]

There were perhaps four thousand Seminole men, women, and children in Florida who would undertake a fight for their homeland against a nation with a population of some fifteen million. Opinion differed with respect to the number of warriors in this tribe, however. The army estimate was fourteen hundred, but President Jackson believed that the figure was closer to five hundred. Jackson's assessment was likely too high as well. It would be safe to say that Osceola probably had no more than three hundred able-bodied warriors—red and black—at his disposal at the start of this war. That figure would increase as more blacks and young men joined the warrior ranks.[4]

Osceola and the outnumbered Seminoles, of course, had no organization for war that could come close to equaling the one that confronted them. It would not be numbers but the determination of the Seminole that would affect the early outcome of the war, however. Osceola knew that his people were heavily in the minority, but he also believed that their power came not from organization but from desperation. The Seminoles must prevail in this conflict or their future as a nation would be in jeopardy—and such a realization could be a potent motivator.

The hostilities in Florida certainly appeared easy on paper for the army to control, but one man who disagreed with that assessment was an old friend of the president. John H. Eaton, the governor of the Florida Territory, warned Jackson that the Seminoles would not simply lay down their arms when the army arrived—they would fight. The governor advised that the best strategy would be to send an overwhelming force of four thousand to five thousand regular soldiers against the Indians. Only by this means could they avoid becoming bogged down in a lengthy conflict.

Eaton was probably correct in his analysis, but he might as well have asked for a nuclear bomb. To ship almost half of the U.S. Army to quell an uprising by a handful of savages seemed silly to Sharp Knife, the conqueror of the Creeks and Seminoles. Moreover, people living in the East Coast states north of Florida felt more vulnerable to a possible threat due to the president's dangerous ultimatum to France than they did to Osceola and his ragtag band of Seminoles.[5]

It was evident that the attacks already so capably carried out by Osceola had not convinced those people that he, not the French, was the real threat. But the Seminole war leader did not intend to rest until he had forced the government to abandon its plans to remove the tribe from its rightful homelands. Only three days after the raid at Fort King in which Wiley Thompson was murdered and Major Dade and his men were killed, Osceola would have the opportunity to display his strength as a military leader in a full-scale battle.

General Duncan Clinch, commander of the Florida army regulars, bore responsibility for regaining control of Seminole country and protecting the nearby farms and plantations. Clinch had been born in North Carolina in 1787 and joined the army as a lieutenant in 1808. He had served during the War of 1812, and seven years later had risen to the rank of colonel and placed in charge of the Eighth Infantry Regiment. This huge man, who was described by an orderly as "fat and lusty, gray and muscular," was not merely a soldier—he moonlighted as a planter, with plantations in both Florida and Georgia. He was a man of deep spiritual beliefs and treated his men with kindness—though not so his slaves. His wife had recently passed away in Alabama while he was on Florida duty, leaving him with eight children to care for.[6]

After the surprise attack against Wiley Thompson, Clinch ordered his 250 regular army troops to abandon Fort King and move to his plantation, Auld Lang Syne, an area about four miles square, with the surrounding fields planted with sugarcane. Accommodations at this makeshift base were less than appealing, however. The troops were lodged in old slave quarters, where they were plagued by lice, rodents, and insects, while the room where the general slept was above a pigsty.[7]

It has been suggested that Clinch moved his troops to his plantation solely to concentrate the force for an attack against the Seminoles in their hideaway along the Withlacoochee River. Fort Drane, however, was no closer than Fort King to Osceola's stronghold in the Cove of the Withlacoochee. A more valid explanation for this move may be that Fort Drane was fifteen miles closer to a natural supply point at the town of Micanopy, which made the new fort more practical for logistical reasons.[8]

Captain Augustus Drane, commanding the Second Artillery, supervised the building of a defensive wall twelve feet high around the buildings, enclosing a compound 150 yards long and 80 yards wide, with a blockhouse mounting one cannon at the east end. When it was completed, Clinch gave the fortification its builder's name and the result was christened Fort Drane.

Captain Drane, who fancied himself a swashbuckler, bragged that he could take 60 men and march through Seminole country without suffering casualties. Apparently the white settlers in the vicinity did not agree with that braggadocio's opinion. Once the stockade had been constructed, at least 150 local citizens scurried from their homesteads and packed the fort to overflowing. In their haste, these people had neglected to bring along an adequate store of food or enough clothing, which put a strain on military supplies and meant huge profits for traders who took advantage of the situation.[9]

On Christmas Eve 1835, General Richard Call, a friend of Andrew Jackson from the Creek War, arrived at Fort Drane after a march from Tallahassee and reported to General Clinch. Call brought with him a detachment of about five hundred mounted territorial volunteers. The term of these Florida volunteers was scheduled to end on New Year's Day, one week away. Both generals understood that it would be necessary to send them into action immediately or an opportunity to strike the Seminoles with a large force would be lost.[10]

It was commonly known that few, if any, of these volunteers would reenlist after this term of enlistment had expired. The militiaman's service in the territory was one of extreme drudgery and hardship, and the volunteers were eager to return home and get on with their lives. Also, it was the opinion of the militia to a man that this Seminole uprising should be managed by the federal government. In other words, the U.S. Army, not militiamen, should be on the front lines of this war against Osceola and his hostile warriors. The volunteers, by the same token, also resented these army troops. They regarded the regulars as a bunch of crude misfits who had no vested interest in the welfare of Florida Territory.

True, the basic army enlisted man of the day was usually uneducated, unskilled, and uncouth—dredged up from the outcasts and maladjusted of society. Most of them were foreigners who had recently arrived in this country and found the transition from Europe to America most difficult. Jobs were scarce for such people, many of whom spoke little or no English. The quality—and perhaps desperation—of these men can be substantiated by the fact that at the time a civilian laborer could earn $1 a day but an army soldier was paid only $5 a month.[11]

The shoulder arm was the weapon issued to the foot soldier. For the most part, these troops had been issued a flintlock muzzle-loading musket of a standard .69 caliber. This weapon was fired by a flint and steel mechanism, loaded with powder and ball downward through the muzzle, and had no rifling in the bore. It was by no means a modern firearm—percussion firing mechanisms, breech-loading, and rifling already existed. The army had a small quantity of these newer rifles—.52 calibers that fired four times faster than the musket and kicked like a mule—but the ratio was one rifle to twenty-two muskets.[12]

Generals Clinch and Call decided that they would move their combined force against the Seminoles without delay. They would attempt to take the war to the Seminoles' home ground by attacking their villages in the Cove of the Withlacoochee River—Osceola's western Florida stronghold and a place few white men had ever entered.

On December 29, Clinch with six companies of regulars, about 250 men in all, and Call with his 500 Florida volunteers, marched south toward the Withlacoochee. Progress was slow as the cumbersome supply wagons bogged down in the mud and turgid water, horses rebelled, and the foot soldiers complained and cursed as they trudged along the narrow and swampy path that led to the river. Clinch was impatient to arrive at their destination and pushed his troops mercilessly. It was imperative that they locate and engage the Seminoles before the hitch of the volunteers expired.[13]

Osceola had expected—and probably welcomed—an attack by the army in retaliation for his actions. He wanted to draw them out of the fort and was pleased that they were on the march. Unbeknownst to them, the Seminole war leader had these approaching white soldiers from Fort Drane carefully scouted. He was aware that General Call and his volunteers had joined Clinch's regulars and that the column had marched from Fort Drane on the morning of December 29. It was apparent to him that the soldiers intended to cross the Withlacoochee River, with their destination being the Seminole villages.

Osceola promptly held council and advised his lieutenants that they would ambush the army column well before the troops became a threat to their homes and families. He then set out at the head of a force of about 150–200 Seminole warriors and perhaps 50 blacks, to meet General Clinch wherever he might be found. Alligator was his second in command, while old Chief Micanopy remained in the swamp with a handful of warriors and the women and children.

On December 30, Osceola led his war party to a well-known and popular ford on the Withlacoochee, the place where he was certain his enemy would choose to cross. It would be difficult for the soldiers to ford farther downstream in deeper water, and the depth at this point was only about two feet. The Seminoles settled into the brush and waited near the ford that night in anticipation of ambushing the troopers when they arrived the next morning.

The army, however, was experiencing a tough march to the Withlacoochee, and had covered only twelve miles on the first day. The wagons were bogging down in the mushy earth, the heat was oppressive, and the column made so much noise that it could be heard hundreds of yards away. The soldiers had brought along scores of dogs, and the barking, howling animals added to the clamor. It was as if Clinch and Call were dispatching a continuous report of their whereabouts to the enemy.

Osceola, depending on the word of his scouts, still remained confident that the soldiers were headed for this most convenient ford on the river.

On the night of December 30, the army column halted about three miles from the banks of the Withlacoochee. Clinch ordered his men to camp without fires—he wanted to keep their position secret. At four A.M. on the morning of the last day of the year, however, the bugler blew reveille as usual. Even if they could have silenced the dogs and quieted the column, all hope of the army executing a surprise attack had been dashed with those familiar bugle notes. In the predawn light, 750 men tramped away from their bivouac on their mission to search for the hostile Seminoles and engage them in battle.[14]

White army officers, with few exceptions, lacked the knowledge and experience for fighting in this type of tropical wilderness. Their troops, no matter how brave and motivated, knew even less about how to deal with their enemy. The entire army really did not know what to expect from a confrontation with their Native American enemy, but they would soon learn—the hard way.

The column would typically march in formation, two abreast, which, due to the terrain and numerous obstacles, would often cause the men to become separated or straggle along the trail as far back as a quarter of a mile. It was not just the troops that found the going difficult. The baggage wagon train, which was not at all suited for the soft soil, drastically slowed progress. The large wheels of the heavy wagons would crack through the earth and become mired in the soggy soil beneath. A detail of men would utilize sturdy poles, along with back, leg, and arm muscle power, to pry the wagon loose and push it onto more solid earth so it could resume its journey.

The men did not bother to apply camouflage of any sort—either a substance smeared on faces or special clothing to blend in with the surroundings—but in this instance it would not have mattered anyway due to the noise of the march. The tactics employed by the army in this place of swamps and thick woodlands were the traditional European battle formations that depended on attrition—killing more of the enemy than army losses—for success.

Osceola was aware of these tactical disadvantages. He understood that one Seminole warrior concealed behind a tree was worth five white soldiers marching forward in formation with their bulky equipment and inferior firearms. His small, light guerrilla unit could move on a moment's notice, skillfully conceal themselves within the leafy brush, easily outmaneuver a much larger force, and swiftly attack or withdraw when the opportunity or need arose. And the Seminole leader was about to exploit these known army weaknesses when the troops appeared at the ford of the Withlacoochee.

The army column eventually arrived at the river about three miles from the shallow ford that had been its intended destination—the place where Osceola waited. General Clinch was in charge of the entire force, with subordinates Lieutenant Colonel Alexander Fanning, who commanded the regulars, and General Richard Call, who led the militia. The three men debated about whether to attempt a crossing at this point or to resume marching upriver.

The river ran about fifty yards wide at this point and much deeper than the other ford. The sky was brightening the landscape, and any intention of crossing in the dark to try to preserve their element of surprise had now passed. In addition, it could take hours to march the distance to the other ford given the overgrown, unpredictable trail to traverse, and that could cost them the better part of the day. The term of enlistment for the volunteers was expiring soon. There was no time to waste. Clinch needed to act as quickly as possible.

One of Clinch's troopers had taken the initiative to swim across the river. He located an old canoe lying along the shoreline, bailed it out, and paddled it back across to the waiting general. This evoked a loud cheer from the troops, much to the chagrin of Clinch, who had ordered that the least amount of noise be made.

The acquisition of the canoe evidently contributed to Clinch's decision about fording the river at this point. Although not the most sound or safe tactic, Clinch ordered the regulars to start crossing the river in the flimsy canoe. Two paddlers would ferry across up to eight men, who would bail furiously as they went. General Call and his volunteer horsemen were ordered to reconnoiter the area and find an acceptable place for the horses to swim across.

Clinch's scouts returned from a reconnaissance of the area to report that they had spotted an Indian sign on the southwestern bank of the river. The general, however, was more concerned with the crossing than with what faced him across the river. He would deal with the Indian sign after his troops had successfully crossed.[15]

Meanwhile, Osceola's Seminole scouts watched from the brush while the soldiers were being transported in the canoe at this most improbable crossing point. After making certain that the entire column was serious about crossing at that location, the scouts hurried to report this change in the army's plans to Osceola. The war leader was assuredly surprised and likely baffled to learn that the soldiers were crossing at such a dangerous place. Nonetheless, he immediately ordered his force to move swiftly downstream to this new location.

General Call, who remained on the north side with the main body of volunteers, ordered a detail of men with axes to start the process of building a bridge at the narrowest point. The canoe, although leaky, held up well enough to carry across a steady stream of regulars to the south side of the river. By then, nearly 250 of them had been transported to the other shore.

After crossing, the troops were told to march inland. About four hundred yards away from steep bank of the river where they landed, they found a U-shaped space with the open part aimed at the river. This grassy field was surrounded on all sides by a hammock, which was thick enough to afford excellent concealment for hostile riflemen. Surprisingly, Clinch, who must have been oblivious of any danger, ordered that the regulars, after arriving in their tiny ferryboat, were to march into this field, stack arms, and await further orders. Twenty-seven militiamen had thus far been ferried across to the south side to join the 250 regulars.[16]

It was late morning when Osceola and his 250 Seminole warriors cautiously approached on the south side of the Withlacoochee. From within the deep underbrush, the warriors could observe the soldiers struggling with the river crossing, which must have been a source of humor to them. Osceola also watched the odd actions of the white men who were lounging around the open field after they had crossed the river. He must have wondered about this curious habit of stacking weapons and allowing soldiers to relax when they had to know an enemy force was somewhere nearby. His heart would have soared with anticipation as he watched this detachment of exposed soldiers, who were dressed in their winter field uniform of now soiled sky-blue kersey fatigues, white crossbelts, and shiny black patent-leather caps as they lounged about with only several sentries on duty who carried firearms.

Osceola commenced deploying his warriors at intervals into the densely wooded hammock to maximize their fields of fire, and told them to hold their fire until he gave the order. He wanted to make certain that every soldier who planned to cross had joined his comrades in the open field.[17]

As has been the case with many battles throughout history, the Seminole were better armed than the army. Nearly every Seminole warrior had a rifle, as opposed to a musket. Although no Seminole rifle of the period has been preserved, it is presumed that they were effective small-bore Spanish weapons manufactured in Cuba and purchased from traders who worked the Florida coast.[18]

Even though the Seminoles had better firearms, the average warrior had received little training in marksmanship and was less than proficient with his weapon than the average soldier. They would take careful aim with the first shot, but after that would become careless and even fail to load the weapon properly. To load the weapon, the warrior would hold a cluster of balls in his mouth and spit one into the barrel on top of a powder charge, but he often did not measure the right amount of powder. Some improperly loaded shots had such little force that they had been known to strike a soldier and bounce off harmlessly or not even reach the target.[19]

The principal weapon of Osceola's men might have been firearms, but they also carried knives and tomahawks secured from white traders. The warriors had to rely upon white men for those weapons but also had their native bows and arrows and wooden war clubs. And they could use their bows with great effectiveness. The arrows, each measuring about four feet long, were made of cane stalks, the tips hardened by fire or occasionally fashioned from some metal.

The traditional Seminole fighting techniques were intended not only to kill as many of their enemy as possible but also to strike terror into their hearts at the sight and sound of them. A number of warriors would paint their bodies with red and black streaks and symbols and go into battle naked except for a loincloth. Other warriors would wear captured military uniforms or their traditional costume of feathers and shiny medallions. The primary tactic used to cause sheer terror was the war cry. A warrior would shriek at will and often each time he fired a shot, which might not have helped his aim but certainly unnerved his enemy.[20]

Osceola was not entirely ignorant of the way his enemy fought. John Bemrose, the young hospital orderly and later historian who had been stationed at Fort King, described what he had seen:

Where I stood amongst a group of [the Indians] watching our men at target practice, I could not help but see that they knew and felt their own superiority. Also, when the (white) men were drilling in the woods at Indian fighting, [the Indians'] faces would express to each other a sense of the ridiculous, intuitively conveying to me their knowledge of our inferiority if opposed to them in the native wilds. And I cannot help thinking that during these five peaceful moons they saw too much and formed their plans accordingly. How common it is for civilized and trained combatants to teach themselves to despise these wild men, thereby entailing upon themselves defeat and disaster! The true policy is never to despise an enemy.

Osceola was an attentive student being taught the white man's tactics right there at Fort King. He would now attempt to use that knowledge to defeat his enemy.[21]

It was nearing noon. The bridge construction was coming along fairly well. It would not be too long until the main body of the militia could begin crossing the river. Osceola, who had donned a blue army officer's greatcoat, likely as a show of contempt, was aware that he needed to attack before that bridge was completed. The soldiers on this side of the river were probably about equal in number to the Seminoles—250 apiece, with the odds in Osceola's favor because his warriors were not lounging about but were concealed and prepared to fight. The element of surprise was certainly in his favor. He gave his warriors a hand signal to begin creeping in around the open field where the soldiers apparently were paying no attention to their surroundings.

Emerging stealthily from the dense hammock, the warriors, led by Osceola, crept forward through the tall grass to move within better range. Closer and closer they came, remaining undetected by the several sentries. Osceola planned it so that when the Seminoles were in position, the soldiers would be surrounded on three sides with their avenue of retreat to the rear blocked by the river. They would be virtually trapped. And he knew the soldiers across the river under General Call would not be able to fire without hitting their comrades.

The warriors had advanced almost to the edge of a large hammock before one of Clinch's sentries detected their presence. The man turned to flee toward the troops, all the while sounding the alarm. "Indians! Indians!"

Osceola gave the order to commence firing—a shrill, terrifying war whoop—and the Seminole warriors and their black comrades screamed in reply. They then poured a withering blast of rifle fire into the mass of unsuspecting army troops.

The confused and terrified soldiers began scurrying about this way and that, trying to find somewhere to escape the hail of bullets. The panicked troopers dived to retrieve their stacked arms while readying their ammunition. Within moments, the sound of musket fire could be heard as the soldiers began to fire at real or imagined targets in the dense underbrush around them. After a brief period of fighting every-man-for-himself style, the officers were able to form most of the men into ranks, which improved cohesion. But this act also bunched them up and made them easier targets for the concealed warriors.

Osceola carried his bullets in his cheeks, spitting them out into the rifle barrel and onto a powder charge before carefully aiming and firing. He stood several paces in front of his line of warriors and repeatedly stepped out from behind his cover to choose his target. His bravery and accuracy with his rifle proved an excellent motivation for his warriors, who watched his every move out of the corner of their eyes. Osceola would occasionally call, "Take away the wounded, never mind the dead!"[22]

The soldiers had fallen back about one hundred yards after the first volley. The thickets were now hazy with wisps of gray smoke, and visibility was becoming a concern. Osceola intently watched the positions of both his warriors and the distant soldiers to make certain he could counter any tactic attempted by the army. He felt sure that he had the soldiers pinned between the field and the river but was cautious nonetheless.

One by one, the soldiers were dropping under this fierce Seminole rifle fire. The warriors could snipe effectively at the exposed troops from their places of concealment, but the soldiers could only fire randomly at the muzzle flashes blinking from inside the thickets. Although Osceola could not know it, the constant screaming of his warriors was becoming as unnerving and deadly to many of the troops as the concentrated fire.

Lieutenant Colonel Alexander Fanning, a small, feisty man who possessed only one arm, urged General Clinch to allow him to lead a charge. This was the only way, Fanning argued, that the troops would gain relief from the hidden fire that was piling up the casualties. Finally, Clinch, with no other alternatives, gave his permission. Fanning commenced assembling his men for the assault.

Fanning was quite noticeable as he exposed himself to enemy fire while readying his troops. Osceola had climbed up onto the lower branch of a tree and intently watched this little man through the thick smoke that hung over the battlefield. He could vaguely hear the lieutenant colonel shouting to his men over the din, not knowing that the officer was ordering the soldiers to fix bayonets. Osceola called to nearby warriors, telling them to aim their rifles at this group of men but to hold their fire until he gave the word.

Finally, Fanning and his tight formation of soldiers—their bayonets glistening in the sun, their screams filling the air—surged forward toward the Seminole warriors secreted in the hammock.

Osceola gave the order to fire. His warriors complied. The soldiers from Fanning's charge were stopped in their tracks by the blistering barrage of bullets. Twice more Fanning urged his soldiers forward with bayonets leading the way. At Osceola's order, the Seminoles fell back from each charge, and then came forward again to fire their weapons into the formation with murderous effect. The soldiers were crushed and began to bunch up into small groups. Fanning lost two-thirds of his men in the three ineffective charges.[23]

Osceola could not help taking aim and firing at General Duncan Clinch, who was such a large and inviting target on horseback. The round fired by the Seminole leader zipped through the general's coat sleeve but failed to strike him. Clinch would also discover a hole in his cap at battle's end.

General Clinch quickly dismounted after this close call. He yelled out orders repeated by his officers that called for the troops to spread out. The men obeyed the order and rolled and crawled in the moist grass to put more space between each other along the perimeter. Another detachment of troops had been organized by the fiery one-armed Alexander Fanning and was preparing to charge once again.

Osceola was instinctively aware that if he could turn either flank and attack from the rear, he could create havoc and inflict great damage to the army regulars. He was not worried about the soldiers on the far side of the river. He could see that General Call, fearing an attack on his rear, had ordered those men into a defensive formation. Consequently, those soldiers had their backs turned to the fighting taking place across the river. They had essentially removed themselves from the battle.

Osceola called out to Alligator to attack the troops on the right flank. General Clinch successfully countered this move by directing fire to this flank. Osceola then ordered his warriors to attack the left flank. Clinch was able to counter this move as well.

Osceola ordered another charge by the main body of his warriors, which impelled the soldiers to fall back and keep going. Clinch had not ordered a withdrawal, however, and whipped the remnants of his force back into a skirmisher line, where they laid down an effective base of fire.

Osceola once again got the attention of Alligator and pointed to the right, where he could make another attempt to flank the soldiers and force them closer to the river, where they would be even more vulnerable. Alligator turned to leave with a band of men, when, suddenly, the war cry that Osceola had offered to inspire his men was abruptly cut short.

Alligator noticed that the right sleeve of Osceola's army uniform coat was turning crimson—a musket ball had struck him in the arm. Osceola backed away into the dense foliage, clutching his injured arm. Alligator ran to his side and scooped up mud to plaster the wound and ripped a coat sleeve to make a bandage.[24]

Once again, the army troops were charging. Lieutenant Colonel Fanning had formed another detail and, waving his sword with his good arm, led the advance of his men.

Alligator looked to Osceola for orders. Osceola could see that the bayonet charges were beginning to have a negative effect on his warriors. Bullets were one thing, but for some reason those gleaming blades evoked greater fear. Many of his fighters were backing away as they fired, moving from tree to tree and shifting their position in a gradual retreat. Part of the reason for this reaction by those warriors near Osceola was concern for his welfare. It had been disconcerting for them to see this great man covered with his own blood.[25]

Although Osceola's gunshot wound was a painful, bloody mess, it was far from life-threatening or a reason for abandoning the field. But this battle that had raged for a little over an hour was for all intents and purposes over. The soldiers had assumed a defensive position, and the warriors could only snipe at muzzle flashes. There was no time like the present for the Seminoles to fall back. Osceola knew that his warriors had inflicted serious damage to the soldiers, and his own losses had been minimal. There was no sense pressing the issue.

Perhaps Osceola hesitated briefly to contemplate the temptation to drive the soldiers into the river. But he had been watching his warriors withdraw of their own accord, especially from Fanning's bayonet charges, and finally gave the order for everyone to fall back into the cover of the hammock and head for home. The warriors swept back into the leafy thickets, making sure to carry away their wounded and dead with them. Alligator later said that the reason for the Seminole retreat was the injury to Osceola, that their leader was disabled and needed medical attention. Make no mistake about it, however: Osceola was in charge until the very last bullet was fired.[26]

General Clinch watched his enemy retreat and vanish into the hammock. He had no intention of pursuing them into the dark and tangled recesses of the forbidding Florida swamps. Thus, the Battle of the Withlacoochee River, the first major engagement of the Great Seminole War, had officially come to a conclusion.

Osceola and his Seminoles had accomplished their primary purpose, which was to stop Clinch's mission to destroy their homes in the Cove of the Withlacoochee. In the process, the Seminoles had lost three dead and five wounded—although Clinch would later claim that he had killed at least thirty of his enemy. Osceola's wound would prove to be inconsequential and would not adversely affect him in any way.

Two of the dead and three of the wounded Seminoles were black. Blacks had constituted less than one-fourth of Osceola's force but had sustained more than half the casualties. The two dead Black Seminoles who were killed had been from Micanopy's household, which greatly saddened the head chief. He pleaded with his blacks to be more cautious in future battles.[27]

Clinch might have held the field in the end—a military prerequisite for victory—but that field was blood soaked and littered with the bodies of his dead and wounded. The army's casualties included four regulars killed and fifty-nine wounded, one of whom would later die. An officer later recounted, "The firing was heavy, and the bushes literally cut up around us, how it was that more were not shot I cannot tell."[28] Apparently Osceola's warriors needed intensive marksmanship training.

Only a small number of General Call's Florida militia volunteers had crossed the river to engage the warriors, but those men later bragged that they had made the difference in the battle. They claimed that Osceola and his warriors were aware of the presence of the volunteer force across the river and were therefore hesitant to mount an all-out assault on the soldiers in that open field. In other words, the volunteers had acted as a deterrent—otherwise the Seminoles would have slaughtered Clinch's regulars. Nothing could have been further from the truth. Osceola and his warriors could only have been encouraged that the militia had not crossed the river to reinforce Clinch and instead set up a perimeter with their backs to the action.[29]

As soon as the log bridge spanning the river had been completed, Clinch and his weary troops marched across to the safe side, leaving behind a cache of weapons and ammunition in their haste. The weary and beaten column returned to Fort Drane, where the Florida volunteers were discharged from service.[30]

Naturally, Clinch claimed victory, but he must have known—as did his officers and men—that he had been embarrassed by Osceola. And the general had no one to blame but himself for his troops being ripped to shreds by Osceola's surprise attack.

Clinch never should have attempted the impulsive and foolish crossing of the swollen Withlacoochee at that location. He should have marched on until he had reached the proper ford. Osceola might have been waiting in ambush at that other ford, but the water was only two feet deep and the troops could have been deployed more effectively. The soldiers surely could have accounted for themselves much better there than the predicament in which Clinch had been placed them, regardless of the ambush.

In addition, there can be no justification for Clinch dividing his force at the river. It was not as if he had a bridge or even a worthy boat to transport the men across. The two sides were connected by nothing more than a flimsy canoe and were virtually stranded on either bank when the firing commenced. Equally difficult to understand is why the general permitted his soldiers to lounge around in that open field. They should have immediately set up a perimeter and remained alert with weapons at the ready and aimed outward toward the surrounding foliage.

Perhaps Clinch had been under the mistaken impression that the Seminoles would be waiting for him at the doorsteps of their homes and he could simply invade the town, kill the inhabitants, burn all the structures, and be done with the war. If anything, there can be no doubt that the general—as well as the entire subordinate chain of command and the common soldiers—was greatly surprised by the military skills of Osceola and now realized that their enemy had been gravely underestimated. The Dade Massacre had not been an aberration—these Seminoles knew how to fight.

General Clinch did not escape criticism from one of his own officers for his handling of the battle and the subsequent report he sent to the War Department. General Richard Call found serious fault in the tactics Clinch employed, outlining the abovementioned blunders and then summing up his personal feelings for his commanding officer: "The fictitious reputation and vainglorious boasting of this individual has long excited my mirth."[31]

One interesting side note concerns Lieutenant John Graham, Osceola's old friend from Fort King, who was present at this battle. John Bemrose cared for the wounded soldiers after the engagement, and he recalled that "Company D were lucky in possessing a Lieut. John Graham in their midst for everywhere he was stationed the balls flew less thickly. This was owing to Graham's former friendship with the savage chief Osceola. Afterward in communication with the Indians we learned that Osceola had given his warriors orders not to fire upon Graham who was a good mark, being a very big man, so he protected him in battle."[32]

Osceola returned with his warriors from the victorious battle to his camp within the Withlacoochee swamp. His people were situated as comfortably as conditions would permit at their enclave in the Cove, the Wahoo Swamp. This swamp was a vast, mysterious wilderness that would intimidate even the most stouthearted outsider. The terrain was an excessively wet and tangled maze of foliage and trees, reverberating with the hiss of alligators, the howling of wolves, the screaming of panthers; infested with rattlesnakes and other poisonous snakes; and teeming with countless more natural dangers. The fact that these Seminole people had chosen to live in this swamp over relocation to the West demonstrated the lengths the people would go, the misery they would endure, and the depth of their commitment to gain justice and remain on their land that they had inhabited for so many years.

The war leader could look out from his hut of palmetto thatch and find solace at the sight of the small fires burning outside the family huts of his fellow Seminoles. The aroma of corn gruel, meat, and fish cooking over those fires wafted across this temporary refuge as smoke drifted up through the trees. The makeshift camp was primitive even by Seminole standards, but they would make do as best they could. These proud people had been driven there by the white man with the knowledge that death and the destruction of their nation were distinct possibilities. But they valued freedom more than life. They would take up residence in that unpleasant swamp and endure miserable conditions until order could be restored to their broken society and they could live freely and in peace once more.

Osceola had accepted the scepter of leadership with passion and determination. Among the Seminoles of Florida, no one else possessed his level of influence. He now bore virtually sole responsibility for the survival of his people. He had his council of chiefs—Alligator, Jumper, and Micanopy, in particular—with whom to seek guidance. But in the end, every final decision was his to make, and any decision could prove to be a fatal mistake. This war was his war to fight. The will and motivation of his people to face their enemy in battle came primarily from him. He had now even marked a battlefield with his own blood. The gash from the musket ball that had ripped through his arm was a badge of honor. Osceola, however, let it be known then and always that he clearly abhorred bloodshed and wanted this conflict to be over. Nearly every contemporary account supports the premise that Osceola hated this war and believed that it had been thrust upon him by the refusal of the whites to recognize basic Seminole rights.[33]

A key to Osceola's genius was his uncanny ability to galvanize and inspire the entirety of his people—men, women, and children. The warriors would follow him to the ends of the earth and the children idolized him. Osceola had apparently turned the women into a smoothly functioning domestic supply and comfort faction of the tribe, which had been their traditional role in war and peace. Army officer John Sprague wrote, "In Osceola was combined a nerve, activity, and intelligence, which seemed to diffuse itself among all classes. The women gave a most hearty co-operation, and though obliged to abandon their homes, they cheerfully encountered fatigue, and congregated in places of safety, where they supplied provisions indiscriminately to the warriors, as they went to and from the field of battle."[34]

One of Osceola's trusted confidants was now Abraham, who was perhaps forty-five years of age. Abraham, the former slave who could read and write proper English and who had been falsely accused of misleading the tribe with the Treaty of Payne's Landing, became one of Osceola's valued wartime interpreters and aides-de-camp.[35]

At his new home deep in the swamp, secluded from the outside world, with the smells, sounds, and sights of the Battle of the Withlacoochee still filling his senses, Osceola beckoned to Abraham. He asked his interpreter to write a message in black vegetable paint that would be carried to General Duncan Clinch by a sympathetic slave or friendly Seminole.

"Tell this to the white chief," Osceola said. "You have guns and so do we; you have powder and lead and so do we; you have men and so have we; your men will fight, and so will ours until the last drop of the Seminoles' blood has moistened the dust of this hunting grounds."[36]

Osceola had once again boldly thrown down the gauntlet in challenge.

Seven

Generals in Confusion

※❖※

Accounts of the Battle of the Withlacoochee were front-page news across the nation, and Osceola became the object of great curiosity. Despite his violent actions against the white man—the Dade Massacre, agent Wiley Thompson's assassination, and his latest victory on the Withlacoochee—he became an overnight sensation throughout parts of Florida and the country. It must be considered strange and perhaps unprecedented that so many whites viewed the Seminole tustenugge thlocklo with such morbid admiration. Some Americans even described him as a visionary of sorts.

Typical of the praise for Osceola is an editorial in the *St. Augustine Herald*: "The character of this chief is but little known and not sufficiently appreciated. He is represented to be a man of great tact, energy of character, and bold daring." And quoting from the *Floridian, Niles' Weekly Register* wrote, "Osceola, the head of the hostile Seminoles, is likely to figure in history with Philip of Pokanokee or Tecumseh, possessing all their noble daring and deep love of country, with more intelligence, and perhaps, more ferocity."[1]

A measure of this regard for Osceola sprang from public sympathy for what many believed was a noble cause embraced by the Seminole. A letter from a Washington, D.C., resident to the *Journal of Commerce* adequately sums up this widespread sentiment:

> This is the last and most desperate struggle of the Indian. He fights now glorious and gallantly, with the spirit of a thousand lions in his breast—for the soil on which he was born, and which was a just inheritance from his ancestors. We, by a forced and corrupt treaty, call it ours. We send armed men—men armed with a whiskey bottle, a weapon more terrible than the rifle—to persuade them to abide by a treaty which they never made, and to cross the Mississippi River never to return. The spirit of their tribe—the Great Spirit walking in the sky—tells them they must perish. The voice of their fathers calls them to their home—the only home which the white man has left them—the grave. Preparations are making not for the defeat of the Seminoles, but for their extermination.[2]

This grimly passionate assessment failed to take into account the fact that at the moment Osceola was winning the war. But with all the resources available to the army, most observers were aware that it would be only a matter of time before the Seminole people would cease to exist as a nation.

It can also be assumed that most of the positive sentiments toward Osceola and the Seminoles were of Northerners and those who had no attachment to the faraway war. Public outrage in Florida over the battle losses and dismal forecast for the war overwhelmed praise by a large margin, however. Colonel James Gadsden wrote a letter to President Jackson on January 4, 1836, that expressed the panic that was sweeping through most of Florida:

> I must say that we the People of Florida are in a most distracted and distressed state—We are literally without a Government; without concert of action . . . a universal distrust seems to pervade the whole Community . . . all seem distracted in the general cry of something must be done, while all oppose every measure that can be suggested.

The Army of volunteers & Regulars have met the Enemy at the Withla-
couchey & after a sharp contest for one hour separated, as it were by
consent—The Army retiring to their old camp at Lang Syne, & the
Indians remaining on the field of Battle—Since when the Volunteers
have returned home leaving Clinch with his regular force reduced 40
or 50 by death or wounds in a position on the frontier—In the meanwhile the Indians have been encouraged & have burnt & destroyed
the whole country to the St. Johns River. . . . Thompson the Agent
I presume you have heard has been killed & the whole country of Tomoka, Lower Allachua, &s Destroyed & laid waste—the People of the
East are in truly deplorable state & something must be done & that
speedily to relieve them.[3]

No doubt Osceola had been informed by his numerous spies that his violent actions had turned the territory of Florida upside down. The general
public was in a panic, the army was demoralized, and the Seminoles were
making their mark as a dissident force with which to be reckoned. Osceola at
present controlled the entire Withlacoochee region, and he was not about to
relinquish his grip or moderate his efforts anytime soon.[4]

Contemporary army officer John Bemrose wrote, "The daily tales of murder and scalping, first in one direction and then in another, possibly 100
miles apart, showed plainly that the enemy was terribly on the alert, nothing
escaping his vigilance, causing us to be filled with many forebodings. Now
all began to see we had got into a hornet's nest, many miles from the sea-
board, and consequently not over safe in keeping out scalps. Tales of horror
filled all minds; discipline became most rigid, for all saw the necessity of
proper care."[5]

The perilous situation in Florida elicited a rapid response from Congress. When word of General Clinch's engagement on the Withlacoochee
reached Washington in mid-January 1836, another $500,000—in addition
to $120,000 already appropriated—was allotted to put down this uprising. It
was common knowledge that part of the reason for spending this much

money and the heightened attention to the conflict was that the War Department, likely at the urging of the president, had vowed to protect the rights of slaveholders. No treaty terms would be offered to Osceola and his dissidents as long as even one slave remained in the hands of that tribe.[6]

The War Department also responded by appointing War of 1812 hero and future presidential candidate Brevet Major General Winfield Scott to assume command of Florida Territory. Scott was not a West Pointer; he had worked his way up the ranks as a proven and skilled commander. He was fifty years old and stood an imposing six foot four, although one shoulder drooped from a severe wound suffered in the War of 1812. Scott was known as "Old Fuss and Feathers" due to his propensity for strict military protocol and discipline. He also favored the finer things in life—elaborate uniforms, marching bands, custom furniture, and rare wines, all of which he brought with him wherever he was stationed.

General Scott was told that no expense would be spared to subdue the militant Seminoles and their wily leader. He could request as many volunteers as he needed from the governors of Alabama, Florida, Georgia, and South Carolina, and draw weapons and equipment from their arsenals. Scott would order that thirty-seven hundred citizen soldiers—two battalions of infantry and three mounted—be mobilized from those states. Congress issued strict orders, however, that he was not to negotiate with the Seminoles whatsoever until they had given up all the runaway slaves they were protecting, and that the preferred result would be unconditional surrender or destruction. Scott predicted that he would crush the uprising within three months.[7]

The general had recently authored an army manual, *Infantry Tactics*, which basically reflected the European style of combat. Battles, according to Scott, were fought in a precision manner, like choreographed dance moves, with the combatants lined up on opposite sides of the field prepared to engage in exhibitions of marksmanship followed by frontal assaults. If General Scott followed the instructions outlined in his respected manual, he would be playing right into the hands of Osceola and his guerrilla tactics.[8]

Unbeknownst to Scott, his nemesis, Major General Edmund Gaines, commander of U.S. forces in Louisiana Territory, had learned about the Dade

Massacre and decided to respond on his own. After all, the western part of Florida Territory was within his jurisdiction—overlapping Scott's command—and he believed it was his duty to take action. Gaines, fifty-nine years of age, was of average height but scarecrow-thin, with a gaunt, weather-beaten face topped by a shock of bristly gray hair. He was outspoken, quick to criticize, and not easy to get along with. Gaines had opposed Jackson's policy of Indian removal, which was part of the reason the president had picked Winfield Scott rather than Gaines to put down the uprising in Florida.

On February 4, 1836, Gaines and a body of Louisiana volunteers put to sea from New Orleans and arrived two days later in Pensacola. When he reached that city, Gaines was informed of the appointment of General Scott, which did not sit well with him. He had coveted that position for himself and resented both Scott and Jackson for this rebuff. Scott and Gaines had been vying for the top spot for quite some time, but Gaines could not control his ill temper and had few allies, whereas Scott was the consummate politician. Gaines and Scott had already feuded during the Black Hawk War several years earlier, when Scott had been sent into Gaines's command area to direct operations. The presence of Scott at that time in that place was a serious affront to the capabilities of Gaines as a commander.

General Gaines and his army traveled by three steamships from Pensacola and debarked in Tampa Bay on February 9. By the time Gaines made it to Fort Brooke, there was a letter from Secretary of War Cass waiting that directed him to take command along the Texas border. The general was in a quandary about whether to proceed on his self-appointed mission in Florida or head toward Texas. At the urging of subordinates—and certainly with designs of showing up Winfield Scott—Gaines chose to remain in Florida.[9]

The general had been joined at Fort Brooke by six companies of the Florida Fourth Infantry. Gaines now commanded a total of about a thousand men, including a full band, and he dragged along a one-pounder cannon. On February 13, Gaines commenced his march into the interior with intentions of visiting Fort King, where he believed 120,000 rations that had been ordered by General Scott were waiting to supply his troops. His men currently carried about ten days' rations. He was guided by twenty-seven "friendly"

Indians as his column headed along the regular wagon road from Fort Brooke to Fort King.

Osceola's scouts were aware of the arrival in Tampa Bay of this large contingent of troops and had been shadowing them as they proceeded down the road on their mission. The Seminole had the distinct advantage when scouting their adversary: large bodies of troops were impossible to hide, but Native Americans could easily disappear into the swampy, wooded landscape. Osceola always enjoyed the freshest intelligence, which allowed him to make his plans while avoiding any trap laid by his enemy.

The route taken by General Gaines retraced the march of Major Francis Dade's ill-fated command less than two months earlier. On February 20, the Gaines column arrived at the site of that massacre. They encountered a grisly scene of mangled human corpses and animal carcasses lying within the breastwork—just the way the men had died at their posts—with other bodies and horse remains sprawled along the road and strewn about the swamp. These repulsive, decaying bodies were unrecognizable due to decomposition and scavengers. Indeed, a flock of buzzards had greeted the soldiers and impatiently circled above to create an even more macabre scene.

This experience must have been horrifying for these men, especially as many of them had friends or acquaintances among those who had perished. These troops were on the hunt for the same Seminoles who had so thoroughly slaughtered their comrades. Hundreds or thousands of warriors could be secreted in the dense hammock at that very moment waiting for the signal to attack. No doubt hearts were beating faster, muskets were clutched tighter, eyes were constantly scanning the surrounding hammock, and there was an urgency to complete their deed here and move on as quickly as possible to the safety of Fort King.

The dead officers were identified by gold fillings in their teeth, rings, and other personal possessions, and were buried together in one grave. The discovery of personal items on those corpses may refute claims that the blacks had looted the field after the Seminoles had departed. The remains of the enlisted men were gathered up and interred in a second and third mass grave. An unserviceable six-pounder cannon that had been recovered from the swamp was dragged on top of the graves to serve as a monument to the fallen. Gaines ordered that the command stand at attention while the band played a funeral march. The shaken troops then resumed their march down the road to Fort King, assuredly on a higher alert than they had been previously.[10]

The Gaines expedition marched through the gates of Fort King on February 22. The general expected to resupply his men and promptly return to the field, but he was shocked and angered to find that the provisions ordered by Scott had failed to arrive. Gaines, who likely muttered a few words about the incompetence of his adversary, realized that he could not continue his pursuit of the Seminoles without additional rations. He dispatched a packhorse train to Fort Drane to procure rations from General Duncan Clinch. Fort Drane, it was soon discovered, was low on provisions as well. Gaines was able to secure enough rations—about seven days' worth—that he calculated would at least take him back to Fort Brooke. His column departed Fort King on February 26 and headed down the route toward Clinch's battlefield at the Withlacoochee River, which he hoped might afford him the opportunity of engaging the hostiles.[11]

Osceola was informed about the direction of the column of troops soon after it moved away from the fort. He held a council with his top lieutenants—Alligator, Jumper, and Micanopy—to discuss strategy. Osceola believed that this large force, as had been the case with General Clinch, was on a course that would lead it to the Cove of the Withlacoochee, which was too close for comfort to their families. He determined that they would go out and strike these soldiers with every warrior available to discourage them from entering Seminole domain.

The excited warriors set about hastily preparing their equipment for another confrontation with their enemy—cleaning rifles and making lead shot, cutting arrows from cane stalks and hardening tips, sharpening tomahawks, and readying clubs. The women busily packed enough food and other necessary supplies to sustain their warriors. Osceola probably moved off by himself, away from the bustle of the camp, to formulate the plan that he trusted would prove to be as successful as his previous attacks. Clinch had made his mistake along the Withlacoochee, he reflected with satisfaction; now it was Gaines's turn.[12]

On February 27, General Gaines's command reached the Withlacoochee River at the same ford, according to his Indian guides, that General Clinch had been seeking but never found two months earlier. Gaines questioned the accuracy of this information. The river at that point was thirty yards across, the opposite bank six feet high, and it appeared to be running deeper than the two feet he had been led to believe was the normal depth. The general ordered that the river be tested to judge their ability to cross. A squad of un-armed soldiers waded into the water. Their companions casually lined the shoreline to watch what could turn out to be a comical scene if the water was indeed deep and swift.

With no advance guard or reconnaissance of the area across the river, Gaines had no way of knowing that Osceola and his warriors had set up a welcoming committee for him at that ford. A large force of Seminoles lay hidden in the underbrush, their rifles trained on the exposed soldiers on the far bank. No sooner had the squad of soldiers stepped into the murky river and moved forward than Osceola gave the signal—a shrill war whoop that filleted the spines of the whites. His warriors echoed the cry and commenced firing at will.

The astonished troops in the water scrambled for shore, while the spectators frantically sought cover from the onslaught. Gaines quickly deployed his men into a defensive position and rallied them to return fire, which sent a barrage of bullets ripping into the brush around Osceola's warriors. The Seminoles, however, were undeterred by the counterattack and kept up their own assault of the army line. Gaines brought up his fieldpiece and commenced spraying the Seminoles with canister shot. Osceola ordered his men to fall back a short distance for safety's sake, but they still maintained their heavy fire.

After about an hour of sustained warfare, without either side gaining an advantage, General Gaines ordered his troops to cease fire and withdraw into the hammock. The army had suffered several men wounded, one of whom would later die. There were no reported Seminole casualties. Gaines had his men establish their bivouac in the trees and thick brush some distance from the river.[13]

As darkness fell, Osceola could observe small fires burning across the Withlacoochee and was impressed by their number. He was once again out-numbered by his enemy—perhaps at present by three or four to one. But the odds might soon change. He was in the process of gathering a larger force. Osceola had been recruiting warriors from across Florida who were arriving daily to bolster his numbers. But for now, he made certain his strategy was designed so that he could avoid placing his warriors in a position where the superior force could affect the outcome of the conflict. Osceola felt relatively safe for the time being under the cover of night and allowed small groups to leave their positions to go back to where the women were and eat and refresh themselves. He was certain that this battle was far from over, and he wanted to keep his men as rested and as ready to fight as possible.

The following morning, February 28, Osceola watched from his hiding place across the river as the column of soldiers broke camp and began march-ing downriver. The Seminole leader moved his warriors parallel to the troops, secreted within the tangled underbrush. General Gaines was heading toward a ford that his Indian guides now swore was the ford with two-foot-deep water and was suitable for crossing.

It could have been that these "friendly" Indians actually had been mis-leading Gaines right from the beginning, while at the same time informing Osceola of the army's movements. No evidence exists for this theory, but an experienced group of guides would not have made the mistake of leading Gaines to the ford that had resulted in the previous day's engagement.

The column of soldiers arrived at this new ford. The lead elements stepped out from the thickets onto the fringes of a wide-open pine barren that extended to both sides of the river. Osceola and his warriors remained within eye contact with the troops but were farther away from the river than previously due to the clearing that stretched back to the underbrush at that location. Gaines figured there would be less chance of an ambush at this open space, and consequently a crossing might be successfully executed. He ordered Lieutenant James F. Izard forward to examine the river to determine that possibility.

Izard waited on the bank, holding his horse, while he sent a squad of men into the water to gauge the depth. At that moment, one of Osceola's best marksmen took aim at the lieutenant. The bullet fired from the Seminole rifle slammed into Izard—entering his nose, passing behind his left ear, and exiting out his left temple. The lieutenant fell to the ground in grave condition, but remained alive as he was dragged back into cover.[14]

The soldiers formed a skirmisher line, and both sides then commenced firing at the other. The army on the northern bank and the Seminole on the southern bank of the Withlacoochee engaged in furious bursts of gunfire and arrows. Specific targets on either side were almost impossible to sight in on due to the distance caused by the openness of the ground and the thick cover of cypress, oak, and mahogany trees and palmetto thickets beyond. The battle lasted until about noon, when the army chose to withdraw. The soldiers had sustained one killed and two wounded in this fierce skirmish. Osceola had all along shrewdly singled out officers as the objectives of his top snipers, and Gaines had lost one dead and one wounded officer thus far.

The general put his soldiers to work felling trees to be utilized as a fortification, a bridge, and rafts. He had no intention of retreating. He would hunker down until he could cross the river and crush his enemy. A quadrangular breastwork was soon partially erected about 120 yards from the river around a small pond, which enclosed an area about 250 yards square. The makeshift log fortress was christened "Camp Izard" in honor of Lieutenant James Izard, who lay severely wounded but still clinging to life.

The general dispatched a courier to Fort Drane, thirty-two miles away, with orders for General Clinch to bring reinforcements and supplies without delay. Gaines told Clinch to cross the river ten miles upstream and execute a surprise attack on the Seminole warriors from the rear. Gaines was low on provisions but decided that if Clinch and the additional troops and supplies hurried, he could yet defeat his primitive enemy. Gaines also vowed that he would no longer pay attention to anything said by his "friendly" Indian guides.[15]

Osceola would have held a council of his top lieutenants that night. He would listen to the advice of Micanopy, the head chief; Jumper, the chief's brother-in-law and counselor; his trusted kinsman Alligator; and of course Abraham, who spoke for the blacks. Osceola was aware of the immense strength of his enemy camped over there in the darkness, and that they were building sturdy walls around their position for protection. The bridge building and the rafts were a serious threat as well. He also knew that six hundred soldiers waited at Fort Drane to reinforce this detachment and might even be on the march at that moment.

Osceola made the only decision that made sense to him—he would attack. It would not be a frontal assault but rather a controlled siege designed to pin down and kill as many as possible and demoralize his enemy until they went away and left the Seminole in peace.

On February 29, just before daybreak, Osceola separated his warriors into two groups and dispatched one group to the east and one to the west of Camp Izard. These men silently crossed the Withlacoochee at known fords onto the northern side utilizing hastily constructed log rafts. Both groups stealthily made their way through the dense hammock until they met and formed a skirmisher line in the high grass and scrub palmetto across their enemy's rear. Camp Izard, which was not fully completed, was now surrounded by warriors on the east, west, and north, with the sole route of escape south toward the river.

Osceola and his men patiently waited. They watched as the men arose from their blankets and ate breakfast before going back to work on their fortification. Osceola had no intention of storming this fortress. Such a strategy would be suicidal for his warriors. Instead, he was more interested in trying to pick off the soldiers one by one as they exposed themselves.

It was midmorning when the time was finally right. Osceola could observe soldiers with axes hacking into logs and others hewing them or tying them together to finish the fortress, as well as some men constructing rafts and a bridge at the riverbank. A majority of the troops, perhaps as many as two-thirds, were now outside the fortification. Osceola gave his trademark signal to attack, that nerve-shattering war cry.

The Seminole marksmen answered with their own war cries and opened fire, dropping a number of the surprised soldiers with this initial volley of hot, angry lead. The troops assigned to the raft and bridge details raced for the breastwork, pausing only to drag their stricken comrades along with them. Those who could grab their nearby muskets covered this frantic retreat. The soldiers eventually laid down an effective base of fire, which had the Seminoles ducking for cover and slowing their own rate of fire.

Osceola had another trick in his bag, however. He had his warriors set fire to the dry grass and brush. The flames crawled along the ground and eventually reached the logs of Camp Izard, which posed a major hazard for those inside. The soldiers did their best to douse the fast-moving flames that also carried choking smoke into their midst, but it was quickly growing out of control. Osceola's marksmen surged forward within the smoky haze to take better aim, at times shooting from nearly point-blank range. The besieged men—stunned by how close the Seminoles had approached—were now compelled to fight smoke and flames and at the same time fend off their enemy.

Osceola had taken advantage of this perfect fire to execute an unexpected tactic. Rarely would anyone brazenly charge a fortification manned by regular army troops. Osceola had contradicted his own strategy of not attacking with a frontal assault. In this instance, however, the opportunity to inflict serious harm on the army—both physical and psychological—outweighed caution.[16]

General Gaines sat in a chair inside his fortress and skillfully deployed his men both to repel the shocking attack and to snuff out the fire. He likely cursed himself for not having sent sentries farther out in listening posts during the night to prevent this bold assault from the rear. All of a sudden, Gaines was struck in the lower lip with a bullet that tore through his flesh and knocked out two of his teeth. He reportedly said, "It is mean of the redskins to knock out my teeth when I have so few!"[17]

Eventually, a shift in the wind turned the fire back onto ground already burned, where it quickly died. This natural act of fate forced the warriors to retreat and spared the army camp from being consumed by the raging inferno. Osceola repositioned his warriors, and the Seminoles continued to pour devastating rifle fire into the breastwork.

After about two hours of sustained battle, Osceola decided to pull back his warriors. This lull afforded Gaines the opportunity to dispatch another courier to Fort Drane with orders for General Clinch to hurry with reinforcements and supplies. The military men also redoubled their efforts on the breastwork of Camp Izard. This skirmish had cost the army one dead and thirty-three wounded, including General Edmund Gaines.

There are no estimates of casualties for Osceola's Seminoles engaged in the fight to this point, but the soldiers reported seeing blood and the warriors carrying away comrades after creeping close to the fortification behind the flames. Perhaps Osceola's rash tactic of leading his warriors up to the doorstep of Camp Izard had been a mistake. That night, his counselors questioned their war leader about continuing this fight. They held the opinion that it might be best to go back home before those reinforcements arrived. Osceola, however, loudly argued—supposedly an army officer across the river heard and recognized his shrill voice—that they maintain the siege. Finally, it was agreed by everyone to remain there and keep the enemy pinned down. But Osceola had to promise not to order another frontal assault of Camp Izard under any circumstances.

The siege resumed in earnest on the first day of March. The Seminole warriors stayed in position while they sniped at any soldier who dared expose himself. This constant shooting was accompanied by those bone-chilling, heartbeat-accelerating war cries that penetrated deep into the soul and psyche of every soldier who gripped his musket and hugged those log walls. It was bad enough to dodge flying lead, but those demonic cries added a surreal factor to the setting.

Conditions at Camp Izard rapidly deteriorated. Rations were dwindling, and the troops were hungry. After three days, all that was left for consumption was the corn brought to feed the horses. Gaines distributed a pint of this corn to each soldier and then began butchering horses and roasting the meat. Camp dogs suffered the same fate. Lieutenant Prince recorded that "a quarter of dog meat sold for $5." Those men who refused horse or dog meat, and there were a number of them, had nothing to eat.[18]

Ironically, at the same time as the siege of Fort Izard, another more famous siege was under way at a mission in San Antonio, Texas. On February 23, Mexico's Santa Anna had brought an overwhelming force of soldiers to Texas and surrounded the Alamo, where 188 mostly American volunteers had taken refuge. This standoff would last for thirteen days, when, on March 6, the Mexican army would storm the Alamo and kill nearly everyone inside.[19]

After five days of the Florida standoff, the namesake of the makeshift army camp and its inspiration, Lieutenant James Izard, finally died from the gunshot wound he had sustained.

General Gaines was running out of options. He could watch his troops starve to death, or he could attempt to retreat with the warriors harassing and sniping at them. Either way, it was apparent that this expedition was headed for a disastrous conclusion unless General Clinch and the Fort Drane reinforcements arrived to save them.

The Seminoles, on the other hand, were not living in luxury by any means, but their women had been busy cooking and molding bullets. The warriors were provided for as well as possible, but the families living in the swamps were beginning to feel the effects of hunger and illness. In addition, Osceola was becoming anxious about this conflict. He had come to the conclusion that the U.S. Army could withstand a long war more easily than could his people.

He also had been informed by his scouts that Clinch and a column of troops were on their way from Fort Drane—as many as 450 infantrymen and 150 cavalrymen—which made him uneasy about present circumstances. Although he held the upper hand in this siege, he had promised not to assault the fortification, and waiting for the men inside to starve to death or make a break for it did not appear to be a possibility before Clinch made his appearance. Osceola did not intend to fight both Gaines and Clinch.

Thus far, the Seminoles had lost three men killed—including one black— and five wounded. This number was far less than the army's casualties, but any bloodshed by his people was too much in Osceola's estimation. He first and foremost wanted peace. With that premise in mind, he dispatched one of his black interpreters, John Caesar, a member of Micanopy's household, to approach Camp Izard under the immunity of a white flag with the task of arranging a parley.

General Gaines had been besieged for eight days and had lost a total of five men killed and forty-six wounded. He could not sustain such casualities for much longer, nor could he endure watching his men starve; hunger had so weakened them that they would be hard-pressed to walk out of there, much less fight their way out. The general could not even be certain that Clinch had received his messages. He could be completely on his own. Consequently, he agreed to a meeting with his Seminole adversaries at ten o'clock the following morning.[20]

At the assigned time on March 6, Captain Ethan Allen Hitchcock and several other officers carrying a white flag departed the safety of Camp Izard and walked out into the open space. Gaines apparently would not dignify the Seminole with his presence and instead sent emissaries. The army officers were met there by Osceola, Jumper, Alligator, Holata Micco, and interpreters Abraham and John Caesar. One of the officers was said to be a man named Chamberlain, who had been friendly with Osceola at Fort King. The two men shook hands and briefly conversed in a cordial manner.[21]

Osceola told Hitchcock and the other officers that the Seminoles wanted not only a truce but also a permanent end to hostilities. He would cease fighting altogether if General Gaines would guarantee that the army would march away and not attack the Seminoles ever again. Further, the general must promise that the Seminoles would not be forced to leave their homeland. Hitchcock told them he did not have the authority to agree to those terms but would pass them on to his superior officer.

General Gaines, of course, did not have permission to agree to any demands made by his enemy, much less to negotiate. The best he could hope for was to maintain this cease-fire until Clinch and reinforcements arrived. To the credit of Gaines, who was not a patient man, he was somehow able to extend the cease-fire and peace talks between the two sides for two more days.

On March 8, the army officers and the Seminole leaders met once again in the open clearing. Osceola was becoming impatient. Gaines was in a quandary. He did not possess the authority to arrange a peace treaty with Osceola, yet if he refused to negotiate there was a good chance that he and his men would die at that place. The general passed the word that he would consider ending hostilities if the Seminole would abandon the area around the Withla-coochee, promise never again to attack whites, and attend formal treaty talks to settle matters once and for all.

Osceola had just agreed through his interpreter that the Withlacoochee should be the boundary line between the Seminoles and the United States when, suddenly, both parties were shocked by bullets whizzing past them.

General Duncan Clinch's column had arrived. His lead troops, not realizing that a parley was in progress, had fired a volley at the exposed Seminoles.

Osceola and the chiefs raced away into the surrounding hammock. The war leader ordered the warriors to retrieve their families and possessions and retreat into their remote camp in the swamp. Osceola deployed a few warriors concealed in the palmettos to guard the Seminole withdrawal but told them not to shoot unless necessary. The siege of Camp Izard had been lifted, and this first attempt by Osceola for a negotiated peace had ended in a hail of gunfire.

General Clinch had brought along with him forty head of cattle and rations of bread and pork to feed the starving survivors of Camp Izard. There can be no doubt that Clinch's timely arrival had saved Gaines's troops from being wiped out. The peace talk had been at an impasse, and Osceola would have soon realized that Gaines was simply buying time with empty promises.

General Gaines did not praise or thank Clinch for his timely arrival, however. Quite the contrary. Gaines proclaimed to Clinch that the Seminole War was over, and he—General Edmund Gaines—had been the victor. At that time, he turned his command over to Clinch for evacuation until the arrival of "the officer charged with the diplomatic arrangements of the War Department," meaning his nemesis, General Winfield Scott.

Two days later, on March 10, the exhausted men who had garrisoned Camp Izard limped away on their arduous journey toward Fort Drane, carrying their wounded—and their terrifying memories—with them.[22]

On March 13, after being delayed by terrible weather, Edmund Gaines and his entourage rode into Fort Drane, and he came face-to-face with Winfield Scott, "the officer charged with the diplomatic arrangements." Instead of an explosion of personalities, the two officers went out of their way to avoid each other. John Bemrose wrote, "I noticed a cold salutation passed between them. There was no companionship and evidently there existed a distaste, a repelling power proving that when interests clash, two of a trade seldom agree." The tension at Fort Drane lifted the following morning when General Gaines departed. Gaines, the "victor" of the Seminole War, would decline public testimonial dinners in Mobile and New Orleans on his way back to Texas.[23]

General Winfield Scott was now free to implement his own strategy, which called for a three-pronged pincer movement to trap the hostiles. Three separate detachments of infantry and cavalry, with supporting artillery attached to each, would attempt to catch the Seminole warriors at the Cove of the Withlacoochee and then surround and destroy them. The artillery would lay waste to the hammock; the infantry would flush out the warriors; and the cavalry would ride them down. Scott was confident that his plan would overwhelm his primitive enemy and have them begging for a peace treaty in no time at all.

The right-wing column, commanded by General Duncan Clinch, would converge on the objective from Fort Drane. The left-wing column, under the command of Brigadier General Abraham Eustis, would ascend the St. Johns River from St. Augustine, cross at Volusia, and traverse the peninsula. The center column, led by Colonel William Lindsay, would march north from Fort Brooke at Tampa Bay.

The three columns, about forty-eight hundred men in total, would approach the Seminole refuge on a predetermined schedule—Clinch across the Withlacoochee, Eustis at Peliklakaha, and Lindsay at Coacoochee. The columns would remain in contact with each other by firing a cannon shot in the morning and another in the evening. At Scott's command, they would simultaneously drive into the Cove of the Withlacoochee and wreak havoc.[24]

Once again, Osceola's scouts were positioned in every nook and cranny of the territory. When an army column marched, the Seminole war leader would soon be informed and could formulate his strategy accordingly. He had already decided to separate his warriors into smaller, more mobile bands that could harass and confuse the enemy and quickly vanish into the hammock. Osceola would fight only when he had the advantage, and his record of success in choosing when to hit and when to run had been remarkable. The Seminoles had sustained casualties, but far fewer than they might have had without the skillful planning of the tustenugge thlocklo.

General Abraham Eustis, commanding about fourteen hundred volunteers, marched his column to the St. Johns River, arrived at Volusia on March 17, and bivouacked for five days. When Eustis finally made the decision to send his troops across the river, the Seminoles were waiting for them. Two companies crossed and, oddly enough, as had been the case with Clinch at the Withlacoochee, the soldiers casually stacked their weapons and were less than attentive to their surroundings. The Seminole warriors "crept within 25 yards of the sentinel before being perceived," and then opened fire on this exposed group of soldiers. Eustis dispatched additional troops across the river to reinforce their comrades. The Seminole ambushers eventually broke contact and withdrew, carrying away one dead warrior. The army, however, lost three killed and another several wounded—two hit by friendly fire when the confused soldiers shot wildly in the opening moments of the attack.[25]

Two days later, those persistent soldiers crossed the Oklawaha River. For unknown reasons, Osceola decided not to set up an ambush to prevent them. Around dusk that day, Brigadier General Joseph Sheldon and a scouting party went to investigate the distant glow of fires that could be observed from the army camp. Sheldon and his men happened upon several Seminole men at a campsite. A duel of sorts ensued between Sheldon and Chief Yaha Hadjo, one of the signers of the Payne's Landing treaty. The chief shot Sheldon through the hip but ran out of ammunition and was subsequently killed. General Sheldon and his party then made good their escape and returned to the column.[26]

The troops then marched toward Okihumpky and Peliklakaha (the latter also known as Abraham's Town), both of which were Chief Micanopy's principal towns. Seminole people who had remained in those places were compelled to flee for their lives toward the Wahoo Swamp as the army approached. On March 30 near Okihumpky, a party of fifty warriors ambushed a cavalry unit, killing three and wounding one before disappearing into the dense brush. This token resistance did not deter the column. The following day, the soldiers set fire to the town of Peliklakaha and took particular pleasure in burning the largest residence, which was said to belong to Chief Micanopy.

General Eustis then—for reasons known only to him—turned his column south toward Tampa Bay rather than west toward the Seminole stronghold. Apparently he believed that his field duty was over, at least for the time being. Osceola and his people could breathe a little easier. Eustis had done them a favor by removing some measure of pressure by taking fourteen hundred men away in the opposite direction from their homes.[27]

Colonel William Lindsay, commander of the center wing, had served with Andrew Jackson in 1818. He was a proud Alabaman, and his column was dominated by fellow Alabamans—750 of the wing's total of 1,250 were from that state; the others came from Louisiana. Lindsay, an artilleryman, decided that there was a need for a supply depot and set about having his men construct a stockade on the road from Fort Brooke to Fort King where it crossed the Hillsborough River. True to form, this stockade was christened "Fort Alabama," which likely was meant as an appeasement to his troops who had a contentious relationship with their colonel. Lindsay had forbidden the sutler from selling liquor to the men and issued other petty orders that the volunteers believed were unreasonable. Lindsay, however, was undeterred by the attitude of his troops. He intended to command a sober, disciplined fighting force, not a herd of ruffians, and the grumbling of the malcontents did not faze him. The colonel garrisoned Fort Alabama with about seventy troops and then led his main column temporarily back to Fort Brooke.[28]

On March 25, Colonel Lindsay received his marching orders from General Scott. He immediately set out from Fort Brooke toward Coacoochee, his assigned point of departure to the Cove of the Withlacoochee. His progress was delayed at times by a constant harassing fire from Seminole snipers secreted in the hammock. Osceola had sent small bands of warriors to monitor and hound each column. When this wing finally marched, the Seminole leader had reinforced his original war party and given orders for them to shoot at the column at every turn but not to stand and engage them.

This bedeviling action provoked a pitched battle on March 26, when Seminole riflemen opened fire from deep cover and brought the column to a halt. The warriors liked their odds and remained in position until the army responded. Lindsay employed the cannon and followed the canister shot barrage with a bayonet charge. At that time, the Seminole warriors broke contact and disappeared into the swamp. Lindsay, however, had lost two men killed and another two wounded in this minor skirmish. The column eventually reached Coacoochee on March 28 and settled in to await further orders. Colonel Lindsay dispatched scouts and fired his cannon but was unable to immediately establish contact with the other two wings.[29]

On March 26, General Scott, with General Duncan Clinch as his second in command, had led the right wing—about two thousand men—from Fort Drane to Camp Izard on the Withlacoochee. Scott's column carted along flatboats that would enable the troops to cross the river easily. Scott, who never marched without his band, had the musicians entertain the troops during supper that evening after they had bivouacked. Osceola's warriors were listening to the serenade on the other side of the river. At its conclusion, instead of applause, the Seminoles opened up with a volley of rifle fire that killed two soldiers.[30]

Osceola recognized the threat of Scott's steady advance and moved his force farther upriver toward the Cove. He allowed Scott's wing to cross the river relatively unmolested, other than harassing them with a few snipers, a trip that the army accomplished on March 29. The general then pushed his column along the same trail that Osceola and his people were using to retreat upriver. Along the way, the soldiers happened upon a deserted camp and an abandoned town, and burned them both to the ground.

This march was particularly challenging for soldiers more accustomed to parade grounds than swamps. Water and mud were virtually everywhere in the alien cypress swamp, and the going was most treacherous. No one could escape the filth that coated clothing, invaded bodies, and fouled equipment. And then there was the fright factor. The men had heard about the alligators and snakes and panthers and wolves, and had felt the bite of the bloodthirsty insects. Their ears were filled with haunting screeches and growls, both near and far, that echoed throughout the eerie landscape. They shivered at the thought of unknown creatures that might be lurking beneath the still, dark water, kicking up those ripples and bubbles. And predators might be watching from those tree limbs dripping with moss or silently stalking them across the mushy ground. Additionally, the soldiers were always mindful that Seminole marksmen could be concealed in ambush anywhere within this quagmire and unexpectedly open fire.

These unnerving natural elements probably had an effect as well on Colonel William Lindsay, who was becoming quite agitated. He had waited anxiously for three days at Coacoochee, firing his cannon morning and night as ordered, but had not been contacted by either of the other two columns. Finally, with his provisions dwindling—he had taken along ten days' rations—Lindsay made the decision to return to Fort Brooke. On March 31, he marched his column toward Tampa Bay, pausing only at Fort Alabama, which was under siege, to frighten away the Seminole attackers.

Colonel Lindsay and the center wing arrived at Fort Brooke on April 4 to await further orders. An additional twelve hundred soldiers had given up the hunt for Osceola and his Seminole warriors. Now only one prong of the three-pronged pincer movement remained in the field.[31]

General Winfield Scott was also frustrated with the progress of his right wing. He had been futilely chasing the Seminole through those forsaken swamps, where his men were at times barely able to traverse the soggy terrain. The troops would stumble over rotted tree trunks and grasping vines, and occasionally had to wade through murky water up to their necks while holding their weapons and ammunition over their heads. At night, they were soaked and shivering from the chill and could not always find dry wood to build a fire. Many of the soldiers had become ill with measles, mumps, and fever. Worse yet, they were regularly losing men to Seminole snipers who would fire a killing or wounding shot and then seemingly vanish before the muzzle flash extinguished. And as if snipers were not bothersome enough, Osceola had yet another more serious vexation in mind for General Scott.

The two-thousand-man column had resumed its march up the Withlacoochee on the trail of the retreating Seminole. Osceola and his scouts watched from the nearby hammock as the army column approached. He called out to the army advance guard, Billy, a Native American, and Nero, a black interpreter.

Osceola told the two men to pass the word that he wanted to meet with General Scott.[32]

Winfield Scott was thrilled with the proposal for a parley and happily agreed. He withdrew his men to a Seminole camp that they had recently burned and waited for morning. Finally, Scott believed, the Seminole had realized they could not run for long from the might of the United States Army. Scott probably boasted to Duncan Clinch that it was evident that this large force coming at them from three directions had convinced the enemy to surrender. The campaign would end in victory. It was now only a matter of time until Scott returned home a hero—the man who had subdued the savage Seminoles of Florida.

The new day dawned, but no Seminole negotiators appeared. General Scott, likely more angry than disappointed, marched his troops down the trail to seek and destroy his belligerent foe.

Osceola had used the night to safely spirit away those Seminole families in the path of Scott's advance back into the Wahoo Swamp—all the while positioning his warriors in the brush and palmetto thickets along Scott's route. When the soldiers came slogging along the trail, the Seminole marksmen unleashed a fierce fusillade of bullets and arrows. The surprised troops dove for cover and returned fire as best they could at their unseen enemy. Scott deployed his cannon, which had a devastating effect on the hammock but nothing else.

Osceola, satisfied that he had once again demonstrated his ability to strike anytime he chose to keep the army off balance, called for a withdrawal. He led his warriors back to the safety of the Cove of the Withlacoochee, leaving behind a demoralized and rattled enemy.

Scott was fed up with his inability to coax his enemy into a fair and honorable battle—a stand-up battle as outlined on the pages of his infantry manual. These sniping and hit-and-run tactics employed by Osceola were impossible to defend against. From a practical standpoint, he could look at the miserable condition of his men, and hear the complaints from his officers, and know that every one of them had endured more than enough of these devilish swamps and their wily enemy. This latest unsatisfactory confrontation had been the last straw. He knew he could not win this hazardous game of hide-and-seek. The army had been outwitted at every turn.

Consequently, the general grudgingly, yet with no alternative, decided to abandon for the time being his pursuit of Osceola and the hostile Seminoles. He marched his battered and beleaguered right-wing column in a south-westerly direction, heading for Tampa Bay and Fort Brooke. On April 6, they gratefully arrived at their destination to rendezvous with the other two columns. One participant wrote, "The campaign, so far, had been a complete failure. The enemy had not been found in sufficient numbers to induce any thing like a general engagement; and when met and defeated, he had always succeeded in effecting his escape."[33]

Major General Winfield Scott—the best the army had to offer—had met his match in the hellish Florida swamps, as well as in the ruler of that soggy domain, Osceola, the Seminole warrior.

Osceola had masterfully dodged the three heavily armed wings, attacked with his small bands when and where he pleased, and moved his people and warriors out of harm's way deep into the swamp, where Scott and his soldiers would never dare venture.

Osceola, however, took little pleasure in his latest victory. This particular maneuver, the three-pronged pincer movement, might have resulted in failure, but the Seminole war leader knew that General Scott was not ready to quit for good.

Nor was he—and the war was just heating up.

» *Eight* «

Osceola Defends His Territory

»❖«

G eneral Winfield Scott reported to the adjutant general that his expedition had returned from the field not by any means on account of being
defeated by the enemy but solely due to a lack of supplies. He was not giving
up, but he needed time to recuperate. The horses had suffered dreadfully
from weather and hard use, and there was an epidemic of measles and mumps
among the men. The Seminoles had broken up into small mobile bands,
which made it extremely difficult to corner them. It was time, Scott realized,
for an adjustment to his strategy.

The general was convinced—given the testimony of a captured "mixed
Indian"—that the families of his enemy were located in the vicinity of Pease
Creek. If he was unable to trap the warriors, he reasoned, perhaps he could
strike a severe blow by finding and capturing their women and children. The
warriors would surely surrender or stand and fight to save their families from
the clutches of the U.S. Army.

Scott organized another expedition, this time with only two prongs. The
Louisiana militia commanded by Colonel Persifor F. Smith would sail south
to Charlotte Harbor and the mouth of Pease Creek. Colonel S. C. Goodwyn
would lead his South Carolina volunteer cavalry overland toward the upper

part of the creek and scout the south bank, the general location where these families were said to be hiding. Scott figured that the women and children were not as adaptable as the men and could not flee as quickly or as effectively. He had a better chance of trapping them or overtaking them when they fled.

The two columns advanced toward their objective as planned. But after what they believed was a thorough search of their target areas, neither one was able to locate even a trace of the families. The going had bordered on treacherous, as usual, with both the men and their mounts struggling through the swampy, wooded terrain. The way they were forced to traverse the tricky vine- and stump-filled morass had once again ruled out any chance of surprise. The Seminoles camped where they knew that nature would serve as an early-alert system to warn them of an approach. And Osceola's unseen scouts were always shadowing the columns and would lead the women and children out of harm's way when necessary.

Goodwyn's men did find and burn a deserted three-hundred-hut village, but they could have done more damage had they been more aware of their surroundings. The column unwittingly overlooked a heavily populated Seminole town that lay within two miles of their route. This town either had not been warned of the army's approach or had not been able to evacuate quickly enough. Only fate—and the terrain—had saved those Seminole families from possible disaster. One army officer later wrote, "This fact speaks volumes as to the character of the country, and the difficulty of finding the savage in his fastnesses [remote locations], and of bringing him to battle." Another expedition had returned home empty-handed.[1]

Scott was perturbed by yet another failure, but he believed in his strategy and was determined to locate those elusive Seminole families. He dispatched the wings commanded by General Duncan Clinch and Colonel William Lindsay with orders to sweep through the territory drained by the Withlacoochee River. It was there, Scott was certain, that the women and children would be hiding and ripe for capture. Clinch would head toward Fort Drane as he scoured the swamps, and Lindsay would return to Fort Brooke when his mission had been completed.

Osceola was informed about these two columns soon after each had taken to the field. He continued his tactic of not directly attacking a strong force, instead striking around the edges, sniping from the hammock, and withdrawing when the soldiers formed to mount a counterattack. Osceola's hit-and-run tactics with various bands of warriors far from each other were achieving great success. In the course of two weeks in early to mid-April, he had small war parties striking virtually everywhere there was a soldier around the Withlacoochee area. They harassed Camp Cooper, a makeshift fortification in the heart of the Cove of the Withlacoochee; attacked the Louisiana volunteers who were manning Fort Alabama, killing one soldier and wounding two; and outwitted and tormented the two columns ordered to seek out Seminole families.

In another assault, Osceola surprised a burial party from Fort Barnwell at Volusia, which subsequently resulted in the court-martial of the officer in charge. Major William Gates was accused of leaving two dead bodies lying outside the fort for a full day while he took refuge from the attacking Seminole warriors. Winfield Scott testified at the court-martial and took a swipe at General Gaines by stating that commanders seemed to have a habit of remaining inside forts instead of being aggressive and going after their enemy. Major Gates was found guilty and cashiered from the service. He was later restored to duty when it was determined that he was correct not to risk living men to rescue dead ones. Gates retired as a brigadier general thirty years after the court-martial. Scott's testimony against Gates demonstrated his frustration with this war; he also was likely setting up his subordinates as future scapegoats for the miserable affair, if necessary.[2]

On April 4, Major John McLemore established a blockhouse on the lower Withlacoochee about twelve miles from its mouth as a supply base for General Scott's expedition. Fort Drane was forty miles away through country controlled by the hostile Seminoles, so there was a need for a resupply point in the field. McLemore—the doctor who led the ill-fated charge at the Battle of Black Rock, the first engagement of the war—had garrisoned the blockhouse with Captain James M. K. Holleman and fifty Florida militiamen.

On the morning of April 12, Osceola and about two hundred warriors approached this blockhouse through the thick hammock and palmetto scrub. When the Seminole war leader gave his high-pitched war whoop, his men opened fire on the pine log structure, which might have had a stockade around it. For two hours, the warriors battered this blockhouse fortress with a multitude of bullets but were unable to penetrate its walls or hit a human target.

This unsuccessful attack did not discourage Osceola. He intended to remain there and lay siege to the new blockhouse for as long as was necessary. The following day, one soldier was killed by a Seminole marksman. Several days later, Osceola assembled about 450 warriors and once again sent volleys of rifle fire slamming into the blockhouse to try to find a weak point. Three soldiers were wounded, but Osceola also lost several men either killed or wounded.[3]

On the night of April 20, while maintaining his siege of the blockhouse, Osceola dispatched another force to attack the depleted Fort Drane while General Clinch and his wing were still away in the field. His men rushed the pickets under the cover of darkness but were beaten back after a vicious fight that wounded three soldiers. The Seminole warriors remained in the brush outside the fort for several days, keeping a constant harassing fire at the garrison. Finally, on April 24, Clinch and his column came riding to the rescue, and the Seminole attackers quickly withdrew.

The fact that Osceola had ordered a nighttime assault on the blockhouse was remarkable in itself. He had again broken the rules of Seminole warfare, which did not necessarily forbid but had traditionally discouraged fighting in the darkness. They were fearful that the souls of those killed might wander aimlessly for eternity. But this action served additional notice to General Scott that he might try anything. The army had no idea what the Seminole war leader would throw at them next, which was just the way Osceola wanted it. He understood that the psychological aspects of warfare could be just as damaging as his arrows and bullets. The ways of the Seminole were a mystery to white men, who had heard many rumors of spiritual and supernatural powers possessed by these native people. Osceola would use bullets and arrows and the element of surprise to keep his enemy off balance and apprehensive, but also working in his favor were the myths, legends, and superstitions that whites at the time associated with Native Americans that put fear into their hearts.

The return of General Clinch to Fort Drane coincided with the arrival of Colonel Lindsay and his wing back at Fort Brooke. The two wings had endured another exhausting expedition in the field, with both men and horses now in poor condition, and they had nothing to show for their efforts. They had fought only a few insignificant skirmishes with the warriors and had not come close to locating any hideouts of the Seminole women and children. Both Clinch and Lindsay would be subjected to harsh criticism from people— both public and military—who believed they should have penetrated the Cove of the Withlacoochee and rooted out Osceola and his ragtag band of hostiles. Apparently those critics had never visited the Cove to see for themselves the obstacles and challenges involved in such a bold action.[4]

On April 23, Osceola ordered two dozen of the warriors who had been laying siege to the blockhouse on the Withlacoochee to coat their arrows with pitch. These arrows were then set afire. The warriors aimed these special fiery arrows at the blockhouse roof. On Osceola's command, they shot in unison. The impact was immediate—the roof was totally consumed by fire. To Osceola's dismay, however, the fire did not spread and there was no additional damage. It was just too moist in the swamp to use fire to bring down the stockade. The fusillade with bullets and arrows continued, but the warriors had no success cracking the defenses of the militiamen. Two more Floridians were wounded, but, according to army reports, the Seminoles also sustained an unknown number of casualties.

On May 3, blockhouse commander Captain James Holleman was killed by a random bullet. Lieutenant L. B. Walker assumed command of a unit whose situation was becoming more desperate by the day. Provisions had been reduced to little more than parched corn and, to make matters worse, ammunition was running low. The men were ordered to fire only when absolutely necessary in order to conserve their ammo.

Osceola had kept his pledge not to charge any fortification—at least in daylight—which in this instance could have worked to his advantage. It is probable that an assault would have forced the soldiers to expend the remainder of their ammunition trying to fight off the superior number of warriors. But Osceola, who was unaware of the militia's ammunition shortage, was not about to lose even one man in an attempt to dislodge fewer than fifty men from their fortress. His scouts assured him that no other army detachments were in the area or were on their way to rescue the trapped soldiers. He would continue to wait them out.[5]

After some deliberation, General Scott made the decision to abandon Fort Alabama, the supply depot that had been constructed in March of that year. His campaign was winding down, and he did not want to leave the structure standing for habitation by the Seminoles. Colonel William Chisholm received orders from Scott via Colonel William Lindsay to evacuate the sick and wounded from the fort and then destroy it. On April 26, Chisholm rode out of Fort Brooke toward Fort Alabama at the head of a column of about 750 men made up of his own Alabama volunteer regiment and a detachment of army regulars commanded by Colonel William S. Foster of the Fourth Infantry.

The column approached Fort Alabama around sunset on April 27. Osceola and about two hundred Seminole warriors were waiting to welcome them.

The warriors opened fire from close range, which panicked both the men and their horses. Many horses reared, throwing their riders, then raced around, creating general confusion and preventing the men from establishing a base of fire. Eventually, the officers were able to maintain order. They deployed their riflemen and brought the cannon into action. With the troopers pouring fire at muzzle flashes in the hammock and canister shot bursting all around, the Seminoles fell back. Chisholm ordered a bayonet charge, and the soldiers—their blades gleaming menacingly—raced across the Thonostassa Creek to root out their enemy. Osceola prudently withdrew his forces for good, leaving behind five soldiers killed and twenty-four wounded. Seminole casualties are unknown.

Colonel William Chisholm regrouped and went on to evacuate the garrison of Fort Alabama as ordered. But he decided not to destroy the log structure, at least not right away. Instead, he fashioned a simple booby trap—two strings running from the trigger of a loaded musket with its muzzle buried in a barrel of gunpowder. If this device, nicknamed the "infernal machine," was tampered with, it would blow up the fort's powder magazine. Chisholm's column was a few miles down the road from the fort when a loud explosion echoed to their ears. It was later found that the fort had been blown to pieces, with logs and debris strewn everywhere. It has never been determined how many Seminoles, if any, were killed or injured in the blast.[6]

There had been no change in the siege at the blockhouse supply base on the lower Withlacoochee River. The Florida militiamen remained inside, and Osceola's Seminole warriors remained outside. Shots were occasionally fired, but no harm had been done to either side. The men inside were starving, however, and needed immediate relief. Unlike desperate military men in conventional wars, surrender was not an option.

Finally, after nearly two weeks of being trapped inside, one daring soldier managed to escape from the blockhouse. He made his way undetected through Seminole lines and arrived in St. Marks on May 20 to let the outside world know that these fifty—minus a few—brave Florida militiamen were under siege in that remote blockhouse. Four days later, a rescue party led by Major Leigh Read of the Florida militia reached the blockhouse and liberated the defenders without a shot being fired by either side. Osceola had moved on when word reached him that the militia detachment had taken to the field.

The angry men who survived the siege blamed General Scott for abandoning them, as did civilian critics who at the same time praised the resoluteness of the heroic Floridians. Scott, who likely did not even know the blockhouse existed, deflected the blame for this debacle. The blockhouse had not been manned by regulars from the army, he pointed out, but rather by militiamen. Therefore, to Scott's way of thinking, it was the negligence of local militia commanders that had led to the siege and abandonment. The U.S. Army was blameless. As might be imagined, Scott's words did not sit well with militia officers.[7]

Osceola had deployed small, mobile bands of his warriors virtually everywhere the army was garrisoned or chose to travel within this land he regarded as Seminole territory. And, although usually greatly outnumbered, the warriors would let their presence be known with harassing fire, whether at soldiers in the field or those behind the log fortifications of a fort. The soldiers were never safe from the ingenious guerrilla tactics or free from the effective reconnaissance operation that Osceola had masterfully put in place.

One incident typifies the closeness of Osceola's surveillance and how the warriors would seemingly appear out of nowhere. General Duncan Clinch had called a halt to await supplies one day while patrolling in the field. He had removed his sword and belt so that he could comfortably rest beneath a tree. When the general departed, however, he forgot to take along his gear. He discovered his mistake some four miles down the road and sent a six-man detail back to retrieve the sword and belt. These men approached the tree to find that a group of Seminoles—one of whom was wearing the sword and belt—had gotten there first. The soldiers were forced to retreat when the warriors commenced shooting at them.[8]

Winfield Scott continued to spread around blame for his inability to formulate an effective strategy to subdue his foe. This time he turned on the volunteer militia troops, after he had already vilified their commanders for ignoring the blockhouse siege. He wrote a letter to Colonel Roger Jones, the adjutant general of the army, the chief administrative officer, stating that it would require three thousand soldiers to end the hostilities in Florida, but these must be "good troops (not volunteers)." This insulting message was soon leaked, and the good people of Florida, especially the volunteer militiamen and their families, were outraged. To make matters worse, Scott added in his Order Number 48 that the panic in Florida occurred because "the inhabitants could see nothing but an Indian in every bush" and referred to "the planters in the recent case near Tallahassee, who fled without knowledge whether they ran from squaws or warriors."[9]

The populace did not take kindly to being called cowards when there was a real threat of violence from the hostile Seminole element that Scott had not been able to conquer. Newspapers far and wide condemned the general, and he was burned in effigy by protesters in the streets. Major Leigh Read of the Florida Volunteers wrote that Scott had been wrong to employ "the shreds and patches of the obsolete system of European tactics where they could not possibly work." Another writer blamed the failure on Scott's "incapacity, presumption, and ignorance." It was evident that Winfield Scott was grasping at straws to cover up the fact—and the embarrassment—that he was being outmatched by a cunning Native American war leader named Osceola and an untrained, undermanned fighting force.[10]

With his ambitious campaign against the Seminoles of Florida in shambles—some might call it an unmitigated failure—there was nothing left for Scott to do but pack up his stellar reputation and move on to another challenge. Secretary of War Lewis Cass offered a convenient way out for the beleaguered general. He informed Scott that his services were required to put down an uprising of Creeks in Alabama who were also resisting removal to the West.

On May 21, Scott departed Florida after first sending a letter to Secretary Cass, saying, "If I can be convicted of having committed one blunder in theory and practice since I left Washington to conduct the War in Florida, let me be shot." By that time, there were plenty of irate Florida volunteers—and citizens, for that matter—who would have fought over the privilege of serving on Scott's firing squad.[11]

The logical successor to Scott would have been General Duncan Clinch, the next highest-ranking officer and a man who was experienced in Florida warfare. President Andrew Jackson offered the command to Clinch, but the general declined and instead resigned from the army after twenty-eight years of service. He had tired of this exasperating and interminable conflict, and returned to his plantation in Georgia to care for his eight motherless children.[12]

With Clinch out of the picture, Jackson turned to an old friend, Brigadier General Richard Keith Call of the Battle of the Withlacoochee fame. Call had earlier been appointed to the post of governor of Florida Territory while former governor John Eaton was sent to Spain as foreign minister. The new commander was a forty-four-year-old Virginian who had been homeschooled by his widowed mother and went on to become a prominent lawyer. He had come to the attention of General Andrew Jackson during the Creek War and had worked as acting secretary of West Florida under Governor Jackson. Call had roomed with Jackson and Eaton while they served together in the Eighteenth Congress. The general was an ambitious man, with a powerful voice and intimidating mannerisms, and even his friends were said to have feared his fierce temper. Jackson, who had introduced Call to his future wife—against her parents' wishes—was pleased to have one of his inner circle of cronies now conducting this frustrating war in Florida. General Call, however, had accepted the position only as acting commander and with the proviso that Major General Thomas S. Jesup would take charge at some point in the near future. Jesup was at present stationed in Alabama on a campaign to force the Creeks to move West.[13]

In the summer of 1836, both Osceola and the military turned their attention toward the forts. Instead of conducting full-scale field operations, the army contemplated the closure of selected forts due to widespread illness among the troops. The intense heat, high humidity, and fever-bearing mosquitoes had caused chills, muscle pain, and a high fever. This condition, known as country fever—probably malaria—had struck down large percentages of men in military garrisons across Florida. Quinine was still decades away from its introduction—the men would simply "sweat out" the fever and hope to survive it. In late May, Fort King, established in March 1827 near Gad Humphreys's agency, was the first post to be abandoned.

In early July, the surgeon at Fort Drane informed General Call that 99 of the 289 soldiers in the garrison were ill and recommended that the facility be evacuated. Call had no choice but to accept the doctor's advice before the fort lacked enough able-bodied men to adequately defend itself. On July 19, the evacuation of Fort Drane commenced. Osceola and about two hundred warriors were waiting when the first wagon train of supplies departed that fort. He ambushed the twenty-two-wagon supply train and sixty-two-man escort a quarter of a mile outside Micanopy. His sharpshooters inflicted serious damage before being chased away by reinforcements riding to the rescue from Fort Micanopy. Five soldiers were killed and six wounded in this incident known as the Battle of Welika Pond.[14]

Fort Drane was completely abandoned by early August. At that time,

Osceola and his warriors took up residence at the fort on General Clinch's former plantation, Auld Lang Syne, and made it their base of operations. They discovered that more than ten thousand bushels of corn and fields planted in sugarcane had been left behind by the soldiers. Osceola had his men carry a portion of the precious food to the women and children, who remained hiding in the swamps. After moving in, Osceola branched out from his base at the fort. His small guerrilla bands attacked settlers—burning their houses and chasing them away—while continuing to strike companies of soldiers out on work details or reconnaissance patrols.

On August 21, Osceola and his people were enjoying their new quarters at Fort Drane when his scouts informed him that a column of soldiers was heading toward them from Fort Micanopy. Major Benjamin K. Pierce had learned that Osceola and his warriors had taken over Fort Drane and was marching with 125 troopers and one cannon with intentions of dislodging the squatters. Osceola secreted his warriors—about three hundred in number—outside the fort in the thick palmettos. The Seminole marksmen opened fire on the soldiers as soon as they appeared, and a spirited firefight ensued. Pierce brought his cannon into action but soon realized that he was outnumbered and ordered a retreat. The army lost one killed and sixteen wounded in the hour-long skirmish. Within days of this engagement, the garrison at Fort Micanopy was also evacuated due to the disease that had been making its way through the ranks of the army.[15]

The justice-seeking Seminoles now controlled the region around the interior and the Withlacoochee swamps like never before. The entire peninsula south of Black Creek and Newmansville and west of the St. Johns had been for all practical purposes vacated by the army and white settlers. The Seminole could now freely go wherever they pleased without fear of being attacked by a military force.

It had been eight months since Osceola had taken up arms against the United States, and his hit-and-run tactics had paid off with victory after victory. He had inflicted many casualties on the army, while his warriors had suffered minimal losses. The Seminole war leader, however, was not deceived into thinking that the war was anywhere near over. He had learned from his informants that Congress had recently appropriated more than $2 million for the war effort, which translated into weapons and ammunition, food, equipment, and other supplies—and most of all, pay for additional men to carry arms against the Seminole. Osceola knew that the army would at some point awaken from its summer-long hibernation and wage war once more in earnest against his people.

Osceola's primary concern at this time, however, might not have been the U.S. Army. The Seminole war leader had picked up the same fever that had caused the soldiers to abandon Fort Drane and the other forts. This illness, probably malaria, had rendered Osceola's physical condition less than one hundred percent. Osceola might have treated his fever with bleeding, perhaps slashing his legs or arms to release the poison. Bleeding was a ritual with the Seminole, but it was used mainly at ceremonies where they might cut themselves for purification and not necessarily as a remedy.

The illness might not have been the only factor causing Osceola to suffer. Alligator stated that the wound Osceola had sustained in the hand at the Battle of the Withlacoochee was bothering him. No other evidence can be found to confirm that premise, but wounds certainly often became infected and were slow to heal given the tropical climate and filthy conditions.

Additionally, it is not known as fact but can be presumed that other warriors at the fort contracted this debilitating fever, which would have reduced the number of able-bodied men available for war parties. Osceola knew it was imperative that he fight through this nagging illness. He was the only one who could lead and inspire his people. All would be lost if he should become incapacitated.[16]

In July, Osceola and his warriors abandoned Fort Drane—the site of such unhealthiness for both the white man and the red man—and headed for their camps in the Withlacoochee swamp. Before their departure, however, they burned every structure and left only the sugarcane growing in the fields.

General Richard Call had intended to mount a summer campaign against the Seminoles. His plans had been dashed, however, due to typical army logistics and the illness that had become an epidemic throughout the army. General Call himself had contracted the fever and wasted much of the

summer lying in a sickbed. The total of field-ready men he could muster fluc-
tuated depending on how many were ill at the time. He could not chance going into battle against a proven dangerous enemy without enough firepower.

The general, who was eager to take to the field, apparently could hear the
footsteps of General Thomas Jesup, the heir apparent, approaching. He worried that his chosen successor would arrive in Florida before his own campaign had a chance to succeed and thereby reflect negatively on his ability to
command. He wrote a letter to Jesup and offered to step down immediately
and turn over his command. Jesup, although nearly finished with his duty
against the Creek, magnanimously refused the offer and instead volunteered
to serve, if needed, in a subordinate capacity to Call until the present campaign had been completed. Call was impressed by the professionalism of
Jesup: "He is a soldier of the first merit and is worth a battalion of your other
generals." General Richard Call was now free to conduct operations against
Osceola and the hostile Seminoles.[17]

On September 19, General Call, commanding 1,200 Tennessee volunteers—
fresh from fighting the Creeks in Alabama—and 140 Florida militiamen, departed Tallahassee for the Suwannee River and arrived six days later. After
the men had crossed the river, Call split up his command into two detachments. He ordered Major Leigh Read to travel with his militia and a handful
of regulars aboard the steamboat *Izard* to the mouth of the Withlacoochee
River, thirty miles distant. Two barges laden with provisions would be towed
behind the *Izard* and taken upstream for twenty miles, where Read would establish a supply depot. General Call would lead the main column with ten
days' rations on a dash toward Fort Drane with hopes of catching those Seminoles who were reportedly living there.[18]

On October 1, Osceola was surprised when a group of his warriors,
some wounded, rode into camp whooping and hollering. These men had
been camped ten miles away when the lead elements of a huge army column
had attacked them. Several of their comrades had been killed in the one-
sided skirmish. This news disconcerted Osceola. He did not readily have a
defensive strategy planned or enough warriors necessary to repel this ad-

vance. The only course of action for the moment was to gather his people and seek safety deeper within the Cove of the Withlacoochee. After the summer's respite, the war had resumed.[19]

When General Call's column arrived at the deserted Fort Drane, he was disappointed to find the place a charred ruin without any supplies other than cane growing in the fields—and the Seminoles had vanished. He had thought there might at least be corn for the horses, but Osceola had fed his horses and cattle with all available forage. Therefore, Call was obliged to postpone his mission while he pastured and rested the tired horses there for a week.

On October 8, Major Benjamin K. Pierce and two hundred regulars rode into Fort Drane and reported to General Call. Much to the delight of the hungry, grumbling troops, they had brought along a few days' supplies. Call now had about 1,350 men at his disposal. He assembled his fighting force and set out from the fort in search of Osceola and the hostiles who had taken refuge at the Cove of the Withlacoochee.[20]

Not all the Seminole bands that were scattered across the region had been informed of the presence of the soldiers. Evidently the uneventful summer had lulled the Seminole people into a sense of security. On October 12, Call's advance guard happened upon a Seminole encampment some four miles north of the Withlacoochee. There are conflicting reports, but as many as fourteen of the forty or fifty people in this camp were killed and four women and seven children captured. These prisoners would likely have been the first captives taken by the army since the start of the conflict.[21]

Osceola understood that he must display a strong show of force to counter this campaign and send an emphatic message to General Call that the Seminole had not quit fighting. The war leader shook off the effects of his illness and went into action. He sent runners to alert surrounding Seminole villages and camps of the army's advance, while at the same time organizing a war party. He and his men hurried to the banks of the Withlacoochee, where they found their enemy waiting on the other side opposite the Cove. Osceola could take some satisfaction that the flooded river was running a full two hundred yards across, resembling a lake more than a river. Any crossing by the soldiers would be highly dangerous, if not impossible—both from the swollen water with its floating driftwood and debris and from the marksmen whom Osceola had deployed along the shoreline.

General Call must have been reminded of his previous visit to the Withla-coochee a year earlier, when he was stuck on that side of the river while Clinch ferried troops across in a flimsy canoe. That engagement had ended in disaster for the army. Call did not intend to make those same mistakes on this day. Unfortunately, he had no rafts, not even an old canoe, and had ne-glected to bring along a sufficient number of axes for his troops to use felling trees to construct rafts.

Undeterred, the general dispatched a double column of horsemen into the river to gauge the depth. By the time the lead horses were swimming, Osceola's warriors had commenced shooting at the exposed troops. The rid-ers had no choice but to wheel their mounts and head back to shore. Addi-tional attempts to cross on horseback were equally futile. During the course of the day, Osceola and his men held their fire and watched with astonish-ment as several horses and their riders became victims of the swollen river. It should have been apparent to the general that the Withlacoochee was im-passable, but he had chosen to learn that fact by losing men and mounts.[22]

General Call had sent a detachment of four hundred Tennesseans under the command of Lieutenant Colonel Josephus Guild downstream to recon-noiter the river for an acceptable crossing point. On a fork where a trickling stream meandered into the Withlacoochee, the soldiers found a town occu-pied mainly by black people. One source states that one of the women pris-oners led them to this town, which could be true, but it was more likely that their guide, Billy, a Black Seminole, knew of the place.

Regardless, the black inhabitants and a small number of Seminoles were aware of the approaching troops and had time to prepare for their arrival. Dozens of armed men waited in ambush behind a wall of foliage along the stream bank. The first person targeted was Billy, the interpreter, who had willfully betrayed his people. Billy's body was riddled with bullets. After that, the blacks turned their attention to the remainder of the column and laid down a withering barrage that stopped the soldiers in their tracks.

The volunteers regrouped and repeatedly charged the entrenched defenders, but they were beaten back each time by the murderous fire. After about an hour and a half, the Tennesseans had lost two men dead and eight wounded. Black casualties were said to have been light—the soldiers reported seeing one black man shot from a tree—but an elderly black man who was later captured claimed that eight Seminoles and five blacks had been killed and many others wounded in the skirmish.

Lieutenant Colonel Guild could not make any headway in this standoff and chose to withdraw his column. He reported to Call that the enemy had been "driven from his position . . . with considerable loss."[23]

Meanwhile, General Call was once again stranded on the banks of the Withlacoochee. He could not cross the overflowing river, and his men were running low on supplies. There was no other choice but to move the column along the river toward the supply depot that Major Leigh Read should have set up by now. Call followed this course for a couple of days, with Osceola and his warriors shadowing him from the opposite bank. The march was taking a severe toll on the horses; the animals were dying in great numbers due to a lack of adequate forage. Men who had signed on to ride were now foot soldiers—infantry—which was a source of discontent for any self-respecting cavalryman. When a horse died, the rider burned the saddle and other tack to keep from having to carry the items. Call dispatched scouts to locate Read's position, but apparently the major and his depot had vanished into thin air. The patrol returned to report that they had found no sign of human habitation for miles.

Call was desperate for rations to feed the troops and forage for the horses. In a moment of utter frustration and anger, he halted his advance, wheeled the column around, and headed for the safety of Fort Drane. For the second time in less than a year, General Richard Call had been forced to temporarily abandon his expedition along the banks of the Withlacoochee River. On October 17, the starving, weary column arrived at Fort Drane without the main body having engaged the enemy in even one skirmish.[24]

Two days later, General Call welcomed reinforcements to the fort. Seven hundred and fifty Creek volunteers under the command of John F. Lane had arrived in Tampa Bay by ship and marched overland to the interior to join the fight against their hated enemy, the Seminoles. In an insidious alliance, the Creeks had been promised by the government that their reward would be "such plunder as they may take from the Seminoles." The "plunder" that had lured them to Florida were the blacks they were told they could capture and keep as personal property. Killing Seminoles was secondary to the opportunity to return home with a cash crop of valuable former slaves and free blacks that could be sold. These Creek warriors would wear white turbans on their heads to distinguish themselves in battle from the Seminoles.[25]

While General Call dispatched Tennessee mounted volunteers 105 miles to Garey's Ferry to obtain supplies, Major Read struggled to establish the supply depot on the Withlacoochee. The steamer *Izard* had run aground and broken up, which caused a delay in Read's being able to transport the supplies to his destination. The major finally had the depot in place on October 22, but that was far too late—Call was already on his way back to Fort Drane. Read blamed the naval officers in charge of the *Izard*—one of whom was Raphael Semmes, who would later serve admirably in the Confederate Navy—of incapacitating their craft. The officers countered that the grounding had been an unavoidable accident.[26]

Osceola was now faced with a new challenge to his leadership abilities. Word had reached the Seminoles that the Creeks had invaded their territory. The Seminoles were furious that these Creeks had formed an alliance with the white man in Florida. These were the same Creeks and their descendants who had fought against the Red Sticks twenty years earlier and had driven Osceola and his Tallassee neighbors away from their traditional homeland in Alabama. Not only that, but many of these warriors had accompanied Andrew Jackson on his raid through Florida in 1818, when Osceola had been taken prisoner as a child. This faction of the Creek tribe had also agreed to sell their homeland to the United States and had come to Florida after fighting against their own people who had resisted removal from Alabama. It can only be imagined what Osceola thought about how these Creek would be paid.

Osceola knew that his battle tactics must be altered to accommodate the presence of the Creeks. His new enemy could live off the land, move more quickly and quietly than the army, and follow the faintest trail, and they possessed excellent fighting skills. He would caution his hot-blooded warriors not to be overly aggressive due to their hatred of the Creeks but to follow his orders explicitly. The Creeks added a new dimension to the ability of the army to fight, and their unique talents would need to be treated with the utmost respect and caution.

General Richard Call did not waste any time taking to the field. On November 10, he marched out of Fort Drane at the head of a column of mounted Tennessee volunteers, Florida militia, Creek warriors, and a number of regular army soldiers—almost twenty-five hundred men in all. Three days later, Call and his men crossed the Withlacoochee, which had receded and was now fordable, without any opposition from the Seminoles. Four men, however, drowned while crossing the 220-yard ford.

Osceola could not risk mounting a full-scale attack against such a superior force. And he feared for the safety of the families. He ordered that the villages around the Cove be abandoned and the people moved into the swamps. The Seminole would make a last stand, if necessary, in the Wahoo Swamp.

The army soon located three large deserted villages and put the torch to them. Many of the log dwellings had been recently constructed and, judging from the workmanship, had probably belonged to mostly blacks, who were said to have been better builders than the Seminole. The former slaves had likely learned construction skills from their masters during their bondage. An elderly black man who had remained behind told the soldiers that his people had not been able to plant crops and were living off cattle and whatever they could pillage or find growing wild.[27]

General Call decided to split his troops into two wings. Call would assume command of the Tennesseans, the Floridians, and a detail of regulars, and would march along the north bank of the river. Colonel Benjamin Pierce—who had been brevetted to that rank for his actions at Fort Drane on August 21—would lead the main body of regulars and the Creek volunteers down the south bank, on the Seminole side of the river. The two wings would sweep the area and rendezvous at the Dade Massacre site.

Osceola could not simply hide out and expect to protect the Seminole women and children in his stronghold. These noncombatants could not travel through this maze at great speed for any length of time. The children especially would need to rest. The army would simply march through the swamps after them no matter the obstacles and at some point run them down. His warriors would be greatly outnumbered, but they must still make an attempt to stop the advance of their enemy.

Osceola also knew that any conflict could now be their final fight for their survival. The army held the advantage in firepower and manpower. His strategy must take into consideration not only inflicting harm on his enemy to halt their invasion but also protecting the lives of the vulnerable families. Scouts had already informed him of the separation of the command into two wings. Osceola wisely chose to fight the wing commanded by General Call in order to avoid the Creeks, whom he regarded as a much more formidable foe.

On November 17, Osceola chose an ambush site and ordered his warriors, who might have numbered around five hundred to six hundred, to shoot as soon as the soldiers came into sight. The Tennessee volunteers led the way for the column and received the initial volley of lead from the warriors. These soldiers, however, steadfastly maneuvered their way through the barrage and charged into Osceola's position. This bold action routed the warriors, who disappeared into the hammock. The soldiers pursued and, often fighting in waist-deep water, managed to kill twenty of the Seminole and capture a few horses and some supplies. Army losses were one killed and ten wounded.

The next day, Osceola had secreted his warriors in the palmetto scrub facing a clearing and tried to lure the army into a frontal assault. General Call, however, sent detachments to attack at the flanks of the Seminole line. After about thirty minutes of heavy gunfire from both sides, the soldiers broke through the resistance and charged Seminole lines. Osceola was compelled to break contact once again, this time leaving behind twenty-five dead warriors and many others who had been wounded, including Chief Osuchee (Cooper). Army casualties were reported as three dead and twelve wounded.[28]

Osceola was not shaken or dispirited by his losses, and neither were his men. His warriors had fought bravely and were eager to return to action.

Osceola ordered that the families move deeper in the swamp while he and his warriors resupplied themselves with bullets, powder, and other necessary provisions. His scouts had told him that the soldiers were running low on supplies and none were on the way. If the army chose to fight once more on this campaign, it could be the decisive battle of the war.

When General Call and Colonel Pierce joined forces at Dade's battleground on November 20, Osceola and his men—about six hundred strong, two hundred of them black—were on the move through the thick cover to meet them.

Osceola deployed his outnumbered warriors in the lush, green hammock at the edge of Wahoo Swamp. He watched as three columns of his enemy weaved their way toward him through the brush. On the right were the Tennessee volunteers, on the left were the Creeks, and in the center were the regulars and the Florida militiamen. In the background, Osceola could observe a group of horsemen being held in reserve.

When the soldiers approached within rifle range, Osceola gave the order to shoot. His warriors blasted away at the exposed men as fast as they could shoot and reload. The soldiers dived for cover, settled in, and returned fire. Osceola, according to his plan, then had his men stop firing their rifles and withdraw. Although the Seminole appeared to be running away in a disorganized fashion, the warriors were in truth racing to their next position on a hidden trail that allowed them to avoid obstacles.

The soldiers followed the Seminole warriors' retreat into the marsh, struggling through a quagmire of mud and wading through black and sluggish waist-deep water. It was about an hour later when the troops had finally traversed the quarter of a mile through roots, vines, and decaying vegetation to come within sight of the new Seminole position. Osceola and his men had moved across a shallow creek and secreted themselves behind stumps and fallen logs.

Osceola watched as the advance elements of the army stepped forward to show themselves. He was delighted with what he saw—the Creeks were in the lead.

The Creek warriors, led by chiefs Paddy Carr, John O'Poney, and Jim

Boy, halted at the creek, not knowing if it was fordable or too deep to cross. Depths could be deceptive in the swamp. Major David Moniac, the first full-blooded Creek to graduate from West Point, stepped forward to measure the water's depth. Osceola gave the signal. His war whoop echoed throughout the Wahoo Swamp. His selected marksman opened fire first. Moniac was struck by a multitude of bullets. His lifeless body collapsed and sank into the morass. The exhilarated Seminole warriors then unleashed a vicious fusillade of bullets.

The Seminoles and the Creeks traded ferocious volleys of rifle fire with each other for nearly an hour. Finally the regulars and Tennesseans, who had been bogged down by the swampy terrain, arrived to lay down a base of fire. Colonel Benjamin Pierce took command and ordered that the Tennessee volunteers prepare for a bayonet charge into the Seminole position. The volunteer commander, Robert Armstrong, however, protested that such a charge would be too risky, and Pierce grudgingly scrapped the plan.

Osceola and his warriors remained in position, shooting only sporadically and waiting for the army to make its next move. That move never came. General Call deemed it too dangerous to proceed with operations. There were too many hiding places for ambushes in this desolate swamp, his men had been on half rations for several days, and ammunition was running low.

At nightfall, Osceola and his warriors watched with wonder as the column of army troops and their Creek allies commenced a lengthy withdrawal. The army had given up its pursuit once again. The Battle of Wahoo Swamp had concluded with Osceola holding the field.[29]

General Richard K. Call was satisfied that he had administered a damaging blow to the Seminoles. Upon his return from the field on November 27, however, there awaited a letter addressed to him from Secretary of War Benjamin F. Butler. On behalf of President Jackson, Butler criticized Call for not being more aggressive, for not establishing a base of operations, and for embarking on a campaign without adequate supplies. Furthermore, and most important, Call had been relieved of his command. The general was stunned by the harsh words, especially from his friend, the president, whom he believed had judged him unfairly on hearsay evidence. He made an effort to salvage his reputation by writing a letter outlining the reasons for his actions, but he would not receive a second chance to correct his mistakes.[30]

The new commander, Major General Thomas Sidney Jesup, would be taking charge of operations as soon as he arrived in Florida. Jesup, who was known to employ whatever means were necessary to achieve his objective, would implement a bold new strategy in an effort to subdue Osceola and the Seminoles.

Nine

Jesup's New Strategy

》 ✦ 《

After the battle, Osceola and his warriors rode triumphantly into their camp in the Wahoo Swamp. They were welcomed there by their loved ones, who had reassembled from the various hiding places where they had fled to escape General Call's advance. The final battle of this campaign had created many anxious moments for the women and children, who had heard that Osceola was determined to make a final stand and fight to the last man. The soldiers had never penetrated that far into the swamp before this battle, and the noncombatants had not known if they would see the warriors alive again after the firing had ended. Now was a time for relief, thankfulness, and celebration.

The families who had fled from the destructive march of the army up the Withlacoochee also returned to their camps or homes to discover what, if anything, remained of their lives. General Call had burned to the ground several large towns, and nothing could be found there but charred debris and ashes. Those blacks and Seminoles who no longer had a town to call home took up residence with relatives or friends at another town or sought safety in a swamp camp. It was too early to start rebuilding. The army would not give up this territory easily. They assuredly would return and burn down any structure that stood.

A victory dance took place that night at Wahoo Swamp to celebrate yet another remarkable defeat of the U.S. Army. Osceola, however, might not have participated in the festivities to the fullest. He had been suffering from the prolonged illness he had contracted at Fort Drane, which had left him physically weak. In addition, the warriors under his command had sustained more casualties than ever before in this campaign—at least forty-five had been killed. He would have privately experienced great sadness at seeing the sorrow of the wives and mothers. But Osceola knew he must dismiss from his mind the thought of those warriors who had gone to be with the spirits. He had opposed this conflict, but the loss of life in war was inevitable. Those Seminoles had sacrificed lives for their cause, and the tribe had not been vanquished. In fact, they had chased away another general officer who had underestimated their determination and fighting abilities. Perhaps now the United States would seriously consider accepting the notion that the Seminole deserved to be left alone in their Florida homeland.

Osceola was also dismayed that the army had captured some Seminole women and children, which he regarded as a cowardly act. He had always preached to his warriors that they were forbidden to wage war on the women and children settlers. There was an occasional violation of this order, but for the most part the Seminoles obeyed the wishes of their leader. The tribe held no white prisoners with which to trade or barter, which was the way Osceola wanted it.

Osceola found it judicious at this time to delegate more authority to his top lieutenants and trusted leaders. He never knew when the nagging fever might incapacitate him and there would be a need for new leadership. Moreover, he had decided to form a number of smaller war parties that could swiftly move on a moment's notice to wherever they were needed. To that end, Osceola separated his combined warriors into bands of between 120 and 200 each. In addition to maintaining one larger band for himself, he assigned leadership roles of the other bands to Micanopy, Abraham, Alligator,

King Philip with his son Coacoochee, and Osuchee (Cooper). These bands would be spread across the territory, all within a day's march of each other, and be ever on the alert for movement by their enemy. Micanopy, Abraham, and Jumper had advised Osceola that the entire tribe should hide out in the Everglades, but this suggestion had been quickly silenced. Osceola would defend the area around the Withlacoochee and flee to the Everglades only as a last resort.[1]

At this time, Osceola, who could not shake off his illness, moved with his family to the Panasoffke Swamp on the Withlacoochee (present-day Lake Panasoffke) to live in a black village. He appreciated the devotion the black people held for him and felt safe within their midst. Osceola had never wavered in his efforts to protect the Maroons, the runaway slaves, the tribal slaves, or the free blacks who were in constant danger of being captured and enslaved by the white man. The Seminole war leader considered these black people to be as much a part of the tribe as he—especially with the possibility that his wife or wives were black—and would never relent on his vow to keep them away from the clutches of the slave chasers. For this reason, more and more blacks had joined forces with the Native American warriors to fight under the command of this man who championed their cause.

The tide had turned in the country at large, however, and the Florida War was no longer a popular undertaking. Antislavery newspapers rose to the defense of the Seminoles and chastised the government for fighting a war against brave people who were harboring runaway slaves. In the Northern states, home to most of the country's abolitionists, Osceola was regarded by the public as an honorable and noble warrior. He became the subject of countless illustrations for newspapers, magazines, and advertising posters. The artists often portrayed him in a togalike garment similar to the costume of the ancient Romans. A popular toast at dinner clubs was to the health of Osceola, "the great untaken and still unconquered red man" who was bravely fighting to remain in his homeland.

Within military circles, the word was spreading among the servicemen that duty in Florida was an assignment to avoid at any cost. Returning soldiers told stories of the horrible conditions under which they had lived and fought—the diseases, the poisonous snakes, the substandard living quarters, the arduous marches through swamps in murky, waist-deep water and, most of all, a resolute, relentless enemy who did not fight fair according to European rules of engagement. There was nothing to gain and much to lose from this dangerous, miserable duty.

Henry Hollingsworth of the Tennessee volunteers summed up the plight that he and his comrades endured: "So little demand has one for mind here—helter skelter, rough and tumble, march all day, eat if you have it, then fall down on the earth and sleep like a beast soundly until day, or until the drum beats for the men to rise, which on a march is generally 4 A.M., and go through the same routine. This is a picture of the soldier's life! A life of dirt and toil, privation and vexation, and the poorest pay in the world $6 per month."[2]

Officers in particular were at a premium for service in Florida. Records reveal that 103 company officers resigned their commissions during 1836, and there were few officers on hand to replace them. The only trained engineers in the United States were graduates of West Point, and those officers were needed for infrastructure projects, such as bridges and railroads, and consequently were not available for duty in Florida. Lieutenant Colonel Benjamin Pierce reported that his table of organization called for fifty-five officers, but he had only six officers to fill those positions. Part of the reason for the exodus could be attributed to the fact that many officers blamed the residents of Florida for provoking the war by stealing livestock, land, and slaves from the Seminole. This attitude among the officers was not conducive to a total commitment to fight the enemy—which certainly could affect the outcome of the war.[3]

Andrew Jackson was completing his second term as president before turning over the White House to Martin Van Buren, his vice president, who had been elected in 1836. One of Jackson's final acts as president, in addition to relieving General Duncan Call of his duties, was to dispatch Thomas Jesup, who had been waiting in the wings, to take command in Florida and fight the Seminoles. Jackson no doubt regarded himself as the best man to subdue the Seminoles, but approaching seventy years of age, he had evidently retired from Indian fighting.

Major General Thomas Sidney Jesup was a forty-eight-year-old Virginian by birth who had moved to Ohio as a youth. He had been commissioned a second lieutenant in the army at the age of twenty-two and was soon brevetted to colonel "for gallant and distinguished skill" after being wounded in the War of 1812. Following that war, Jesup was assigned to the position of quartermaster general of the army and promoted to the rank of major general in 1828. He had been ordered to Florida not due to his connections to influential politicians but on account of his record as a leader of fighting men. Jesup had replaced the ineffective General Winfield Scott during the past summer's campaign against the Creeks in Alabama. He had achieved immediate success by crushing Creek resistance and inducing the tribe to emigrate west. The War Department had great confidence that this man whose military career had demonstrated competence with every assignment would duplicate his Alabama victory in Florida.[4]

In October, following a five-year superintendence by Lewis Cass, President Jackson appointed his attorney general, Benjamin Butler, to also preside over the War Department. General Jesup arrived at his new command with specific orders from the new secretary of war: "The hostile Indians having been discovered in considerable force on the banks of the Wythlacoochie, and it having been also ascertained that their principal Camps and settlements are situated on the south side of the river, you will immediately make all suitable arrangements for a vigorous attack upon their strongholds, and for penetrating and occupying the whole country between the Wythlachoochie and Tampa Bay. . . . The above direction to attack the enemy in his strongholds and to possess yourself of the country between the Wythlacoochie and Tampa Bay . . . you will regard as a positive order, to be executed at the earliest practicable moment."[5]

Jesup assumed his command knowing that the strategies of the previous commanders had failed. He intended to be as aggressive as possible and would ideally have liked to engage the Seminole warriors in a full-scale battle, but he knew the history of that tactic. Four generals in the past year—Gaines, Clinch, Scott, and Call—had marched their armies to the Withlacoochee River only to be outwitted by Osceola with his hit-and-run tactics. Not only had the army been embarrassed, it had also sustained a stunning number of casualties without punishing the enemy in kind. The government set the official number of Seminoles killed to this point at only 131. Obviously, it was time for a new strategy.[6]

The general was known as a creative strategist and at times a loose cannon—he had defied an order by General Scott in Alabama in favor of his own plan, which had led to success. Now he had devised a new, devious strategy that he would implement here in Florida. If he could not meet his enemy face-to-face on the field of battle, he would endeavor to capture as many of the Seminole people as possible. He knew that most of these captives would be women and children—the noncombatants—which he believed would demoralize the tribe and influence the warriors to surrender. This plan had in fact already been field-tested with encouraging results.

On December 3, 1836, before Jesup's arrival but under his orders, the Alabama mounted volunteers stormed a black village at the head of the Oklawaha River, burned every structure, and captured forty-one people. This was nearly three times the total number of blacks that had been taken during all of the previous year. Jesup was elated. His plan had worked to perfection. The black warriors who were fighting with Osceola would certainly take notice of this operation that had targeted home and hearth, as would their Native American allies.[7]

The fact that a town of mostly blacks had been chosen to test this new strategy was not accidental. General Jesup wrote to the governor of Georgia three days after those blacks were captured: "This is a negro war, not an Indian war; and if it be not speedily put down, the south will feel the effects of it on their slave population before the end of the next season." The general was also confident that his new strategy would assist in recruiting volunteers from Southern states. He solicited the governors of the nearby states to form new regiments of men who would sign up for a minimum twelve-month enlistment.[8]

General Jesup saw the need for more forts in the region to act as supply depots for his forces in the field. He had heard about his predecessors being forced to abort their marches due to a lack of supplies, and so he envisioned stocked forts at strategic points throughout the area. Only Fort King remained operational, but that was soon to change. At the site of the Dade Massacre, the Tennessee volunteers constructed Fort Armstrong, named in honor of their commander. Fort Alabama was rebuilt and renamed Fort Foster. Fort Drane was regarrisoned. Fort Clinch was rebuilt at the mouth of the Withlacoochee. Fort Dade was erected on the Withlacoochee at the crossing of the Tampa Bay–Fort King road. Jesup would garrison these forts primarily with Marines and sailors, which would leave his combat-ready army detachments free to scour the area for hostile Seminoles.[9]

Soon after his arrival in Florida, General Jesup and his army set out to scout the Wahoo Swamp in search of the elusive Osceola and his allies. His advance scouts found nothing of interest in that area; Osceola had already taken his people away. In addition, by that time, Micanopy, Alligator, and Jumper had moved their bands toward the headwaters of the Oklawaha, Osuchee had settled in the vicinity of Lake Apopka (near present-day Winter Garden), and King Philip and his son were situated south of St. Augustine. The general was not discouraged that he had not made contact at the Wahoo Swamp. He knew the Seminoles remained around the region, and he would hunt them down wherever they set up camp.

On January 10, Jesup and his troops executed a surprise raid on the black village at the Panasoffke Swamp. This village happened to be the one currently occupied by Osceola and his family. The Seminole war leader was compelled to rise hastily from his sickbed and run for his life with only three warriors at his side. Sixteen blacks were captured, but most of the inhabitants of the small village escaped into the dense palmetto scrub.

Osceola, in the company of about fifty warriors and their families, led his people away from the army toward the headwaters of the Oklawaha. There were countless places to hide within this tangled wilderness, and adequate supplies were readily available. This attack by the army had been too close a call. The early-warning system that had always been in place had become a victim of Osceola's part-time leadership due to the reoccurring illness that plagued him. It was essential for their survival that he reestablish his intelligence network, especially now that his health was hampering his mobility.

Osceola would make certain from now on that his scouts shadowed Jesup and any other detachments in the field in order to avoid what had been a life-or-death situation at the Panasoffke.

Intelligence was also on the mind of General Jesup. His strategy of capturing Seminole people had paid off with vital information. One of the captured blacks near Panasoffke was a man named Primus, who had been with Osceola's band since last spring at Camp Izard. Primus revealed to Jesup that Osceola was ill and could probably muster only about one hundred fighting men to take to the field. At the same time, Jesup learned that Micanopy and Jumper had taken refuge at the headwaters of the Oklawaha, and Osceola was on his way to that location. If he hurried his army on the march, he might be able to strike a serious blow to the leadership of the dissident Seminole.[10]

On January 22, Jesup led his troops out of Fort Armstrong toward the Oklawaha River. The first engagement of the march happened the next day when a detachment of Creeks, scouting ahead of the main column, located a Seminole camp near Lake Apopka. Acting without orders, the warriors attacked their hated enemy. Chief Osuchee (Cooper), who had been recuperating from a wound suffered during the Battle of Wahoo Swamp, was killed, along with his oldest son and two other men. The Creeks captured Osuchee's wife and three children, another Seminole woman and her two children, and two black men and their families.[11]

During an interrogation of the captives, it was revealed that Osceola and his band were now on the move in a southeasterly direction toward the Caloosahatchee River. Jesup chose the Marine Corps commandant, Colonel Archibald Henderson, to lead a brigade composed of Alabama volunteers, mounted Marines, and Creek scouts to pursue the elusive Seminole war leader. Henderson's troops climbed Thlawhathee, or White Mountain, as the whites called it, the highest point in Florida, and eventually happened upon a trail made by a herd of cattle—presumably driven by Osceola's band.

On January 27, the brigade found these animals contentedly grazing in an open field. Henderson dispatched a scouting party to locate the camp of the livestock owners. Along the way, his scouts passed more cattle, which were placed under guard, and eventually grabbed a black man who was seated by a campfire. This man admitted that Abraham, whom he identified as an influential black leader, and forty to fifty Seminoles were to their rear, and many blacks were on the move ahead.

While Henderson set out to track this band of Black Seminoles, another army detachment dispatched by Jesup and commanded by Lieutenant James Chambers struck a Seminole baggage train some miles away. Twenty blacks, mostly women and children, along with two Seminole women and three children were captured. The real prize, however, was one hundred Seminole ponies—half of them laden with valuable supplies, household items, and personal possessions.

Colonel Henderson's column eventually arrived at the edge of the Great Cypress Swamp (not to be confused with the one of the same name south of Lake Okeechobee) near Hatcheelustee Creek, which flowed into Tohopekaliga Lake. The vanguard of mounted Marines approached the creek at a place where two trees had been felled across to form a crude bridge. Unbeknownst to the Marines, these trees had been cut to allow the mostly Black Seminole families and their belongings to cross the twenty-yard-wide waterway easily. Moreover, people who had escaped from the baggage train attack had already warned Abraham about the soldiers, and he had immediately deployed his warriors in ambush.

The Marines stepped onto the log bridge and were met by sustained rifle fire. One Marine fell dead and three were wounded in the initial volley. The Marines regrouped and counterattacked, which forced Abraham's warriors to retreat deeper into the swamp. A running gun battle ensued, with the Seminoles assuming a defensive position behind stumps and fallen trees and then withdrawing after firing at their pursuers. One more Marine was killed and another wounded before Abraham led the men far enough away that his enemy could no longer follow through the muddy, tangled swamp. It was reported that two blacks and one Native American were killed during the four-hour skirmish.[12]

This alarming sequence of events must have been quite distressing and frustrating to Osceola. He was accustomed to keeping the army off guard with his ambushes, and here he had almost been captured or killed by his enemy's surprise attack, and other Seminoles across the region were also running for their lives. Further, Osceola was greatly troubled by Jesup's strategy of capturing the noncombatant Seminole people. He could only wonder with dread about the fate of these women, children, and old people, the blacks in particular. It was not as if Jesup were superior in military skill to any of the other generals, at least in Osceola's mind. These recent successes of the army occurred only because Osceola was plagued by the confounding illness that would affect him with a high fever and bone-shaking chills, and weaken his slight body to the point that he could not function properly. And just when he thought he had shaken the sickness, it would return to debilitate him. For the time being, the Seminole were without a dependable leader, which had created a dangerous situation. Osceola was the field general, and no one else could replace him. It was imperative that he regain his health or the Seminole War could be lost.

General Jesup was frustrated as well. His troops had captured a total of 150 Seminoles, mostly women and children, along with cattle, personal property, and community food stores, and he had prevented the tribe from settling anywhere to be able to sow corn now that the planting season was upon them. Not only that, Osceola was ill—how seriously, he did not know—and could not effectively command his warriors. Jesup, however, understood that his own accomplishments were minimal compared to what would be necessary to bring this conflict to an end. He admitted that "not a single first-rate warrior had been captured, and only two Indian men have surrendered. The warriors have fought as long as they had life, and such seems to me to be the determination of those who influence their councils—I mean the leading negroes."[13]

The general had another idea that might accelerate his progress, and it had nothing to do with deploying fighting men in the field. He had been informed that Ben, one of the blacks captured in the Great Cypress Swamp, was a notable voice within the tribe. Ben, who was about forty years old, had been taken with his wife and infant son by the Marines who had been pursuing the warriors from the ambush at Hatcheelustee Creek. Ben had never been a slave, according to him, and admitted to being a part of Micanopy's band.

Jesup saw in Ben the perfect emissary—he spoke English and Seminole, he had the ear of important chiefs, *and* his family was being held hostage.

On January 28, Ben was dispatched by General Jesup with orders to find Jumper, Micanopy, and Alligator, and tell those chiefs that the general wanted a parley. They could come in unmolested under a flag of truce and be free to leave after the talks ended. The general simply wanted them to personally hear what he had to say so there would be no misunderstanding or misinterpretation of his words.

Ben, however, did not seek out those chiefs; rather, he appeared at Abraham's camp. Ben probably felt more comfortable passing the message to a black leader who would know what to do about the general's request. This emissary from General Jesup had come to Abraham's camp at a most opportune time. The subject of continuing the fight had been weighing heavily on Abraham's mind. He had recently taken stock of the situation and come to the conclusion that his people were on a disastrous course. Much of their stores and livestock had been confiscated, including most of their gunpowder. Soon the warriors would be fighting with only the powder that was held in their powder horns. Consequently, Abraham kept the message from Ben to himself and decided to accept Jesup's invitation to meet.

On January 31, Abraham arrived at Fort Dade. An eyewitness describes the appearance of this Black Seminole leader:

> Abraham, who is sometimes dignified with the title of "Prophet," . . .
> is the prime minister, and privy councellor of Micanopy; and has,
> through his master, who is somewhat imbecile, ruled all the councils
> and actions of the Indians in this region. . . . Abraham made his ap-
> pearance, bearing a white flag on a small stick which he had cut in the
> woods, and walked up to the tent of Gen. Jesup with perfect dignity
> and composure. He stuck the staff of his flag in the ground, made a sa-
> lute or bow with his hand, without bending his body, and then waited
> for the advance of the General, with the most complete self-possession.
> He has since stated that he expected to be hung, but concluded to die,

if he must, like a man, but that he would make one effort to save his people.[14]

The arrival of this black man and not one of the Seminole chiefs did not disappoint Jesup in the least. He understood that the black leaders were essential to any agreement made between the two sides. The meeting between Abraham and Jesup was quite cordial—they even shook hands on meeting. But Jesup did not waver from outlining the same terms that the Seminoles had heard for more than a year. The only way this war could end, the general told Abraham, was for the Seminole to emigrate. Abraham, however, wanted assurances that the black people would be free to accompany the tribe to the West. The general was noncommittal about this controversial issue. The positions held by both men might have sounded like the basis for a stalemate, but each of them was encouraged by this initial contact. The meeting ended with Abraham promising to bring in Alligator and Jumper to join the talks. He departed in possession of various gifts, including food and tobacco.

On February 3, an apprehensive Alligator and Jumper arrived to meet with General Jesup, who greeted them cordially. Little of substance was discussed, but the two headmen accepted Jesup's invitation for formal talks to take place at Fort Dade in ten days' time. Until then, both sides agreed that a truce would be honored and all hostilities would be suspended. The two chiefs were encouraged by the tone of the meeting and departed to gather their people for the parley at the fort. At the same time, Jesup assembled his army and headed toward Fort Dade on the Withlacoochee to prepare for the arrival of the Seminole negotiators.[15]

It is doubtful that Osceola heard right away about the parley scheduled by Abraham, Jumper, and Alligator. Perhaps he was too ill to participate or the chiefs had purposely not informed him of the meeting. There can be no question that if Osceola had been in good enough health and had known about the proceedings, he would have been the primary spokesman for the tribe—or, with the soldiers assembled there, he might have attacked Fort Dade. Regardless, any agreement would have to go through the Seminole war leader as long as he lived, and it was unlikely he would accept any provisions that included the tribe leaving Florida.

Jesup's decision to negotiate rather than fight his way out of this war might have been based on his utter distress at every aspect of the conflict. He penned a most revealing letter to Adjutant General Roger Jones that summed up the emotions of a man who understood the extreme challenges of his assignment:

> As an act of justice to all my predecessors in command, I consider it my duty to say, that the difficulties attending military operations in this country can be properly appreciated only by those acquainted with them. . . . This is a service which no man would seek with any other view than the mere performance of his duty: distinction, or increase of reputation, is out of the question; and the difficulties are such, that the best concerted plans may result in absolute failure, and the best established reputation be lost without fault. If I have, at any time, said aught in disparagement of the operations of others in Florida, either verbally or in writing, officially or unofficially, knowing the country as I now know it, I consider myself bound, as a man of honor, solemnly to retract it.[16]

This was quite a statement from a man who should have been exhilarated by his ability to entice these prominent Seminole leaders to the bargaining table.

Word of the suspension of hostilities had either not reached Chief King Philip and his son Coacoochee, or they chose to ignore it. Philip had married Micanopy's sister, but now his best days were behind him. This marriage had assured King Philip, however, that upon his death Coacoochee would ascend to chief of the clan. Before dawn on the morning of February 8, King Philip and a Seminole force estimated at two hundred to three hundred warriors crept through the palmetto scrub to approach a detachment of perhaps four hundred to five hundred soldiers who were camped on the south shore of Lake Monroe (near present-day Sanford). The commander of this column, which was composed mainly of new recruits, was veteran Seminole fighter Lieutenant Colonel Alexander Fanning. The lieutenant colonel had wisely ordered his men to erect a low log breastwork the previous day and had made them sleep with their rifles. The soldiers were also supported by a nearby steamboat, the *Santee,* which was armed with a six-pounder cannon.

At dawn, an alert army sentry noticed movement in the bushes and fired his weapon and yelled to warn his comrades. That single shot was quickly followed by scores of rifles discharging from the hammock as King Philip and his son gave the order to fire. The soldiers scrambled for their weapons and wildly returned fire, which had little effect. Colonel Fanning was eventually able to settle down the jumpiness of these new recruits and direct a counterattack. The riflemen steadied their aim to shoot at muzzle flashes in the brush, while the cannon blasted salvos of grape- and canister shot at the Seminole position.

The warriors maintained a heavy rate of gunfire, which pinned down the soldiers behind their breastwork for about three hours. At that point, King Philip, or possibly his son, gave the order, and the Seminole war party slipped away through the hammock. The army detachment lost one man killed, Captain Charles Mellon, and fourteen wounded, a number of them seriously. The casualties would have been much higher if these soldiers had not erected the makeshift breastwork and had stacked their weapons instead of keeping them in their possession. Fanning's experience and competence had saved countless lives.

A fort would soon be established near this battle site and named Fort Mellon in honor of the fallen officer. This skirmish was also notable for the fact that King Philip's son, Coacoochee, or Wildcat, as he was to become commonly known, had acted as co–field commander for the first time. Coacoochee would eventually become a fierce and respected leader among the Seminole people. This battle had been a training session for the chief-in-waiting.[17]

The next day, army troops under Colonel William Foster happened upon a large Seminole camp some sixty miles west of Lake Monroe on the Gulf. An estimated fifty warriors put up a stiff resistance, but in the end, Foster—aided by sailors who rowed to shore to join the fight—managed to rout the war-riors and destroy the village. The army lost one man killed in this skirmish. Seminole casualties, if any, were unknown, but many people lost their homes and were now destitute and on the run.[18]

General Thomas Jesup became nervous when reports of these engage-ments reached him at Fort Dade. He did want anything to interfere with his planned peace talks. There had been a cease-fire in place, but he knew that communication for both sides was inadequate. His worries were realized when the morning of February 18 arrived and the Seminoles did not appear for the scheduled meeting. Jesup asserted that the reason for their absence was not the recent hostilities during the truce but his treaty demands. "I have required immediate emigration," he wrote. "There would be no difficulty in making peace were it not for that condition. The negroes who rule the Indi-ans are all averse to removing to so cold a climate."[19]

The premise that the Black Seminoles had refused to emigrate due to the weather might have been a slight contributing factor, but that could not com-pare with the fear of being sold or returned to their masters. Abraham, the Seminole leader who had been promoting the treaty parley, however, did not want this opportunity with Jesup to pass without further serious talks. He understood that the might and resources of the United States would eventu-ally prevail in this conflict. Now was the ideal time to negotiate a treaty that could provide favorable terms for the Seminoles, both red and black. He ex-erted every effort to persuade the chiefs not to ruin this chance for peace.

Abraham arrived at Fort Dade on the afternoon of February 18 and made apologies to General Jesup for the absence of the chiefs. He stated that Alliga-tor, Jumper, and Holatoochee (Davy)—who was Micanopy's representative—would show up the following day. Over the next few days, many members of the tribe, both red and black, trickled in to camp around the fort. Finally, Al-ligator and Cloud arrived, but Jumper was said to be too ill to travel.

On February 24, General Jesup held the conference with Seminole repre-sentatives Alligator, Cloud, and Holatoochee, with Abraham serving as translator. Jesup, in response to Holatoochee stating that Micanopy wanted to remain where he was living, once again told them they could not stay in

Florida but must emigrate west of the Mississippi River. This statement about that sensitive subject effectively concluded the conversation for the day. The two sides might have been far apart, but they did agree to meet again on March 4. Jesup realized that nothing could be accomplished without Micanopy, however, and made the negotiators promise that the head chief would attend the next meeting. Twelve Seminole hostages, including Micanopy's nephew, were left at the fort as a gesture of good faith.[20]

On March 4, Abraham, Jumper, and the other Seminole representatives appeared as scheduled. Micanopy was absent, but he had authorized Holatoochee to serve as his representative. Alligator also did not attend but sent two representatives—Cotza Tustenugge (Panther Warrior), who was said to be his nephew, and a Black Seminole named Pease Creek John. These negotiations between Jesup and the Seminole representatives lasted for two days and produced extraordinary results.

On March 6, 1837, the chiefs signed a "Capitulation of the Seminole nation of Indians and their allies by Jumper, Holatoochee, or Davy, and Yaholoochee, representing the principal chief Micanopy." The primary terms of this formal agreement provided that hostilities would end and that the entire Seminole Nation would immediately emigrate to the West. The tribe would withdraw south of the Hillsborough River until they presented themselves to the concentration point at Tampa Bay for removal no later than April 10. They would receive rations from the time they arrived at Fort Brooke in Tampa Bay until they reached their new home, and then for a year thereafter. The chiefs agreed to hand over hostages to General Jesup at that time to ensure their full cooperation.

This document basically reinforced the terms of the Payne's Landing treaty—except for one eye-opening article that addressed a subject that had been heretofore nonnegotiable. Article 5 stated: "Major General Jesup, in behalf of the United States, agreed that the Seminole and their allies, who come in and emigrate West, shall be secure in their lives and property; their negroes, their bona fide property, shall also accompany them West; and that the cattle and ponies shall be paid for by the United States at a fair evaluation." No doubt Abraham had been the driving force behind the inclusion of this stunning provision.[21]

It would appear from an honest interpretation of this article that runaway slaves and free blacks would be regarded as "allies." Taking into account that they had allied with the Seminoles to fight against the army, those slaves would be allowed to emigrate with the tribe. Second, those slaves who were owned or under the patronage of the Seminole people would be called "bona fide property." The tribe had won a key concession—their black comrades would be permitted to travel with them to their new homes in the West.

On March 18, Micanopy visited Fort Dade and personally signed the agreement. General Jesup was delighted with the cooperation of the head chief. He believed that this historic document would truly end the Florida War. The Seminoles seemed sincere in their capitulation, and the blacks among them appeared satisfied with the promise that they would not be returned to their white masters.

Jesup understood, however, that such agreements could be precarious at best. That day, he wrote to the adjutant general, "I now for the first time have allowed myself to believe the War at an end. The same errors, however, that renewed the war in Alabama would renew it here; I mean the impudent violence of the citizens. Should they attempt to seize any of the Indians either as criminals or as debtors the scenes of last year will be renewed. If it should become necessary to protect them from such annoyance, I shall not hesitate to declare Martial law, and send every individual not connected with the public service out of the Country."[22]

Osceola, the most influential Seminole leader, had not been heard from directly. The treaty negotiators had implied that they were speaking on behalf of Osceola, but Jesup did not know for certain. And, veritably, Osceola was not particularly pleased with the agreement. He was skeptical of the truthfulness of the government with respect to the blacks, and he folded his arms and walked away whenever the subject of emigration was mentioned. He remained steadfast in his belief that the tribe should remain in Florida, but that notion was beginning to erode for practical purposes.

Osceola had mixed emotions about this capitulation agreement. He had always been fiercely anti-emigration, but he was perceptive enough to know that the days of winning victories against the army were numbered. Ammunition and gunpowder were becoming scarce, and they lacked the means to secure more. Their access to traders had been blocked. And he was disappointed that his top lieutenants had apparently lost their zeal to fight and chose to negotiate.

The army had also been capturing their livestock, and many people were reduced to eating roots, fallen fruit, and whatever foodstuffs they could steal from whites. Women and children were starving and burdened by the stress of moving from hastily erected camp to hastily erected camp as the troops invaded deeper into the swamps. And many others, in addition to Osceola, were suffering from illnesses caused by malnutrition and the unhealthy climate. If they did not accept the terms of this latest agreement, which now did at least provide for the blacks, Osceola reasoned, there was a good chance that the entire tribe would eventually be exterminated. He desperately wanted peace for his people. He was tired of seeing them suffer so much. But he simply could not bring himself to buy into this new capitulation agreement that he had refused to sign.

Osceola watched with disgust as his people flooded the relocation center in Tampa Bay and the other relocation sites. During April, chiefs Micanopy, Alligator, Jumper, Holatoochee, Cloud, Yaholoochee, King Philip, and others, along with hundreds of men, women, and children, had surrendered, handed over their weapons, and been confined at the centers pending the move west. Osceola was having a difficult time deciding whether to submit and join his tribe in Tampa Bay or gather up all the warriors he could and take to the swamps once more. That choice became easier to make when word reached him of the government's latest betrayal.

The emigration of the Seminole tribe appeared to be going along according to plan, but the one aspect General Jesup had not taken into account was the fury of the Southerners, especially those involved in the slave trade. His document of capitulation had become public, and slave owners across the South were up in arms about the terms—specifically Article 5. Jesup was permitting their property to simply sail away from Florida without any compensation to the rightful owners. The Southern press vilified Jesup daily and denounced the treaty as an insult. The slave owners felt betrayed by one of their own, a native Virginian, and loudly complained to their representatives.

General Jesup began to have second thoughts about Article 5 of the capitulation document. The very institution of slavery would be threatened by allowing the runaway slaves, or for that matter any black who was suspected of having ever been a slave, to emigrate west. This significant event, if it indeed stood, would set a troubling precedent. The more he thought about it and listened to the uproar of his critics, the more he knew he could no longer justify the negative impact and historic ramifications of this article. Did he really want to become known as the man who broke the back of slavery?

In the end, Jesup bent under the pressure of the slave owners. He was aware that he could not come right out and rescind Article 5. Instead, he created a way around the issue—interpretation. The general decided to interpret the document so that runaways who had sought refuge and fought with the Seminoles during the war were not to be regarded as allies, as defined in the document. They would be seized and returned to their rightful owners. Further, taking into consideration that there was no official system for recording ownership of slaves among the Seminoles, virtually every black associated with the tribe was suspect and would be in danger of being taken into custody. In other words, no one could "legally" distinguish which blacks had been living with the tribe before the war and which ones had joined them during wartime. Jesup had for all intents and purposes entirely nullified Article 5 of the capitulation document with his new interpretation. Every black in Florida was now subject to apprehension until proved to be bona fide Seminole property—if that could be accomplished.[23]

General Jesup, however, needed to invent a way to enforce his new interpretation without making it common knowledge, which would scare off the blacks who were at present assembling at the relocation centers. On April 8, Jesup made a secret agreement with several Seminole chiefs, including Coa Hadjo, which he explained in a letter to J. R. Poinsett, the new secretary of war under President Martin Van Buren: "The chiefs entered into an engagement yesterday to surrender the Negroes taken during the War. They will deliver them to the commanding officer of the Posts on the St. Johns."[24]

Coa Hadjo suggested to his Seminole coconspirators that the slaves they captured not be taken to Tampa Bay to be turned over to the authorities. Instead, it would cause less of an alarm among the black population if they were kept away from relocation centers for the time being. In another troubling move, army troops had entered Seminole country to observe the move of the tribe to the centers. And, although Jesup had vowed that he would not "make negro-catchers of the army," the soldiers were also taking possession of fugitive blacks. In fact, many former slaves had heard about the roundup and surrendered to the soldiers. The blacks told tales of harsh treatment among the Seminoles, which, whether true or false, they hoped would lessen the severity of their punishment when they were turned over to their white owners.[25]

In addition to the controversy over Article 5, Jesup was obliged to deal with myriad nagging obstacles in his mission to assemble the Seminoles for removal west. He had to quell a rumor that the tribe was going to be put aboard transports at Tampa Bay and taken out to sea and thrown overboard to drown. And then there was the outfit from Georgia that had sent slave chasers down to Florida with powers of attorney to capture runaways, which kept many Seminoles away from relocation centers. Jesup dealt with the slave chasers by issuing an order that forbade unauthorized white people from traveling in certain parts of the territory that would interfere with the removal.[26]

In time, this secret agreement to hand over the blacks found its way to Osceola's ears. He was outraged by this latest betrayal and declared that as long as he had a drop of blood in his veins, no blacks would be surrendered to the whites. Osceola vacillated about what course of action to undertake next, however. He needed to find out firsthand the sentiments of his people at the relocation centers.

Osceola decided that he and his small band would turn themselves in to Lieutenant Colonel William S. Harney at the relocation center in the vicinity of Fort Mellon near Lake Monroe. He would join the other twenty-five hundred or so Seminoles assembled there who had pledged to emigrate. That way, he could get an accurate account of conditions and weigh his options.

No doubt Osceola's arrival at Fort Mellon caused quite a stir among the soldiers who had heard so much about this savage war leader. Instead of the fierce monster they might have imagined, Osceola was in truth a slight, dignified man with an engaging personality who was not averse to joking with the whites. One night he shared the hospitality of Colonel Harney's tent. It has been reported that he even organized a game of ball. Osceola would have camped near the fort but would not have allowed himself to be confined and would have made sure he could come and go as he pleased.[27]

Osceola would also enjoy a reunion at Fort Mellon with his old friend Lieutenant John Graham, the man who it is alleged he saved from harm at the Battle of the Withlacoochee. This can be verified by an article that appeared in a St. Augustine newspaper that attempted to cast light on Osceola's character: "Toward Lt. Graham he entertained the kindliest of feelings of friendship, not to be broken by the unhappy war which exists between his nation and the white man. During his visit to Fort Mellon, he took occasion to present Lt. G. with a handsome plume of white crane feathers to be worn as a badge of protection in the battle field. This is a remarkable instance of friendship."[28]

It seems odd that this great war leader would give himself up at Fort Mellon without a fight and risk being incarcerated. He knew that Jesup was not beyond any treachery when it came to dealing with the Seminoles. But Osceola had ulterior motives for surrendering. He and his closest ally, Arpeika (Sam Jones), had wanted to visit King Philip and Coacoochee (Wild Cat) at Fort Mellon to determine their interest in continuing the resistance. Osceola simply could not convince himself that the fight was over, especially now that the government had broken another agreement by capturing those Black Seminoles alleged to be runaways or not verifiable property.

General Jesup was growing impatient with the delay in assembling the tribe for removal, and for some unknown reason he blamed Osceola, the most influential leader of the tribe, for part of the problem. He wrote to Colonel Harney, "If you see Powell again, I wish you to tell him that I intend to send exploring parties into every part of the country during the summer, and that I shall send out and take all negroes who belong to the white people, and that he must not allow the Indians or Indian negroes to mix with them. Tell him I am sending to Cuba for bloodhounds to trail them, and I intend to hang every one of them who does not come in."[29]

Osceola was predictably offended by this undeserved threat. The army did not know what was on his mind. After all, he had brought quite a number of his people into the detention center with him. Jesup should have applauded him for that obedient act. It was as if the general was so confident he had won this war that he was taunting the Seminole war leader. Agent Wiley Thompson had found out with tragic results that it was not the best idea to humiliate Osceola. Had General Jesup thrown down the gauntlet in challenge?

Although Osceola had not by any means completely shaken off his illness, he was nonetheless not one to shy away from a personal affront. He would summon all the strength he could muster to execute one more dramatic and brazen attempt to thwart the plans of General Jesup to remove the Seminoles from Florida. The territory would once again be rocked by the audacious actions of its most ardent defender.

Ten

Final Betrayal

»◈«

In the darkness of night on June 2, about two hundred Seminole warriors led by Osceola and Arpeika approached the Seminole detention camp about eight miles from Tampa Bay and Fort Brooke. It was here that most of the chiefs—notably Micanopy, Cloud, and Jumper—and hundreds of Seminole men, women, and children waited for transport to their new home in the West. Osceola had decided that it was time to liberate his people.

Osceola's renegade war party had departed Fort Mellon with weapons and ammunition in hand, in addition to food stores they had been collecting and secretly hiding in the nearby hammock. Osceola had never completely conceded that the tribe would be leaving its homeland. Under his orders, the people had been stockpiling lead and powder and essential provisions just in case the removal process fell through. And the unwitting U.S. Army had been the provider of most of these supplies.

General Jesup had ordered that the Seminoles not be permitted to trade with the sutler at Fort Mellon. Colonel William Harney, however, had partially rescinded the order when taking into consideration that many of the Seminoles were literally naked and in need of clothing and other necessities.

The Seminoles—at Osceola's direction—had taken advantage of Harney's compassionate act by surreptitiously trading for forbidden items and hiding away those and other provisions. Also, there was never a lack of unscrupulous traders passing through the area or within a short distance away who had no qualms about dealing in prohibited goods with the tribe.

Before departing for Tampa Bay that night, Osceola had left instructions for the families at Fort Mellon to sneak away into the wilderness after he was gone. These people would be led away by Coacoochee (Wildcat). Osceola did not want the innocent people who remained at that relocation center to suffer any consequences for his actions near Tampa Bay. So his ambitious plans included emptying two detention centers and freeing most of the tribe.

Days earlier, Captain John Page had feigned illness in order to remain with a group of Seminoles who were on their way to the detention center at Tampa Bay and had camped about twelve miles away. On June 1, Page sent a report to Cary A. Harris, commissioner of Indian affairs, stating that members of the tribe had been "passing backwards and forward" engaged in what he called "mysterious conduct." Other observers in various areas had noticed this mysterious conduct as well.[1]

At about the same time, General Jesup had been informed of rumors flying around of a possible raid on the detention center encampment near Fort Brooke. Rumors were rampant in those turbulent days, and it cannot be determined if this perceived threat was taken seriously or not. Jesup was probably overly confident that his plan was working to perfection and regarded any rumored attempt to disrupt activities on a large scale at Tampa Bay as preposterous.

Captain William Graham, commander of a mounted company along with 120 Creek warriors, had been assigned the task of guarding Micanopy's camp. On orders from Jesup, Graham placed two Creek spies within the Seminole population but failed to discern any advance knowledge of this supposed raid. In truth, the Creek infiltrators might have found out about Osceola's plan but refused to report it to their white commander. The Creek warriors had become disgruntled with the army after learning that their families, who were confined in Alabama prior to relocation to the West, were being mistreated. Evidently, the Creek had come to hate the white man more than their traditional enemies, the Seminole.[2]

Osceola watched from the darkness to determine if there was anything suspicious about the sleeping detention center camp where the chiefs and his people were lodged. Spies were everywhere in this time of great confusion and turmoil. He did not want his warriors to walk into an ambush. His scouts returned to report that nothing was stirring inside or outside the camp. Osceola had his orders passed among the group of warriors once more—no whites were to be harmed, and no dissent would be tolerated by their own people. He knew that some of the chiefs might not want to come along willingly and would need to be persuaded. For that reason, Osceola had given no advance warning of his raid to these detainees.

At about midnight, Osceola and Arpeika, along with a band of warriors, entered the camp to search for the chiefs. They first confronted Jumper, who resisted. Warriors pinned the chief's arms behind his back and dragged him away. Cloud was taken next, without incident. Micanopy was startled awake by Osceola and told that he must go with them. According to the account of an eyewitness from a report written by Captain Page, the chief did not go easily: "Micanopy refused . . . saying he had signed a treaty. . . . They told him his blood would be spilt if he did not go. He threw his bosom open and told them to kill him and do it quickly. They then forced him on his horse and guarded him off."[3]

Osceola then dispatched his warriors throughout the camp to gather up every man, woman, and child. These people were told to quickly and quietly pack their belongings and follow the warriors out of the camp in a northerly direction. Most of these Seminole families were pleased by this unexpected intervention, and few refused to leave their confinement. The majority of them had silently opposed the emigration agreement all along but had not protested for fear of reprisal from both the whites as well as their own chiefs who had agreed to the plan. The elated people now demonstrated their willingness to leave the camp by hurriedly following the warriors into the night. They had feared this impending move to an unknown country and never wanted anything more than to live in peace in their familiar homeland.

Oddly enough, neither of the two Creek spies at the camp, both of whom must have been aware of the presence of the invaders, voiced any opposition or gave the alarm. In addition, army details that should have been patrolling the area had been eluded or were nonexistent. The stealth of the Seminole people in Osceola's well-planned operation, combined with the apathy of the Creeks and the absence of the military guarding the camp, made for a smooth execution.

Remarkably, under the cover of darkness, more than seven hundred Seminole people followed Osceola and Arpeika away from the relocation center without a shot being fired on either side.

This column of Seminole refugees initially headed toward Long Swamp near Peliklakaha, the former hometown of Micanopy. It was Osceola's plan to separate them into smaller groups, which would take up residence all over central Florida. He had chosen the ideal time of the year to spirit away his people. They had been provided new clothing at the relocation center, and there were some crops in the fields ready to harvest. Also, the white soldiers would not take to the field to wage war during what they called the summer sick season. Osceola himself intended to settle with Arpeika near Volusia on Lake George. Incidentally, Arpeika would be elected primary chief of the tribe to replace the dishonored Micanopy, while Osceola remained the tustenugge thlocklo, the head war chief. Osceola could have been elected chief had he so chosen, but due to his reoccurring illness he had designated Arpeika as the heir apparent. The people deserved to have a chief who was healthy, and Osceola was satisfied with his role as war leader.[4]

This "abduction" at Tampa Bay, as General Jesup called it, was a mortal blow to the removal process. Osceola had outwitted yet another army general. Jesup was alternately incensed and distraught by this personal humiliation and blamed everyone for its failure but himself. First of all, Captain Graham had been derelict in his duty to guard the camp. Second, the Creek spies had obviously betrayed their employers. Last, the general blamed the greedy slave owners who had badgered him for the return of their property.

The finger of blame from every other quarter, however, pointed directly at Thomas Jesup. He was the man in charge, and there could be no excuse for the ineffectiveness of his command. The general was heaped with abuse from the public and press, not to mention from within the government and military for this latest disappointment. The removal of the Seminoles had been so close. Now the matter was back to square one. People in the North, however, were not the least bit upset by Osceola's brazen liberation. The Seminole war leader's already substantial legend was bolstered by yet another feat of cunning. The abolitionists in particular thought Jesup got what he deserved for modifying Article 5 of his capitulation document.[5]

General Jesup tried to explain away this embarrassing abduction in a letter to Indian Commissioner Cary A. Harris:

Soon after the Indians had begun to assemble in this neighborhood [Tampa Bay] the measles, which had prevailed in the Army during the winter, broke out among them, after which very few came in—the Indian Negroes had been alarmed by the arrival in camp of individuals who had lost their slaves during the war—most of them fled, and but few could be prevailed upon to return. This was the state of things when . . . a party of armed warriors seized Chiefs Micanopy, Jumper, and Cloud in their camp about eight miles from this place on the evening of the 2d instant, and hurried them off to the swamps of the interior. I had received through the Principal Creek Chief on the morning of the 1st inst., intimation that an attempt would be made in a few days by a . . . small band of Seminoles to kill or abduct those chiefs—I ordered Major Graham who was stationed with a mounted company and a hundred and twenty Creek warriors four miles from Micanopy's camp, to send out spies at night and observe the movements of the Indians. The Major sent two Indians into the Seminole camp on the night of the 1st and though he ordered them to go out again on the night of the second they either disobeyed the order or failed to report. The mounted force here and at Major Graham's camp was held in readiness to move at a moment's warning, but it was not until the morning of the 3rd that the flight of the Indians was known. They had twelve hours start, and in the state of the country, and the extreme heat of the weather, pursuit would have been useless.[6]

Jesup, predictably, was devastated by this startling and unfathomable turn of events. He wrote to Adjutant General Roger Jones, "This campaign so far as it relates to Indian migration has entirely failed. . . . I believe the emigration of the Seminoles to be impractical under any circumstances. The country can be rid of them only by exterminating them."[7]

General Jesup, however, questioned himself about whether he had the passion and perseverance to lead such a mission. Consequently, he requested that he be relieved of his command. Major General Alexander Macomb, commanding general of the U.S. Army, understood Jesup's present state of mind and determined that the general was perhaps reacting rashly to recent disappointments. Macomb told Jesup that he could withdraw from the campaign if he chose to do so, but urged the general to reconsider his decision.[8]

There was no shortage of replacements who stepped forward in the event that Jesup accepted this way out of Florida. Major General Edmund Gaines was the first to stake claim to the command, and he was soon followed by Major General Winfield Scott. Evidently both officers were eager to make amends for past failures. Jesup thought about his situation, however, and decided that the only way he could regain his lost honor was to remain there and win the war. This decision was approved by his superiors. The general would be permitted to stay in command of what was now called the Army of the South.

In truth, Jesup had presided over the most successful campaign against Osceola and the Seminoles waged by any commander thus far in the war. Hostilities had decreased dramatically, and travel throughout the territory was relatively safe. The Seminoles had been driven from their traditional strongholds and were hiding out in the interior swamps, away from the white population. And Jesup had come so very close to placing the majority of the tribe on steamers that would have carried them away from Florida forever.

Regardless of small successes, Jesup vowed to abandon his previous strategy of negotiation. In its place, he resolved to defeat the Seminoles on the battlefield once and for all—no matter the cost.

Summertime, however, was not the ideal season to embark on an offensive campaign. Debilitating illnesses such as dysentery, typhus, malaria, yellow fever, and fevers of unknown origin were commonplace. Fort Mellon was abandoned in June on account of widespread sickness. At one point, one company of regulars was down to just eight healthy men, and out of five battalions only one hundred men were fit for duty. General Jesup urged that this crisis situation be kept secret so that the enemy did not take advantage of it and the whites did not panic.[9]

One of the areas in which Jesup had achieved moderate success was the capture or surrender of Black Seminoles. Jesup reported to the new secretary of war, Joel Poinsett, who had taken over for Benjamin Butler in March, that the Seminole in Florida would always have blacks among them who would "form a rallying point" for runaway slaves—another reason for extermination. He went on, "I enclose a list of the Indian Negroes captured during the campaigns." Jesup called this document "Registry of Negro Prisoners captured by Thomas S. Jesup, owned (or claimed) by Indians, 1836–1837." This list included 103 names, with the general's comments regarding each one. Eighty-eight of the ninety-three blacks whom the general identified as being runaway slaves had been returned to their white owners. Examples of the entries on this list with Jesup's comments:

BEN   Owner, Micanopy, Age, 40. Father. [The mother of nine children follow on the list.] One of the most important and influential of the Negroes.

INOINOPHEN   Age, 45. Husband. Commander of the Negro force on the Withlacoochee. Chief counselor among the Negroes, and the most important character. [Wife, Eliza, and two children on this list.]

TONEY BARNET   Age, 36. Claims to be free. Said to be a good soldier and intrepid leader. He is the most cunning and intelligent Negro we have seen. He is married to the widow of the former chief.

DICK   John Hicks Town. Said to be the property of Colonel Gad Humphreys.

ABRAHAM   Age, 50. Claims to be free. The principal Negro chief. Supposed to be friendly to the whites.[10]

The general intended to keep Abraham around and use him as an interpreter and guide, but he did not entirely trust this influential black leader. He wrote, "I have promised Abraham the freedom of his family if he be faithful to us, and I shall certainly hang him if he be not faithful."[11]

During the summer, more blacks—mainly disgruntled runaway slaves—had tired of their life among the sick and starving Seminoles. They surrendered to the whites and told tales of their days of hardship. They had been reduced to eating coontie roots (arrowroot) and alligator tails and, they claimed, had been regularly beaten by tribe members. No doubt life had been difficult for the Seminole people—red or black—but once again it is suspected that these former slaves embellished their stories in hopes of receiving less punishment when returned to their owners. Slave owners were delighted to have solid proof that these blacks were better off as slaves than as free people.

General Jesup turned the incident to his advantage by offering freedom to all runaway slaves who abandoned the Seminoles. This edict had an immediate impact on increasing the number who surrendered. At the same time, he told the citizen soldiers under his command—and later included his entire force—that they would be compensated for each black they captured. This policy became counterproductive when blacks who sought to turn themselves in were usually grabbed by soldiers before they could reach an army fort, which scared away many others.[12]

In September, Jesup moved his headquarters from St. Augustine to Tampa Bay as he prepared to conduct a fall campaign against the Seminoles. His primary concern was the availability of adequate horses and mules. He spent $1,500 of his own money for horses after the highly contagious equine disease glanders broke out and killed many animals. Mules were superior to horses for heavy drayage, but Jesup found it impossible to buy enough of them. The general preferred the Dearborn wagon, with its large, wide wheels and watertight body that could be used as a boat when necessary. The quartermaster was able to secure a number of Dearborns that he promised would be delivered in time for the campaign. Jesup planned his mission with precision, listing hundreds of items that he would need, from wagons and livestock to maneuver across the marshy terrain to pontoons and steamers to traverse rivers. He had been appointed quartermaster of the army following the War of 1812 and knew what equipment was available and how it would fit into his plans.

The respected author and historian John K. Mahon describes the task that Jesup faced in his procurement of the proper equipment and supplies to outfit his army:

He [Jesup] was willing to try new firearms, such as Colt's revolvers and Cochran's repeater. But the mountain howitzers sent him were of no use whatever under Florida conditions. [A mountain howitzer is a heavy gun mounted on a large two-wheeled cart. It immediately sinks into mud.] Shotguns were needed for use by the light companies. More Mackinaw boats were needed, flat-bottomed, with a double set of oars, each capable of carrying twenty men. Barricades should be prepared to fit the sides of three small steamers. Haversacks, wall tents, common tents, hospital tents, camp kettles, mess kits, canteens, axes, spades, and hatchets—all must be provided in time. Large-size sheets of rubber cloth, sheepskins for saddle blankets, halters, hobbles, wagon harness, whips, sadler's tools, and a few thousand horseshoes must be on hand for the mounted men. Parched corn meal would be useful, as would "portable" soup. Three ounces of soup, a little rice, and a half a pound of bread would make a day's rations weighing no more than three quarters of a pound. Light astringent wines would be good in this climate, so would garlic and onions; but the present ration was wholly unsuited to Florida.[13]

There can be no question that Jesup spent a considerable amount of time corresponding with the various supply departments of the army and with the secretary of war for approval of his purchases. The appropriation of finances was not an issue. The government had made available its considerable resources in unprecedented amounts to provide the army with enough supplies to end this war once and for all. The war had gone on for too long, according to most of the American public and press. The constant conflict without significant progress had demoralized the army, especially the officers' ranks, with high casualties and a loss of respect for the fighting abilities of the soldiers. Many abolitionists, as well as the public at large, believed that the Seminole had been punished enough and it was time to negotiate a treaty that would finally bring peace to Florida.

Meanwhile, Osceola waited to determine what method of tactics the whites would implement in this latest campaign against the Seminole before he moved his people or readied his warriors. He had chosen to fight a defensive war and had no intention of changing that strategy. Osceola knew that the army was preparing for an extended expedition into central Florida in the fall, and he dreaded it. It would mean more suffering for his people, who were already starving and weary of moving at a moment's notice. He wanted peace, but the white man refused to recognize the basic rights of the Seminole. It was only just and fair that they be allowed to remain in their homeland. The territory was big enough for both white settlers and the Seminole people. If only the government would offer them a tract of land on which to settle, this war could come to an end. Was it asking too much, he contemplated, simply to want to live in peace and raise their families?

General Jesup decided that he no longer required the services of the Creek regiment. In his opinion, they had let him down during Osceola's raid on the detention center near Tampa Bay. He arranged for the warriors to be transported to Pass Christian, Louisiana, where Major W. G. Freeman would muster them out of the service. There was of course the matter of compensating the tribe for the eighty blacks they had captured during their time in Florida. Jesup wrote to the secretary of war and explained, "The Creek Indians have been promised a reward for the captures they should make of Negroes belonging to citizens of the United States. Had compensation not been promised they would have taken no prisoners, but would have put all to death. I compromised with them by allowing twenty dollars for each slave captured. To end all difficulty on that subject, I have purchased the Negroes from them on account of the public, for eight thousand dollars. . . . I respect-fully request that the purchase be sanctioned."[14]

There was one problem concerning this payment, however. By allocating the $8,000, whether hidden within an obscure piece of legislation or stand-ing on its own, Congress would be putting the government in the business of buying slaves. This situation was extremely delicate, to say the least, and if leaked to the press would probably escalate into a national scandal. Addi-tionally, the Creeks were not satisfied with the amount of money and wanted more for their plunder. In the end, Congress did not have to vote on the mat-ter. The payment was handled privately and discreetly when individuals in the slave trade came forward with $15,000 to pay off the Creeks. What could have been another disaster for Jesup had been averted.[15]

The Creek fighting force had achieved some measure of success in sev-eral skirmishes, but Jesup now wanted a more savage detachment of Native Americans—Miamis, Delawares, and especially Sioux—northern Indians who would ruthlessly kill the Seminole warriors and seize the women and children. He would promise to pay them with everything they could confis-cate from the Seminoles—livestock, blacks, and other items of worth—and would entice them by telling them that the Creeks had been able to earn $15,000 for their efforts.

The government approved the general's request and promised that he would receive those additional Native American warriors from various north-ern tribes who were motivated to fight the Seminoles for whatever bounty they could take. This practice of recruiting Native American mercenaries into Florida for combat duty was not well received by the public or by many in the ranks of the military. The objective had been to remove Native Americans from the territory, not invite more to move there, even temporarily. Also, some members of the military, especially militiamen, viewed this recruitment as a slap in their faces for not being able to subdue the Seminole on their own.

Other people opposed the employment of Native Americans on moral grounds. Samuel Forry, a surgeon who was stationed at Fort King, reflected this opinion when he wrote, "The head of the War Department has granted

Gen. Jesup the following Indian force: four hundred Shawnees, 200 Delawares, 200 Choctaws, 100 Kickapoos, and 100 Sacs and Foxes. We shall then
have war to the knife. Every warrior shall be killed, and all the women and
children become slaves to the captor! How magnanimous is a civilized and
enlightened Republic of the 19th century! In the catalogue of earth's nations,
the name Seminole shall be erased! They have been weighed in the balance,
and found wanting! The edict has gone forth!" Forry's overly dramatic tirade
would be all for naught. Only a small band of Delawares and Shawnees would
ever serve with Jesup, and they would prove to be ineffective.[16]

In addition to wanting more ruthless Native Americans, General Jesup
vowed to become more ruthless himself when interrogating captured Seminoles and blacks. He put in place a policy of threatening his prisoners with
hanging if they did not provide relevant information. Although most captives
had freely volunteered whatever they knew about the whereabouts of the
various camps and who and how many resided in them—mainly to curry favor with their captors—this added pressure of the rope might have paid off
for the army. There is no evidence that the threat was ever carried out and
that any captured Seminole or black was hanged. But as a tool of warfare, any
psychological edge could provide untold benefits.[17]

On the subject of informants, John Philip, a slave belonging to King Philip,
the Seminole chief, surrendered to authorities at St. Augustine. This Black
Seminole and his wife had become weary of the hardship associated with living as fugitives in the swamps. In the course of his interrogation, John admitted, perhaps under the threat of hanging, that he could lead the white men to a
deserted plantation south of the Tomoka River near Dunlawton Mill, twenty-
five miles away, where King Philip and his followers were camped. The capture of this influential Seminole chief would be quite a prize. Jesup immediately
put a plan into motion and called up a detail of soldiers to execute it.

On September 8, captive John Philip led 170 regulars and militiamen—
including Osceola's friend Lieutenant John Graham—under the command of
Brigadier General Joseph M. Hernández toward the encampment of King
Philip. Hernández was a native Spanish Floridian from St. Augustine who
had pledged his allegiance to the United States after Spain ceded Florida. In

1822, he had been appointed the first congressional delegate from the territory and served for seven months. His had been a loud voice in the legislature
promoting the idea of removing the Seminoles from the territory. Hernández
commanded the East Florida militia, which he organized. He soon became
the right-hand man of General Jesup, who could trust his subordinate general
to carry out any mission without question or comment about its propriety.[18]

The ride of Hernández's command was difficult, with horses bogging
down to their bellies in the swamps. Finally, at sunset, the column halted at
the Dunlawton Plantation, which was in the vicinity of the hostile camp.
From that vantage point, smoke rising from fires into the thick hammock
could be observed. John Philip and a detachment of scouts were dispatched
to reconnoiter the campsite where Chief King Philip was said to be residing.
They returned to confirm the presence of the camp.

At about midnight, Hernández ordered the Florida volunteers to dis-
mount and assume positions on foot enclosing three sides of the camp. The
regulars would remain mounted and execute a surprise attack into the unsuspecting hostiles. The troopers remained in their positions throughout the
night. The Seminole camp was apparently blissfully unaware of the danger
surrounding them—not a horse whinnied, not a dog barked, and no soldier
made an unnecessary noise.

Jacob Motte, a surgeon attached to the unit, described the scene from that
night: "Silently and cautiously we wended our way through the old woods,
where possibly a civilized being had never before voluntarily ventured. A
deep and beautiful serenity pervaded nature; for all was silence, save when at
long intervals the cry of some solitary bird broke on our ears with startling
shrillness; or when a rustling among the dry branches made us pause in
breathless silence, till a deer, bounding across our path, would plunge into
the opposite thicket: while we dare not send a bullet after him, lest the report
of our guns should alarm the wily enemy."[19]

At dawn, General Hernández tightened the noose. His men crept closer
and closer to the camp, until finally the general ordered the charge. The
mounted troopers assailed the village with pounding hooves while the foot
soldiers stood up and fought their way through the thick hammock. The in-

habitants of the camp were taken completely by surprise and had no time to reach their weapons and fight. In a bloodless assault, almost every Seminole in residence there—about twenty—was captured. King Philip was said to have been knocked down into the mud by a charging horse, but otherwise no one was harmed. Only King Philip's eighteen-year-old son escaped. His favorite son, Coacoochee, had not been present.

Jacob Motte wrote, "We soon found ourselves unexpectedly in the presence of royalty, for there stood King Philip . . . naked as he was born, except the breech-cloth; and covered with most unkingly dirt. . . . There were also a number of women and children captured; the former miserable, blackened, haggard, shriveled (smoke-dried and half clad) devils; the latter, ugly little nudities."[20]

One of the Seminole men taken prisoner was named Tomoka John. He let it be known to General Hernández that Seminole Chief Euchee Billy and his followers were camped only about six miles away. Tomoka John volunteered to show them the way. The following night, the general employed the same tactic that had been successful in taking King Philip's camp. He had one hundred men crawl through the dense cabbage palm to encircle the sleeping inhabitants of Euchee Billy's camp. Nothing could be heard but nature's night sounds—and the pounding heartbeats of men about to go into combat.

At dawn, barking dogs alerted the camp to the advancing troops, and the attack was sprung. This time there was moderate resistance. Lieutenant John Winfield Scott McNeil was shot and wounded, and died on the way back to St. Augustine, the only army casualty. One Seminole warrior was killed and several others were wounded. But the result was the same as the previous day—Chief Euchee Billy and his brother Euchee Jack were taken prisoner.

Brigadier General Hernández and his column arrived triumphantly back in St. Augustine and paraded the captives through the streets in front of a cheering public. Hernández would be feted by several balls and dinners to celebrate his great victories. General Jesup was thrilled with the operation that had brought back forty-seven prisoners. He wrote that the captured King Philip, Euchee Billy, Euchee Jack, and John Philip "are worth fifty common Indians and negroes."[21]

King Philip requested that his family be permitted to join him at Fort Marion. Jesup viewed the proposal as a guarantee that if the chief's wife and children were present he would not contemplate escape. It was also a way to add to the number of important Seminole prisoners. Jesup gladly granted the request.

General Hernández, with a mounted battalion, was assigned the duty of escorting King Philip's people from the place of rendezvous, the ruins of the Bulow Plantation, back to St. Augustine. This group would be escorted by Coacoochee, King Philip's son, who did not intend to surrender. Jesup was aware that Coacoochee was a dangerous man who had conspired back on June 2 with Osceola to free the detainees awaiting removal. Hernández was warned to not let Coacoochee, this "Wildcat," out of his sight.

On September 26, Coacoochee and his small entourage—Blue Snake, Tomoka John, and two other warriors—arrived under a white flag at the former Bulow Plantation. In late afternoon, despite windy and rainy conditions, Hernández decided that the party would depart for St. Augustine. On the way, prior to arriving at Fort Peyton, Coacoochee insisted that they halt while he changed into his formal attire. Surgeon Jacob Motte, who was a member of the escort party, wrote, "He soon reappeared in all the pomp of scarlet and burnished silver; his head decorated with a plume of white crane feathers, and a silver band around his gaudy turban. His leather leggings were also superceded by a pair of bright scarlet cloth. He insisted on being mounted on a spirited horse; and attired in his picturesque native costume, he rode with a great deal of savage grace and majesty."[22]

Coacoochee and his companions were on display to a curious public as they rode through the streets of St. Augustine. The young warrior likely enjoyed the expressions on the faces of these white people who ogled at what they would regard as a savage wearing a garish costume. At the end of the ride, however, Coacoochee and his companions unexpectedly found themselves at the gate of Fort Marion prison, where they were placed in irons and incarcerated. The son of King Philip had assumed that his white flag of truce, which had been honored without exception by both sides throughout the war, would be respected and he would be treated accordingly. Instead, General Hernández, on orders from Jesup, locked up the young warrior with his father and the other Seminole prisoners.

This act of treachery by General Thomas Jesup came to the attention of another army surgeon, Samuel Forry, who was in St. Augustine at the time awaiting orders. Forry wrote, "We have received intelligence of Coa-cuchee's being enticed into St. Augustine—that he came under the protection of a white flag, which secured him a position in the old Fort. Can such things be enacted by men who call themselves civilized? I do not, however, credit this report."[23]

The report was true, however. In fact, General Jesup had at first thought about hanging Coacoochee for conspiring with Osceola to abduct the detainees from Tampa Bay and Fort Mellon. After some deliberation, the general decided that his cause would be better served by using the respected warrior to lure other hostiles into the fort. After several days in the prison, Coacoochee was temporarily released to act as a messenger for his father, who asked that his people come in and meet with the army. Jesup made it clear to King Philip that he would be severely punished if his son did not return as scheduled.[24]

In the meantime, Osceola, who continued to battle his own illness, understood that his starving and sick people could not hold out for much longer. They needed a permanent place to call home, and fields in which to plant crops, and the freedom from fear to raise their children. He had discussed the matter with Chief Coa Hadjo, and the two men had come to the conclusion that the only way to relieve the misery of the people and secure their future as a tribe was to negotiate a treaty. Neither man, however, truly believed that the white man wanted peace without first punishing the Seminole. Regardless of the risk, they thought it best to set up a parley to assess the army's willingness to negotiate. Perhaps the government had softened its stance with respect to emigration and would now entertain the notion of a Seminole reservation in Florida.

On October 16, Coacoochee returned to Fort Marion in the company of his uncle and younger brother while more of King Philip's people straggled

212 ⊷ OSCEOLA AND THE GREAT SEMINOLE WAR

toward the fort. At that time, he informed General Joseph Hernández that Osceola wanted to parley. The Seminole war leader would be arriving in a few days to camp near St. Augustine with about one hundred of his people. As a show of good faith, Osceola had sent along a gift of a beaded peace pipe and a white plume for General Hernández.

Hernández immediately informed General Jesup of this unexpected but welcome message from Osceola. Jesup's heart must have skipped a beat at the thought of his nemesis voluntarily leaving the swamp and coming to within arm's reach of the military. This was the man who had tarnished Jesup's reputation, and he was now seeking favors. Jesup wanted to make certain that nothing happened that would spoil this opportunity. He advised Hernández to send his best wishes as well as presents to Osceola, and to tell the Seminole leader that they would be pleased to meet with him. These goods and good tidings were dutifully delivered by Coacoochee.[25]

Once again, Samuel Forry was skeptical of the army's sincerity:

Coa-cuchee returned day before yesterday; and yesterday Gen. Hernandez went as far as Hewlitt's mills, carrying provisions for about 100 of Philip's people, who are approaching from different points. The Gen. met about 50 Indians, and brought to Fort Peyton 79 negroes. My friend, Joe Hicks, was there, and Powell [Osceola] and Coahadjo, they say, will be at Fort Peyton today. The Indians have not the least idea of emigrating. Tomoka John has no doubt held out false hopes to them, declaring that a portion of this territory will be assigned to them. If these people once get into our power, they will be held as fast as the old Fort can make them. They come with a view of having a talk and a ball-play, and eating and drinking. Gen. Jesup and staff got here yesterday, doubtless concocting some direful plans to entrap the poor savage.[26]

On the evening of October 18, General Hernández held a grand ball attended by army officers and the upper crust of St. Augustine society. The main attraction at this formal dance was Coacoochee, who was dressed in his

Seminole finery of fancy feathers, shiny metal, and colorful cloth. The handsome young captive made quite a striking figure, and Hernández took great pleasure in showing him off to the denizens of the city.

Samuel Forry, who provided a most fascinating eyewitness account of this dance, described Coacoochee as being the "lion of the night." White observers conceded that this young man, who was perhaps in his early twenties, was quite handsome, a living Apollo, who was aware of the impact that his presence had on people. There can be no question that the young ladies in particular were pixilated by the exotic Seminole warrior and engaged in a spirited competition for his attention. They fluttered their eyelashes and pursed their lips from behind palmetto leaf fans as they surveyed this attractive young man and flirted as inconspicuously as possible. One lady asked an officer from Fort King if Osceola was as handsome as Coacoochee and was told that the Seminole war leader was even better looking.

Coacoochee, although he might have danced with several of the girls, apparently was not as attracted to them as they were to him. At one point, he was introduced to a newlywed couple and insinuated that the pretty girl was enjoyed by her husband now but after she had a few children she would not be worth the bother. This blatant insult, however, might have been misinterpreted or not interpreted at all.[27]

Osceola and Coa Hadjo arrived the following morning with their people and camped about a mile from Fort Peyton, a hastily constructed log structure on Moultrie Creek. They dispatched a messenger to request that General Hernández meet them at their camp for a parley.

General Thomas Jesup wanted to make certain that Hernández handled this important conference properly and wrote a memorandum of talking points and questions that Hernández should direct at Osceola: "Ascertain the objects of the Indians in coming at this time. Also their expectations. Are they prepared to deliver up the negroes taken from the citizens at once? Why have they not surrendered them already, as promised by Coa-Hajo at Fort King? Have the chiefs of the nation held a council in relation to the subjects of the talk at Fort King? What chiefs attended the council, and what was their determination? Have the chiefs sent a messenger with the decision of the council? Have the principal chiefs, Micanopy, Jumper, Cloud, and Alligator, sent a messenger, and if so, what is their message? Why have not those chiefs come in themselves?" Jesup told Hernández that if the replies from Osceola and Coa Hadjo were unsatisfactory, he was authorized to seize the two men.[28]

On Saturday morning, October 21, 1837, Brigadier General Joseph M. Hernández rode out of St. Augustine to keep his appointment for a parley with Osceola. His column was joined by about 250 dragoons and Florida militiamen under the command of Major James A. Ashby who were garrisoned at Fort Peyton.

According to army officer John Sprague, General Jesup was waiting nervously at Fort Peyton while this mission was being carried out. At one point, he wrote a message to Hernández in the field: "Let the chiefs and warriors know that we have been deceived by them long enough, and that we do not intend to be deceived again. Order the whole party directly to town. You have force sufficient to compel obedience, and they must move instantly. I have information of a recent murder by the Indians. They must be disarmed. They can talk in town, and send any messengers out, if they please."[29]

Hernández responded: "Sir—For the purpose of carrying into effect your instructions, conveyed to me verbally by your aid-de-camp, Lieutenant Linnard, after having left Fort Peyton, that if the answers of the chiefs to my inquiries should not be satisfactory, they were to be made prisoners, I had given the necessary directions to Major Ashby to ensure their capture."[30]

General Hernández and his column arrived at Osceola's camp some seven miles away, where a white flag of truce had been conspicuously raised. The white flag was an indication that the Seminole regarded the parley as a truce, not a surrender. Ashby already had been given orders to deploy his dragoons, and the troops gradually—and as unobtrusively as possible—assumed positions to surround this fair-sized camp. Osceola had been accompanied to the parley by twelve chiefs in addition to himself and Coa Hadjo, seventy-one warriors, six women, and four blacks—ninety-five people total.

Assistant surgeon Nathan Jarvis, who had accompanied the column, recognized Osceola at once as the "principal man." He reported that Osceola wore a bright blue calico shirt, red leggings buttoned on the outside, a bright print shawl around his head, and another shawl over his shoulders. He looked unwell, but "nothing of savage fierceness or determination mark'd his countenance, on the contrary his features indicated mildness and benevolence."[31]

General Hernández faced Osceola and Coa Hadjo, and read the message from General Jesup. He hurled the rapid-fire questions at the bewildered warriors, who either did not answer or had no answer, other than stating that the three missing chiefs in question had measles and could not attend. Hernández, however, had not expected answers and did not care about whether or not these renegade Seminoles responded to his questions. He had orders from General Jesup to execute, and reading the memorandum was merely a formality.

At a prearranged signal from Joseph Hernández, scores of soldiers stepped forward with their carbines raised. At the same time, a handful of their comrades roughly grabbed Osceola and Coa Hadjo and took them captive.

About forty Seminoles were armed, but the action by the troopers had been so swift and shocking that they had no time to resist, which in any case would have been a grave mistake. It was apparent that any warlike movement by the warriors would have resulted in the soldiers opening fire and massacring the entire party.

There was no expression of surprise on Osceola's face and no protest came from his lips. He was accustomed to treachery by the U.S. government.[32]

The white flag of truce waved above the heads of Osceola and Coa Hadjo as they were escorted away to Fort Marion prison.

» *Eleven* «

Gone to Be with the Spirits

»»◆««

The white flag of truce had been violated once again. First it had been Coacoochee who had been tricked; now, Osceola. The white flag had been flown by both sides throughout this Seminole War—as well as during previous conflicts between the U.S. Army and Native Americans—and there had not been one single recorded instance of either party failing to honor its meaning. Nevertheless, on October 21, 1837, this respected—sacred to some—tradition had been ignored and Osceola and his entourage had been taken prisoner.

The ninety-five Seminole captives were placed in a single file between columns of soldiers and marched away toward St. Augustine. Osceola and Coa Hadjo were provided horses to ride, while the other prisoners walked. Osceola rode with the poise of a conquering hero rather than a man who had just been the victim of a treacherous act. Surgeon Jacob Motte noted that Osceola had apparently accepted his capture without protest, and although it was evident that he suffered from some illness, "the fire of his flashing eyes was unsubdued."[1]

On their way to Fort Marion, General Hernández, as was his habit, proudly marched his prisoners through the streets of St. Augustine. The news of Osceola's capture had preceded them, and almost the entire population of the city turned out to gape at the elusive Seminole leader. It can only be imagined how swelled the chest was of Hernández as he led the procession. The farthest thought from his mind was that he had done anything wrong by capturing the Seminole war leader. He had simply followed the orders of his superior when he had ignored that white flag. In the days ahead, however, he would be called upon to defend his position against those who regarded his actions as shameful as those of Jesup. But for now he basked in the glory of delivering the most wanted man in Florida to prison.[2]

Fort Marion had been an old stone Spanish fortress known as Castillo de San Marcos, or Castle St. Mark. The structure had been built in 1672, which made it the oldest fort in the United States, and it had been designed to protect the ocean route of treasure ships returning to Spain. Over the years, the fortress had been repeatedly attacked but never taken by force. In 1821, a dungeon had been located beneath a high turret, with human bones and other evidence that would point to the room having been used as a torture chamber. The grisly discovery was considered to be a "remnant of the Inquisition, and that the punishment was a lingering death."[3]

Upon arrival, Osceola was locked up in the casements, which were large rooms situated in the walls. His cell was located on the southwestern corner of the courtyard and measured eighteen by thirty-three feet. It was bare save a one-foot-wide, three-foot-high platform that rimmed part of the room. The sole source of light was a narrow opening lined with metal bars—called a loophole—some fifteen feet up the side of the wall.

Incarceration in Fort Marion was not as torturous as might have been imagined given the bleak accommodations. Food was plentiful, beds were made of forage bags stuffed with straw, warm blankets were provided, and the prisoners could wander around the courtyard for several hours each day. Osceola's cell mates were Coacoochee; John Cavallo, a black man who had often represented Chief Micanopy; and about twenty other Seminoles.[4]

Incidentally, the prison courtyard was also the site of an occasional Seminole tribal dance, one of which was described by Samuel Forry: "A few nights ago, the Indians had a dance in the fort; the whoops and yells alarmed the city—the Mayor ran to Gen. Jesup and hoped that he would send for more troops, for Osceola would take the city before daylight. The Indians are perfectly secure, and do not dream of escape. A barricade was erected to prevent a rush upon the passage leading to the door."[5]

Soon after his arrival, Osceola requested a meeting with General Jesup. The general ordered that Osceola be escorted to headquarters. The Seminole war leader made no mention of his treatment—either under the white flag or his present conditions—and had only one request. He asked if he could send for his family. Jesup viewed this as a positive sign that Osceola had accepted his imprisonment and had no plans to escape. He readily agreed to dispatch a messenger to locate and escort Osceola's family to Fort Marion. Jesup had been correct; Osceola, who was ill and in a weakened condition, likely had no intention of attempting an escape—at least until his health improved. The same could not be said for Osceola's cell mate, Coacoochee, who would have been obsessed with the notion of escaping as soon as the cell door had clanked shut behind him.

Within a matter of days, the capture of this most famous Seminole had come to the attention of the entire nation. The fact that Osceola had been taken prisoner was not the primary issue, however; rather, it was the manner in which he had been seized. The shameful nature of this proud warrior being taken under a white flag of truce became a cause célèbre for many advocates, especially abolitionists, and sparked nationwide protests against the conduct of the Florida War. The public was outraged by General Jesup's scandalous betrayal of accepted military tradition and called upon the government to take action to remove the general, if not immediately end the conflict. Representatives on the floor of Congress heatedly debated this controversial topic, with about as many legislators defending the general as opposing him. In the eyes of the public, however, the incident had created a martyr, Osceola, and a villain, Thomas Jesup.

Jesup was mercilessly vilified in the national press—and even abroad. *Niles' National Register* wrote in an editorial, "We disclaim all participation in the 'glory' of this achievement of American generalship, which, if practised towards a civilized foe would be characterized as a violation of all that is noble and generous in war." The paper went on to predict that Jesup's treachery would "produce more bloody and signal vengeance than has yet marked their ruthless doings." Meanwhile, Andrew Welch wrote, "Never was a more disgraceful piece of villainy perpetrated in a civilized land." Welch went on to point out that the United States had dealt with the Seminole as a sovereign nation, making treaties with them, and consequently this act of treachery by Jesup was no different from an English general capturing an American general under the white flag of truce. Although countless newspapers trumpeted the call for investigations and the firing of Jesup, the government, which had the final word, stood behind its commander.[6]

Jesup and his defenders presented a number of reasons for the decision to ignore the white flag. Jesup claimed that he had heard from tribal members that Osceola and Coa Hadjo were coming to St. Augustine with intentions of attacking the prison and releasing King Philip, and at the same time massacring all the white people in that city. Not one tribal member or collaborating military man was presented to support this claim. The general also made the assertion that Osceola had at some point killed a messenger under a white flag of truce, and that the Seminole war leader regularly abused the use of the white flag in order to spy on St. Augustine. Specifics of those charges have never been provided, and no evidence exists to confirm them. Jesup then argued that the removal of Osceola from the fight was vital to the expedient end to the war; therefore, such a drastic measure was justified. True, Osceola was the crafty war leader, but white flags of truce without exception had been honored up to and including the highest-ranking member of either side. Further, General Jesup contended that Osceola was aware that the government was through negotiating and that anyone who turned himself in did so with the knowledge that he was surrendering. One piece of evidence—albeit questionable—suggests that there could have been a hint of credibility to Jesup's statement about Osceola understanding that his meeting with General Hernández near Fort Peyton was a surrender.[7]

This premise that Osceola intended to surrender comes from Dr. Robert Lebby, an army surgeon who later wrote about his experiences:

The Indian that accompanied Osceola, when he surrendered to Genl. Jesup, was at Fort Moultrie, with him, a very intelligent man, and I think was the Counselor or Lawyer of the nation—He said repeatedly that Osceola, surrendered himself, knowing and believing that he would not be permitted to leave the camp again.—And he repeated a conversation that occurred between himself and the Chief a day or two before they got to the Genl's Camp—I think this man's name was Coa Hadjo. . . . In the conversation referred to, he said when Osceola met him—he asked if he was going into the Genl:—Hadjo's reply,—yes for he was satisfied that his people could do nothing more—they were worn down by sickness, and starvation, and he was going in—Osceola's reply—that he would go with him—that he was now done—and asked Hadjo, if was likely the Genl would let him come out again and gather his people—Hadjo said, that he was certain Genl. Jesup would not let him go—if he ever went in, and if he wished to gather his people he had better do so before he surrendered,—for he had done a great deal against the whites, and they would not permit him to go out again.[8]

There exist a couple of factors that cast doubt upon Coa Hadjo's statement, however. No matter the circumstances, Osceola would have been accompanied by his family to Fort Peyton for his conference with General Hernández if he had decided to surrender. It would be well over a month after his capture before his wives and children would finally arrive at Fort Marion. He would never have knowingly planned to be separated from his family for so long—if not forever, given the hostile feelings toward him by Jesup. He would have wanted his relatives by his side during such a momentous occasion. Osceola would have known that if he surrendered, the war, and probably his life, would be over. In the event that he did choose to give himself up, he would have negotiated his surrender and been provided promises about his treatment and that of his people long before meeting in person with representatives of the army. Also, it was common knowledge that Osceola's people—and family—were starving, sick, and desperate, but they had suffered from these dire conditions for many months and nothing indicated that they had not vowed to endeavor to persevere even longer. Consequently, Coa Hadjo's assertion simply does not make sense. All the associated evidence establishes Osceola as a dedicated family man who would never consider deserting his wives and children and a leader who refused to surrender his people, much less himself.

Another factor to consider: throughout history there has been controversy with respect to the language translation between Native Americans and whites. Translators of both races have occasionally misinterpreted a speaker for their own benefit, or have misunderstood the intent of the words, or just made a mistake. Native American languages have words and phrases that do not smoothly translate into English, and vice versa. In addition, some Native Americans, for fear of reprisal or simply wanting to please the whites, have been known to say what they thought the white man wanted to hear. When considering the veracity of Coa Hadjo's statement—even if it was correctly translated—it must be noted that this was the same man who had secretly conspired with Jesup to capture Black Seminoles and turn them in to the army, despite Article 5 of the capitulation agreement.

Regardless of reasons or excuses, Major General Thomas Jesup had issued an order that would stain his reputation for the rest of his life and for generations thereafter. There can be no question that the controversial capture of Osceola under a flag of truce stands to this day as one of the most disgraceful acts in American military history.

With Osceola securely locked up at Fort Marion, General Jesup deflected the criticism of his dishonorable deeds and returned to the business of war. He buried himself in the task of fine-tuning his field strategy for the fall campaign. The capture of Osceola, Coacoochee, King Philip, Coa Hadjo, and the other leaders had dramatically crippled the Seminole resistance, but the fighting was by no means over. Jesup had sent out detachments of scouts who returned with valuable intelligence. The general intended to put into the field seven columns that—unlike the three wings in Scott's campaign—would not necessarily rendezvous or depend on any other unit for support.

Colonel Persifor F. Smith, with about six hundred Louisiana volunteers, would maneuver south of the Caloosahatchee River toward Lake Okeechobee. Colonel Zachary Taylor, the future president who had recently arrived in Florida with the fourteen-hundred-man First Infantry Regiment, would patrol in the area between the Kissimmee River and Pease Creek. At some point along Pease Creek, Taylor would establish a supply depot to provide for his column in the field. Navy lieutenant Levin Powell, commanding eighty-five sailors, one company of volunteer infantry, and two companies of artillery, would move into the Everglades. These three columns would endeavor to beat the bushes and, if not actually engage the hostiles, push the warriors ahead of them, where they would encounter the main column of soldiers.

This main column would be composed of four separate detachments. The first would be commanded by General Joseph Hernández, and would travel by steamer to Mosquito Lagoon to await further orders. Colonel John Warren would take his Florida militia and two companies of dragoons and head in a southerly direction between the Atlantic Ocean and the St. Johns River. General Abraham Eustis would advance up the St. Johns River by boat. Last, a column would sweep through the territory between Fort King and the Oklawaha River.[9]

Before Jesup's columns were ready to take to the field against the Seminole, a most surprising development that some believed had the potential to end the war presented itself. It was learned that a Cherokee delegation dispatched by Chief John Ross was on its way to Florida from Georgia for the purpose of persuading the Seminole to cease fighting. Ross, a man of great intelligence who had written the Cherokee Constitution, had been moved to act after learning about the terrible suffering endured by the Seminole people.

This delegation arrived at St. Augustine on November 10 and held a meeting with Seminole representatives the following day in the fort's courtyard. These Seminoles had received another discouraging piece of news on the day before the arrival of the Cherokees. General Hernández had returned from the field with fifty-three more prisoners he had taken at Spring Garden. These captives included Coacoochee's two brothers, sixteen fugitive slaves, and twenty warriors. Needless to say, the Seminole—after first smoking the peace pipe—listened closely to an address from John Ross that was read and interpreted to them that called for a cease-fire and treaty negotiations.

The Seminole response was positive, with Osceola stating that "he was tired of fighting" but not agreeing to any terms to end hostilities. The Cherokee delegation was satisfied that they had made progress. They then departed for Fort Mellon—guided by Coa Hadjo, who would serve as interpreter—where they intended to contact Micanopy and other chiefs who remained at large and pass the message on to them.[10]

On November 29, while Osceola still waited for his family to arrive, a most bold and daring incident took place at Fort Marion prison. The warriors who were locked up in Osceola's cell—mainly Coacoochee and John Cavallo—had devised an escape plan, and this was the night it would be attempted.

The prisoners in that cell had managed to secure a file. Although no one knows for certain how this tool found its way into the hands of the prisoners, it could have easily been smuggled inside by a friendly free black. There were many such blacks living in St. Augustine who were sympathetic to the Seminole cause.

The plan was set in motion when one of the taller warriors stood on the foot-wide, three-foot-high platform along the cell wall. This platform was about twelve feet below the loophole, the narrow opening lined with metal bars. Several of the stronger prisoners took turns standing on this first man's shoulders and were boosted up high enough to work the file to remove two rusted bars from the loophole. It was strenuous work, but eventually the bars gave way. The top warrior then hacked footholds into the stone wall with a knife. The canvas forage bags used for bedding had been emptied of straw, cut into strips, and braided together to make a sturdy rope. The top warrior, with that rope clenched between his teeth, then used the footholds to lift himself gradually until he could grab hold of the ledge of the loophole. He tied the rope securely to a remaining metal bar and tossed the other end, perhaps weighted down by a rock, through the opening toward the muddy moat twenty feet below.

When the rope had been secured and the footholds dug, the most difficult part of the operation was at hand. One by one, the people from the cell were boosted up to the loophole. Once there, it was necessary for them to wiggle and strain—and endure the pain of flesh being ripped from their bodies by the rough stone and remnants of metal—in order to squeeze through what was said to be a tiny eight-inch opening. After making it through the aperture, they lowered themselves down the wall with the rope and finally dropped into the muddy water below.

Twenty people, including Coacoochee, his two brothers and an uncle, John Cavallo, and two women—scraped up and bloody—managed to escape to freedom. The fugitives headed south toward the Tomoka River, where the remnants of King Philip's followers were known to be camped.[11]

Osceola was not among those prisoners who escaped—for unknown reasons. Perhaps he was too ill and feeble to accomplish the laborious act of climbing the wall and enduring the subsequent journey, and did not want to hinder the others by having them assist him. Additionally, his family had not yet arrived and he would not have wanted to risk having them held as hostages and punished for his deeds. He certainly would have encouraged those prisoners who were able to escape and probably advised them about gathering warriors and continuing the war.

On the afternoon of November 30, a caravan of Osceola's family that included at least two wives and fifty other people arrived at Fort Marion under a white flag. Osceola was said to have had four children with Morning Dew and an unknown number with his second wife, but accounts mentioned only two of his children in this group. It can be assumed that many of the other people would have been extended family on his wife's side and possibly a few related by blood to Osceola.[12]

Lieutenant John Pickell, who was on duty at Fort Marion at the time, described the arrival of Osceola's family: "They came with a white flag, hoisted upon a staff or pole 8 feet high and presented altogether a pitiful sight. The bearer of the flag was a fine looking young warrior and the head of the train, which was composed of about 50 souls. . . . The Negro part of the train was a wretched picture of squalid misery. . . . They have been on their way a number of days and were much fatigued when they arrived; they brought two miserable looking Indian ponies with them. From the voraciousness of their appetites when they were supplied with food, they seem to have been nearly starved."[13]

General Thomas Jesup had traveled to Fort Mellon and was present on December 3 when the Cherokee delegation returned from the field. The Cherokees had persuaded Micanopy, Cloud, eleven other chiefs or subchiefs, and a number of warriors to accompany them back to the fort under a white flag of truce. Micanopy told the general that he wanted peace and would agree to emigrate. He pledged to gather up his people, but they were scattered far and wide across central Florida and it would take him considerable time to locate the various bands and then more time for them to make their way to a relocation center.

Jesup became furious with this answer and accused Micanopy of purposely delaying the inevitable. In truth, Jesup was probably upset about the prison break and his own failures and decided to take it out on Micanopy. To the horror of the Cherokee observers, the general once again ignored the white flag and seized Micanopy and his people. He then told the chief that his messengers had ten days in which to reassemble the entire tribe for removal to the West.

Jesup had already tasted public and military outcry and condemnation for his betrayal of Caocoochee and Osceola; now he had made the same mistake again. The Cherokees were astounded that Jesup had acted so treacherously by taking prisoner these Seminoles who had come to talk in good faith. John Ross protested to the secretary of war about the "unprecedented violation of that sacred rule which has ever been recognized by every nation, civilized and uncivilized." Nevertheless, Micanopy and seventy-eight of his people were placed aboard a steamer and shipped off to St. Augustine for incarceration.[14]

General Jesup answered his critics this time with an act of diplomacy. He ordered that Colonel J. H. Sherburne present a proposition for peace to the Seminole leaders in the presence of the Cherokee delegation. This new agreement offered the Seminoles possession of all of the territory south of Tampa Bay between the Gulf of Mexico and the Atlantic Ocean. In return, the tribe would promise to return any runaway slaves that showed up there and would defend that land against foreign invasion. In other words, the Seminoles could have all the swampland in the south of Florida while the good land in the north went to the white man.

The chiefs, other than King Philip, who distrusted the government, heartily agreed to this incredible offer. It was a dream come true for the tribe to be able to remain in Florida. The right to live in their homeland had been their purpose for fighting the war in the first place. Even Osceola was impressed enough to send a white plume from his turban to Colonel Sherburne with a message: "Give this to our white father in token that Osceola will do as you have said."[15]

There was only one problem with this generous proposal. General Jesup had neglected to obtain prior approval from the powers that be in Washington before dispatching Sherburne to make the offer to the Seminoles. The government was adamant that the Seminoles relocate west of the Mississippi River and denied Jesup's request for approval. Consequently, nothing but bad feelings would ever come of the offer.

It can only be speculated whether Jesup had made the proposal in all sincerity or if he had been playing a cruel trick to temporarily pacify these incarcerated people. Perhaps he thought the Cherokee delegation and Chief John Ross—as well as the public—would tone down their criticism of his white flag treachery if they believed he was truly seeking a peaceful solution. In any event, General Jesup had once again demonstrated his uncivil, if not malicious and unethical, behavior toward these beaten but unbowed people.

Meanwhile, Jesup's military campaign was under way. Colonel Zachary Taylor had taken to the field with eight hundred regulars, two hundred mounted Missouri militiamen, and a detachment of Delaware Indian volunteers. Taylor maneuvered down the west side of the Kissimmee River, finally halting near Lake Isopoga, where he built a supply fort. Along the way, the column collected a number of prisoners—including Jumper, who was tired of being a fugitive, and sixty-three of his warriors. On Christmas Day, the army column marched toward Lake Okeechobee, where a recent Seminole camp was found at the edge of a cypress swamp.

Colonel Taylor had stumbled upon the camp of Coacoochee, Alligator, and Arpeika, who were waiting for him. These warriors had learned their lessons well from Osceola. Ten warriors wrapped in moss had hidden themselves in a deep morass of saw grass and palmetto to spy on the approach of the army. The main body of warriors—about 380 men, both red and black—waited in ambush behind trees and stumps and even perched upon high branches in trees.

The Delaware volunteers had refused to take the point for Taylor and had been replaced by the Missouri volunteers. When the Seminole scouts signaled that these soldiers were in range, the secreted warriors rose up and unleashed a murderous barrage of rifle fire. Taylor's surprised forces frantically scattered. The Missouri volunteers, who lost their colonel in the initial volley, fled the field. The infantry commanded by Colonel Ramsey Thompson, however, managed to establish a defensive line and returned fire.

This fierce battle between riflemen raged from noon until about three P.M., when the Seminole warriors withdrew. When the roll was called by the army, it was found that they had sustained 26 soldiers killed and 122 wounded. Seminole losses were said to have been 11 dead and 14 wounded.

Zachary Taylor returned from the field with his battle-tested troops on New Year's Eve. He had suffered considerable casualties—nearly 15 percent of his force—but defended his campaign by pointing out that he had captured 180 Seminoles, 600 head of cattle, and 100 horses. His campaign was judged a success, and he was hailed a hero.[16]

Osceola would have been proud of his chiefs and warriors had he known about this victory in the Battle of Lake Okeechobee. The Christmas Day battle would be the final large-scale battle of the war, and the last one in which Black Seminoles would participate in significant numbers. Osceola could have learned about the fight from the fort's officers or even from the prisoners captured and sent back to Fort Marion while Taylor was in the field. But Osceola had another important issue on his mind at present. General Jesup had judged that the Fort Marion prison was not secure enough, as evidenced by the embarrassing escape of Coacoochee and the other Seminoles. All the prisoners were going to be transferred to another facility, and it was not located in Florida.

On one of the final days of 1837, Osceola was placed aboard the US *Poinsett* for the voyage up the coast to Sullivan's Island, which was situated in Charleston Harbor in South Carolina. His shipboard mates were chiefs Micanopy, King Philip, Cloud, Coa Hadjo, 116 warriors, and around 80 women and children, including Osceola's family. Sullivan's Island was the site of Fort Moultrie, a Revolutionary War–era fortress originally constructed from palmetto logs but rebuilt with brick and mortar. The fort received its name from Colonel William Moultrie, who defended the fort against an attack by the British in 1776. Fort Moultrie would now become the prison home for Osceola and the other Seminoles.

The ship docked on January 1, 1838, and the prisoners were taken to their quarters. Osceola was afforded a room to share with his wives and children that had a fireplace for heat. The fire would have been a comfort for him to lie near when the chills from his terrible illness tormented him. Osceola was also allowed to keep his scalping knife and had permission to roam freely around the fort. At one point, the chiefs were even escorted over to a Charleston theater for a performance of the play *Honeymoon*.[17]

While at St. Augustine, Osceola had been attended to by Dr. Frederick Weedon, and the two men had become friendly. When Osceola was transferred to South Carolina, he requested that the doctor accompany him. Weedon, who knew that Osceola was seriously ill, readily agreed. The friendship between the two men was rather odd, given the fact that Weedon was the brother-in-law of Wiley Thompson, the Indian agent murdered by Osceola.[18]

The Seminole war leader, whose romanticized adventurous exploits were internationally known, was now the most famous Native American alive. Many whites throughout the country had been rooting for him to prevail in his quixotic quest, and the constant press coverage had made him a virtual hero. Thus, Osceola became quite an attraction for the public to view when he arrived in South Carolina. Visitors traveled great distances to pack Sullivan's Island for a chance to catch a glimpse or stand in the presence of this living legend. Osceola received these people graciously, and cordially bantered with crowds of men, women, and children, all of whom treated him with the utmost respect.

Although Osceola and his adoring public could not converse—unless an interpreter had been present, which is not known—facial expressions, body language, gestures, and smiles and laughter certainly would have been sufficient communication. Osceola was said to have occasionally conveyed to visitors the woes of his poor health and the prospects of dying. Another topic that he embraced was the loss of his homelands and the frustration of not being able to assist his people in their ongoing conflict. He certainly had a charisma that shone through his illness and sorrow to captivate his audiences.[19]

Winthrop Williams, a visitor to the prison, described his meeting with Osceola:

Today being Saturday I took leave of the city about 11 o'clock, embarked in a Packet Boat for Sullivan's Island, arrived there at ¼ past 12, visited Fort Moultrie, saw Mickanopy, Oseola, Allegator, Jumper, Cloud, Billy Hix and about two hundred more Seminole Indians— Oseola was the one I was most curious to see. He is about 35 years old, large sized, about 6 feet high, well formed, has every appearance of the Indian, does not speak English, has an intellectual countenance, with a sad expression. He is now in rather bad health. . . . It is a mistake about Oseolas being an educated man. He is no doubt a good Indian warrior and nothing more . . . I can assure you that I have not been so well pleased with any excursion for some time as this today.[20]

The artist George Catlin learned about the incarceration of Osceola and viewed it as an opportunity to paint a portrait of the famed warrior. Catlin arranged to have the War Department commission him to render portraits of the five principal Seminole chiefs locked up at Fort Moultrie. On January 17,

Catlin arrived in Charleston aboard the steam packet *New York* and was billeted in the officers' quarters at the fort. Catlin was probably surprised to discover that the Seminole captives, Osceola in particular, had piqued the interest of many fellow artists, who had made the trek to South Carolina to paint portraits. Perhaps for that reason, the first portrait Catlin painted was of Micanopy, who was more available for posing than Osceola.[21]

Thomas Storrow witnessed the competition to paint Osceola and described the arrangements that were made to accommodate the artists:

When the wishes of these gentlemen were made known to Osceola, he readily consented to sit; and to prepare himself to be drawn in a costume that he thought becoming, he devoted all the early part of a day to arraying himself in a manner which, in his eyes, was best calculated to set off his person to advantage. This was not done after the usual way of Indian warriors, with all the implements of war upon him, his body disfigured with dirt, his face made hideous with paint of many colors; but there was a marked display of what we should call taste, in the arrangement of his whole attire. His face was presented in its natural teint, but his person was arrayed in his best garments, covered with many ornaments, and on his head was a cap adorned with plumes which fell behind with studied grace. In short, if he had not presented a figure to command respect, one might say that he was somewhat of an Indian *élégant,* who desired to attract the gaze of the multitude.

For the convenience of the painters, it was agreed that two should work at the same time in one room, one at each end, while Osceola occupied a seat in the centre, or moved about when he wished to be relieved from restraint. Beside being a relaxation to him, the plan was of great advantage to the artists, by exhibiting his features while undergoing the alternate expressions of action and repose. The room was generally well filled with visitors, who came to see the progress of the work, more probably for the purpose of seizing this favorable occasion of beholding the original; and as the chief moved back and forth in a placid mood, became animated by conversation, or excited by the wondering audience, the artists were able to catch every lineament of his countenance with an accuracy which many of our most celebrated painters often fail to obtain. Osceola was much pleased with the portraits, and often regarded them with marks of evident satisfaction.[22]

Only two artists besides George Catlin who visited the prison to paint Osceola's portrait are known by name. One of them, W. M. Laning, depicted Osceola standing in the foreground of a semitropical landscape of palm trees with a Native American man and boy armed with a bow and arrow in the background. Laning worked in Charleston at that time, but he might not have been from that city. His painting, titled *Osceola, Chief of the Seminoles,* which betrays the artist's limited talent, is in the collection of the Chrysler Museum in Norfolk, Virginia. The other known artist was Robert John Curtis of Charleston, a relatively unknown but quite talented painter. Curtis painted a head-and-shoulders portrait titled simply *Osceola.* The Curtis painting is at the Charleston Museum.[23]

It has been reported that George Catlin and Osceola shared a special relationship, a friendship, during the time the artist painted two portraits of the Seminole warrior. They would sit alone together for long hours, often well into the night after their work for the day had been finished. During his time, according to Catlin, Osceola "became sometimes animated, when he would laugh and talk freely. His thoughts were perpetually turned toward [Florida], of which he spoke with much feeling, and was ever eager to obtain news of the progress of military events."[24]

Osceola when possible did follow the news of the continuing war with great interest—rejoicing at Seminole victories and grieving for the losses. His incarceration, the loss of his homeland, and the frustration of not being able to assist his people in their conflict, however, weighed heavily on his mind and significantly affected his declining health.

Dr. Robert Lebby recorded that Osceola "was extremely sensitive about Florida, and anxious to hear any news from that territory—I am under the impression that when his likeness was taken by Mr. Catlin, he was told of one of the engagements, in which the Indians were represented to have been successful—The effect was electrical—The whole man was changed instantly—He grasped the rifle in his right hand, and while in that position, Mr. Catlin succeeded in taking his picture."[25]

Catlin was greatly impressed by the warrior's physical and intellectual refinement, saying, "I am fully convinced from all I have seen, and learned from the lips of Osceola, and from the chiefs who are around him, that he is a most extraordinary man, and one entitled to a better fate. This gallant fellow," he continued, seemed to be "grieving with a broken spirit, and ready to die, cursing the white man, no doubt, to the end of his breath."[26]

George Catlin immersed himself in capturing on canvas the true likeness and personality of Osceola. He described his subject:

He wore three ostrich feathers in his head, and a turban made of a vari-coloured cotton shawl—and his dress was chiefly of calicos, with a handsome bead sash or belt around his waist, and his rifle in his hand. . . . In stature he is about at mediocrity, with an elastic and grace-ful movement; in his face he is good looking, with rather an effeminate smile; but of so peculiar a character, that the world may be ransacked over without finding another just like it. In his manners, and all his movements in company, he is polite and gentlemanly, though his con-versation is entirely in his own tongue; and his general appearance and actions, those of a full-blooded and wild Indian.[27]

Catlin would paint two portraits of Osceola—one a head-and-shoulders study, the other a full-length work. The head-and-shoulders portrait of Osceola in all his Seminole finery is considered to bear a remarkable resem-blance to the man, fully capturing his grief-stricken eyes and enigmatic smile with exceptional sensitivity. In fact, art critics would later say that of all the paintings the artist had rendered, this portrait of Osceola was George Cat-lin's masterpiece.

Osceola also enjoyed the company of the officers he had befriended at the fort and would occasionally chide them about the Florida War. An early biographer of Osceola, Thomas Storrow, who was present at the fort, writes, "In one of his playful moods he ridiculed our mode of warfare, and gave an excellent pantomimic exhibition of the manner of the White man and the Indian in loading and firing. He evidently possessed a large portion of self esteem, mingled with no inconsiderable share of vain-glory. . . . 'It was always my pride,' said he, 'to fight with the big generals. I wore this plume when I whipped General Gaines; these spurs when I drove back General Clinch; and these moccasins when I flogged General Call.'"[28]

As the days passed, however, Osceola tired quickly and devoted less time to interacting with outsiders. His recurring illness would sap his strength, the fever would return, and he would be compelled to take to his bed. According to Dr. Weedon, part of the reason for the deterioration of Osceola's health was his good nature in agreeing to spend so much time posing for artists and mingling with the public.

By January 26, Osceola was deathly ill and not expected to live through the night. In addition to his ongoing health problems, he was struck with tonsillitis complicated by an abscess—called "violent quinsy" at the time. The severe pain and inflammation of the tonsils caused difficulty swallowing and breathing, and his body temperature rose to 105 degrees. Dr. Weedon found it necessary to prop Osceola up in an erect position to prevent him from suffocating. The public and press clamored to see the Seminole war leader, but he was far too ill to entertain visitors. At one point on January 27, Weedon expected his patient to die within two hours. Osceola clung to life, but his condition did not improve.[29]

During those next few critical days and nights—which would prove to be the final ones of Osceola's life—George Catlin, as well as officers from the fort, held a vigil at the bedside of the Seminole warrior. It was apparent that Osceola had made quite an impression on everyone around him, and a shroud of gloom descended upon the prison. Those people who had not believed that Osceola truly hated war had been won over after experiencing the passivity and charm he displayed to everyone with whom he came in contact. He had always been polite and considerate, and he gained respect for himself and his tribe from those who were supposed to be his enemies.

George Catlin departed Charleston on January 27, 1838, likely with a heavy heart, knowing that his new friend was at death's door. The artist took with him his finished portraits of Osceola, Micanopy, Cloud, Coa Hadjo, and King Philip—all completed over a seven-day period. These paintings would later be placed on exhibition in New York City's Stuyvesant Museum.[30]

On January 29, a mysterious Native American man entered Osceola's room. This man would later be identified as a prophet and doctor that Osceola's family had sent for to minister to him. No one knows exactly what this prophet told Osceola or what remedies he applied with his sacred powers. From that point on, however, the Seminole warrior refused any medical treatment suggested by Dr. Weedon or his associates.

After the prophet had departed, Osceola beckoned Dr. Weedon to his bedside to apologize for obeying his family's wishes that he be healed by the prophet and not Weedon. In a brief conversation, or deathbed confessional, he also stated that he no longer wished to live on account of knowing he would be sent west, where Charley Emathla's friends would kill him. Emathla had been one of the chiefs who had cooperated with the authorities to prepare his people to move before the conflict got heated, and he had been assassinated by Osceola. Osceola then asked that his bones be taken by the doctor to Florida, where they would not be disturbed and could rest in peace. He said he had only one regret—the killing of Wiley Thompson. He did not regret waging war on the United States, which had taken away his people's homeland, their natural birthright. Additionally, if he should somehow happen to live, he would continue to fight against the white man.[31]

Just before six o'clock on the evening of Tuesday, January 30, 1838, three months after his capture, the thirty-four-year-old Osceola realized that he was near death. George Catlin had requested that Dr. Weedon record for him the final living moments of his friend. The doctor wrote:

About half an hour before he died, he seemed to be sensible that he was dying; and, although he could not speak, he signified by signs that he wished me to send for the chiefs and for the officers of the post, whom I called in. He made signs to his wives . . . by his side, to go and bring his full dress, which he wore in a time of war; which having been brought in, he rose up in his bed, which was on the floor, and put on his shirt, his leggings and his moccasins—girded on his war belt—his bullet-pouch and powder-horn, and laid his knife by the side of him on the floor.

He called for his red paint, and his looking-glass, which was held before him, when he deliberately painted one-half of his face, his neck and his throat . . . with vermilion, a custom practiced when the irrevocable oath of war and destruction is taken. His knife he then placed in its sheath under his belt, and he carefully arranged his turban on his head, and his three ostrich plumes that he was in a habit of wearing in it.

Being thus prepared in full dress, he laid down a few moments to recover strength sufficient, when he rose up as before, and with most benignant and pleasing smiles, extended his hand to me and to all the officers and chiefs that were around him, and shook hands with us all in dead silence, and also with his wives and little children.

He made a signal for them to lower him down upon his bed, which was done, and he then slowly drew from his war-belt his scalping knife, which he firmly grasped in his right hand, laying it across the other on his breast, and in a moment smiled away his last breath without a struggle or a groan.[32]

At six twenty P.M., Osceola, the Seminole warrior, had gone to be with the spirits.

Twelve

Osceola's War

»» ◈ «

O sceola, the symbol of Native American valor, had died in prison from the combined effects of malaria, violent quinsy, and—for the romantics— perhaps even by the heartbreak caused by the treachery of his foes. People of all races throughout the world wept at the news. On the day after he died, he was afforded a formal military funeral and buried near the front entrance of Fort Moultrie. A man named William Patton from Charleston supplied a white marble headstone for the grave that bore the inscription:

OSCEOLA

PATRIOT AND WARRIOR

DIED AT FORT MOULTRIE

JANUARY 30TH, 1838

By the time of his death, Osceola had become a larger-than-life character and the most famous Native American in the world. His tragic demise was reported on the front pages of newspapers worldwide, and his fame took on legendary proportions. One testament to how popular Osceola had become was the fact that not long after his death there were towns, counties, steamboats, schools, hotels, and children named after him.

On February 3, 1838, *Niles' National Register* published this elegy: "We shall not write [Osceola's] epitaph or his funeral oration, yet there is something in the character of this man not unworthy of the respect of the world. From a vagabond child, he became the master spirit of a long and desperate war. He made himself—no man owed less to accident. Bold and decisive in action, deadly but consistent in hatred, dark in revenge, cool, subtle, sagacious in council, he established gradually and surely a resistless ascendancy over his adopted tribe, by the daring of his deeds."[1]

The respect that Osceola had gained from the white man was summed up best by the historian Charles H. Coe:

The fearless bravery and manly qualities of this chief, his unusual knowledge of scientific warfare, and, above all else, his unswerving determination to defend to the last his chosen home, had spread his fame throughout the length and breadth of the country, and won for him respect and admiration even in the hearts of his bitterest enemies. . . . The fame of Osceola was well earned; not for that inhuman cruelty such as characterized most of our Western tribes, but for true patriotism and determined effort, against the combined armies of a great and powerful nation, in one of the most remarkable struggles known to history. His fame will never die; centuries will come and go, but the name Osceola will remain as long as the earth is peopled.[2]

There exists, however, one grisly aspect to the death and burial of Osceola. For unknown reasons, Dr. Frederick Weedon secretly removed Osceola's head from his body. Dr. Weedon's great-granddaughter, May McNeer Ward, provided the account that has become family oral tradition: "After the death of the Seminole chief, Dr. Weedon was able to be alone with the body. During this time he cut off the head, but left it in the coffin with the scarf that

Osceola habitually wore tied as usual around the neck. Not long before the funeral Dr. Weedon removed the head and closed the coffin."[3]

At some point during the twenty-four hours between death and interment, Weedon secretly decapitated Osceola, replaced the severed head in the coffin for viewing, and then covertly removed it before the burial. Weedon probably was assisted in this procedure by Dr. Benjamin B. Strobel, an associate who was a teacher of anatomy at the Medical College of Charleston. According to family oral tradition, Weedon embalmed Osceola's head with a formula of his own devising. Incidentally, there can be no doubt that Osceola's head had been removed from his remains. Archaeological digs at the grave site have revealed a headless skeleton in Osceola's grave.

The whereabouts of Osceola's severed head have been a subject of countless rumors over the years. The last place the embalmed head was known to rest was with Dr. Valentine Mott of the Medical College of the City of New York, who owned an extensive collection of Native American artifacts. The doctor displayed it for many years as the remains of a "man of international importance" at what he called the Surgical and Pathological Museum on Fourteenth Street in New York City. The head was reportedly destroyed at that location in a fire shortly after Mott's death in 1865.

Additionally, right after Osceola's death, Weedon managed to persuade reluctant Seminole chiefs to allow him to make a death mask of the war leader's face and upper body. This cast of Osceola was shipped to a collector in Washington, and in 1885 it was placed in the anthropology collection at the Smithsonian Institution.[4]

Captain Pitcairn Morrison, who was the officer in charge of Seminole prisoners at Fort Moultrie, made the decision that Osceola's ornaments not be buried with him. These artifacts, as well as other possessions left behind, were shared by both Weedon and Morrison. Many of these items have been passed around over the years and were lost or hidden away in the hands of private collectors. Quite a number of artifacts, however, have been preserved by a Weedon descendant, including a lock of Osceola's hair that was examined and found to have been infected with head lice.

Other items, including a bag, a sash, and a beaded belt, were in the possession of future president Zachary Taylor, perhaps given to him as gifts for his service in Florida. The sash and belt were eventually auctioned at Sotheby's and brought more than $100,000. The high bidder was the Seminole tribe of Florida, which placed the precious artifacts in their museum. A number of other items purported to be Osceola's personal possessions—shirt, moccasins, turban, gun, knife, tomahawk, feathers, scarf, beads, earrings, pipe, to name a few—have been placed on display at one time or another at museums or claimed ownership by private parties. Most have lacked documentation other than being authentic from that time period. As can be imagined, everything from Osceola's head to his possessions has been the subject of scams by people who try to sell them to gullible collectors.[5]

Not only have Osceola's artifacts been subject to false claims, but the location of his remains has also been in question at times. In 1966, Otis W. Shriver, a Miami city commissioner, claimed to have robbed Osceola's grave and stolen his bones, which he had locked up in a bank vault. Shriver intended to rebury the remains in a shrine at Rainbow Springs. To add credibility to Shriver's claim, the National Park Service admitted that a hole had been dug near Osceola's grave at Fort Moultrie on the night of January 7, 1966. This hole, however, had been made a yard and a half away from Osceola's grave and supposedly missed the mark. Shriver disputed that conclusion, and the press and public demanded answers.

The National Park Service, after waiting for water levels to subside, finally excavated the grave in the summer of 1968. The team removed the wooden coffin, intact and untouched, and discovered inside a skeleton that was missing its skull and the first five cervical vertebrae. None of the personal possessions that had been buried with Osceola were found, confirming the story that Weedon and Morrison had made off with them. Shriver, who might have believed he had dug up Osceola's bones, had actually removed animal bones from the earth.

Osceola's final remains have been involved in a tug-of-war between South Carolina and Florida for decades. Bills have been introduced in the

Florida legislature, and numerous overtures have been made by Floridians to purchase these precious bones. But, contrary to the Seminole war leader's dying request that he be buried in his beloved Florida, his remains to this day rest in South Carolina.[6]

In early 1838, while Osceola's decapitated body lay in a grave in Charleston, his brethren continued to fight the Great Seminole War—Osceola's War. Multiple columns of troops under the overall command of General Thomas Jesup were sweeping down the peninsula on the east side of Lake Okeechobee in an effort to engage Osceola's warriors. Jesup was determined to crush these small bands wherever they were hiding. But with the death of their spiritual leader, these warriors were not defeated or demoralized to the point that they wanted to quit. Instead, they now had extra motivation to resist the army's intrusion into their domain. The name Osceola would be a rallying cry by Seminoles throughout Florida, who vowed not to let this great man die in vain but to keep his dream and fight alive.

On January 10, a force of fifty-five sailors and twenty-five soldiers under the command of navy lieutenant Levin Powell was patrolling the east coast of Florida when they happened upon a trail made by a large force of Seminoles. Powell followed that trail and five days later came upon a woman whom he coerced into leading them to the Seminole camp. The lieutenant observed campfire smoke rising from the swamp and decided to charge into this encampment of unknown size. The warriors were waiting in ambush and met the soldiers and sailors with a deadly volley of rifle fire. Powell rallied his men, and even ordered a charge, but the small detachment soon found itself outnumbered and almost completely surrounded. Powell's troops were then compelled to engage in a rearguard action in order to fight their way back to their boats. The skirmish cost the military five dead and twenty-two wounded.[7]

On January 24, General Jesup anticipated his first taste of personal glory in combat while patrolling east of Lake Okeechobee. It had been reported that a war party of Seminoles was secreted in a defensive position up ahead across a cypress swamp. Jesup ordered a mounted charge, and his troops roared into the swamp, only to find their horses mired up to their girths and foundering. These dragoons dismounted and resumed the charge on foot. The Seminoles fired from their defensive line and kept the attackers at bay. Jesup deployed his artillery, and soon the hammock was rocked with bursts of exploding cannon fire.

The general decided to personally lead an assault against his enemy and called to the Tennessee volunteers to follow him. No sooner had he cried "Charge!" than a bullet struck and shattered his glasses and ripped across his cheek. Jesup abandoned his charge and raced for the rear. The Seminoles who had been positioned in that hammock were not about to remain there in the midst of such devastating artillery fire. They eventually just melted away, leaving the field to Jesup. The army sustained seven killed and thirty-one wounded, including General Thomas Jesup, who had fought his first—and last—battle.[8]

On February 8, Seminole Chief Tuskegee and a younger chief, Halleck Hadjo, held a meeting with General Jesup under a white flag of truce near Cypress Swamp. Halleck Hadjo spoke passionately about how his people were suffering under almost unbearable hardship. He promised that the Seminole would stop fighting if only they were given a piece of land, no matter how wretched or small, somewhere in Florida, perhaps south of Lake Okeechobee.

Jesup was in favor of the request. He understood that it would be a long and difficult struggle to root out the remaining Seminoles who were hiding out in the south Florida swamps. This land south of Okeechobee, he realized, was not suitable for white agricultural purposes and therefore should be disposable. Jesup, however, knew he had to seek approval from Washington before he could make any promises to the Seminoles. The chiefs and their people were told to camp near Fort Jupiter, situated below Lake Okeechobee, and await a reply from the government. About five hundred tribe members assembled at a camp about a mile from Fort Jupiter. As a show of good faith—in an effort to save themselves, and against Osceola's staunch policy—they surrendered 140 blacks, who were subsequently marched to Tampa Bay. Also during this time of truce, the officers from the fort enjoyed dances at the Seminole camp and treated their hosts to copious amounts of whiskey. In fact, there was frequent socialization between the men at the fort and the people in the Seminole camp, and a supply of liquor usually flowed freely to loosen inhibitions.[9]

In the meantime, Jesup ordered that the more notorious of the thousand Seminoles incarcerated at Fort Moultrie be placed aboard the brig *Homer* and shipped off to New Orleans and then to their new home in the West. The manifest read like a who's who of Seminole chiefs—Micanopy, Coa Hadjo, Cloud, and King Philip. Only the name "Osceola" was missing, although his family was aboard the ship. There are no accounts that mention the fate of Osceola's wives, children, or extended family after they arrived in the West. Of course, it was stated that only two of his children had accompanied his wives to Fort Moultrie in November, and it had been previously noted that he had four children. Perhaps two or more of them somehow managed to remain in Florida.[10]

Zachary Taylor had taken to the field during the month of March and encountered little resistance from those Seminoles he happened upon. These people had tired of running; they were weak from hunger and had lost their eagerness to fight. For those reasons, Taylor managed to capture an estimated 513 Seminoles—including 150 warriors with firearms and 161 blacks—who had been hiding north of Lake Okeechobee. Alligator would soon join them with 88 of his people, including John Cavallo and 27 blacks.[11]

On March 20, Secretary of War Joel Poinsett answered General Jesup's request about carving out a reservation in south Florida for the Seminole. The secretary curtly reminded the general that it was the policy of the president and Congress that all Southeastern tribes must be moved west of the Mississippi River, and the Seminoles were no exception. He advised the general to resume his campaign against this tribe without delay.[12]

Jesup summoned the chiefs to his camp to deliver the bad news, but they were wary and refused his invitation. The general immediately ordered Colonel David Twiggs to surround the camp, reportedly after the army had provided the Seminoles with large quantities of liquor. A small number of people managed to sneak away, but Twiggs and his men were able to detain more than 500, including at least 150 warriors. Perhaps the Seminole should have remembered that Jesup had a bad habit of not honoring white flags and been on guard for treachery.[13]

The *Arkansas Gazette* reported in April: "The distinguished Seminole Chief, Jumper, died at New Orleans Barracks on 18th ult., and was buried this afternoon. In his coffin were placed his tobacco, pipe, rifle and other equipment, according to his people's custom. The military, and a number of citizens, attended his funeral, which was conducted with all the honors of war." Jumper, who had signed the Payne's Landing treaty and had been kidnapped by Osceola from the relocation camp at Tampa Bay the previous year, had died of tuberculosis. He had lived out his final days at a miserable refugee camp awaiting transport to Arkansas Territory.[14]

On April 29, General Thomas Jesup was informed that he had been relieved of duty in Florida and could resume his position as quartermaster general of the army. Jesup went about making arrangements for a change of command. He decided to ship off a detachment of regulars to Georgia and Alabama, where the removal of the Cherokees was in progress. Two infantry regiments and four companies of dragoons would remain to fight in Florida. This would reduce manpower in Florida to about twenty-three hundred, the lowest number in quite some time. Jesup would also oversee the transfer of most of the Seminole captives from Tampa Bay to a detention camp near New Orleans.[15]

By May, more than eleven hundred Seminoles—including more than two hundred blacks—had arrived in New Orleans. These people, about half of whom were ill, were then confined in new barracks while awaiting the final leg of their journey up the Mississippi River to Arkansas Territory. At one point, a tussle ensued over the fate of a number of the blacks who had been servants or owned by Seminoles and supposedly had been captured by the Creeks. These people were demanded by a slave trader who claimed he had purchased them. U.S. Marine Corps lieutenant John G. Reynolds had been placed in charge of those black prisoners. He and his associates bravely managed to fend off local slave state attempts at intervention along the Mississippi to see that almost sixty of the ninety blacks captured by the Creeks made it to freedom in Arkansas Territory.[16]

On May 15, 1838, General Jesup handed over the baton of leadership of Florida forces to Zachary Taylor, who had been promoted to brevet brigadier general for his actions at Lake Okeechobee. During Jesup's watch, more than one hundred Seminole warriors had been killed and more than twenty-nine hundred people captured, many of whom had arrived at their new home in the West. Whether his tour of duty could be regarded as successful would depend on whether it was judged on its military accomplishments, which were superior to those of his predecessors, or his conduct of the war, which was often unethical and despicable.[17]

On June 7, King Philip, Coacoochee's father, who had been ill for some time, died aboard a boat headed up the Mississippi. He was buried with military honors featuring a one-hundred-gun salute on the west side of the river near Baton Rouge, about sixty miles from Fort Gibson.[18]

Brigadier General Zachary Taylor, now commander of forces in Florida, decided on a strategy to prevent the Seminoles from entering northern Florida, which would allow settlers to return to their homes. His plan was to construct small posts at intervals across the north connected by wagon roads, and to use larger units to systematically search designated areas. Taylor reported early in 1839 that fifty-three new posts had been established, accompanied by 848 miles of wagon roads. The general also noted that the fall and winter had been an extremely quiet period for hostilities, with only a handful of skirmishes and hundreds captured.

By March 1839, just when Taylor had begun to believe that his strategy was producing results, President Martin Van Buren and Congress decided to move in another direction. The public had become fed up with the war in Florida and clamored for a conclusion to this never-ending endeavor that had dramatically increased the size of the army and racked up astronomical costs. Additionally, many in the country believed that by holding out for so long, the Seminoles had earned the right to a reservation in Florida. On the military side, there was doubt that the tribe could ever be completely conquered and removed from those swamps. In an effort to seek closure, the president ordered that the commanding general of the army, Major General Alexander Macomb, travel to Florida to act as peacemaker and end the conflict once and for all.

In May, Macomb set up his headquarters at Fort King and invited the chiefs to visit for a parley. The Seminoles ignored the request. They had been victimized too many times in the past and were wary of any attempt to negotiate a treaty. Macomb made further entreaties, promising gifts. Finally, a nervous Halleck Tustenugge, carrying a white flag, appeared with seven warriors to meet with Macomb. Soon, Chitto Tustenuggee, who was representing head chief Arpeika (Sam Jones) arrived, and later Thlocklo Tustenugge (Tiger Tail) joined them. John Cavallo had been permitted to return to Florida from the West to serve as interpreter. Macomb had been authorized to offer the terms that General Jesup had presented the previous year that had been denied at that time. The parley featured many gifts and generous amounts of whiskey.

On May 19, General Macomb announced that a treaty had been reached. The tribe agreed to cease hostilities in exchange for a reservation in southern Florida. Macomb was praised far and wide for accomplishing what six generals before him had failed to do. The chiefs departed with the notion that the Seminole would be able to stay in Florida forever. Macomb thought it prudent to leave the word "temporarily" out of the treaty conversations. The chiefs did not directly ask how long they would be permitted to stay; therefore, no answer had been given. Macomb had pacified the chiefs with misleading information and then proclaimed to the world that he had ended the war with the Seminoles.[19]

On the night of July 23, 1839, Colonel William S. Harney and a detachment of twenty-six men were on duty at a trading post being built fifteen miles from the mouth of the Caloosahatchee River. Harney had just returned from hunting wild boar and was preparing to retire when the camp was attacked by heavy rifle fire from about 160 warriors. Harney and some other soldiers dashed down the path toward the river in an effort to escape. The colonel and another man were able to locate a boat and escape downstream. Many of the soldiers—as many as eighteen—were killed. The attackers then made off with several thousand dollars' worth of trade goods, including $1,500 in silver coins and a number of serviceable rifles.

The assault on Harney's post had been conducted by so-called Spanish Indians, who lived deep in the peninsula. The war party had been led by

Chakaika and Hospetarke, who had not participated in General Macomb's peace talks. The U.S. government in its negotiations with Native Americans across the country never understood that only those chiefs who had signed a certain treaty agreement were considered by themselves to be bound to obey its terms. Thus, those chiefs who had not signed, as well as their bands, were not in their own minds violating the treaty by attacking the white man. Not that it would have mattered to Chakaika. He could not have let such a ripe plum as Harney and his post be left unplucked.[20]

For all intents and purposes, General Macomb's treaty had held for two months. The Harney massacre shook Florida and the nation. War had resumed.

In late 1839, the Florida legislature came up with a novel method that had been successful during the Maroon Revolt in Jamaica in 1655–1739. Governor Richard Call, who had been appointed governor in 1835 and had futilely chased Osceola himself, was not above spending money from his own pocket for the war effort. He dispatched Colonel Richard Fitzpatrick to Cuba, where the colonel purchased thirty-three bloodhounds at $151.72 each. On January 27, 1840, these animals that had been expertly trained to track runaway slaves were given to General Taylor to use for tracking Seminoles.

The importation of these bloodhounds created a controversy in Congress and with the public, especially with abolitionists, who claimed they had been bought to chase slaves, not Indians. There were also concerns that the vicious beasts would kill or injure Seminole and black women and children. Secretary of War Poinsett was compelled to issue an order that the dogs would remain muzzled and attached to leashes while tracking. Ultimately, the fuss was over nothing. The sensitive noses of these bloodhounds were unable to detect scent within the swampy terrain. The grand total of Seminoles captured by the expensive dogs was only two.[21]

On May 5, 1840, Zachary Taylor, who had served longer than any other commander in the Florida War, was granted permission to transfer. Taylor was initially assigned to Fort Gibson and then sent to Fort Smith, Arkansas. He had departed Florida Territory but would continue policing the Florida Seminoles in their new western home.

The new man in charge was Brigadier General Walker Keith Armistead, who had earlier served in Florida as second in command to General Thomas Jesup. This fifty-five-year-old, who had graduated at the top of his class at West Point, had served in the War of 1812, where he attained the rank of lieutenant colonel. He was subsequently assigned as chief of engineers and later placed in command of the Third Artillery Regiment. In 1831, he had been brevetted brigadier general for a decade of faithful service. Armistead apparently assumed command without the respect of a number of his subordinate officers. A fellow West Pointer, Captain Nathaniel Hunter, called the general a "grey bearded and imbecile dotard." Major Ethan Allen Hitchcock referred to Armistead as "puerile" and criticized his previous methods of handling the Seminoles.[22]

Armistead, who would command 3,400 enlisted men and 241 officers, wasted no time dispatching detachments to the field to pursue an enemy that was now reduced to fewer than one thousand, including women and children. His campaign was met with one major obstacle—tropical rain. After years of drought, a deluge fell during the summer months. Water filled to overflowing the swamps, streams, and hammocks, which hampered the movement of the troops and supplies.

Despite these conditions, the general deployed small guerrilla-style units that harassed the Seminoles. These troops would encounter their enemy now and then, and on those occasions took captives, confiscated equipment and livestock, and destroyed cultivated fields. At least five hundred acres of crops, including fields in Wahoo Swamp and at Chocachatti where it was thought the tribe no longer dared live, were burned that summer. In one instance, a group of Seminoles celebrating the Green Corn Dance was interrupted by soldiers and forced to flee. Colonel Harney raided one village and captured the mother and daughter of Coacoochee.

Coacoochee was not idle, either. In May, he led an attack on a touring Shakespearean company near St. Augustine, killing three actors and making off with a huge wardrobe of costumes. The Seminoles might have been on the run, but they did manage to kill at least fourteen soldiers during the month of July alone.[23]

In October, two of the most important chiefs still at large—Thlocklo Tustenuggee (Tiger Tail) and Halleck Tustenuggee—requested a parley with General Armistead. Thlocklo Tustenuggee had grown up near the home of a Tallahassee banker and was a genteel man who spoke fluent English and understood the ways of the white man. Helleck Tustenuggee was the polar opposite of his companion chief. He had killed his own sister because she had wanted to emigrate, and when a member of his band had insulted him, he bit off the man's ear. Halleck ruled his band with an iron fist and threatened to kill any of them who favored emigration.[24]

On November 10, Thlocklo Tustenuggee and Halleck Tustenuggee, with forty warriors, met with General Walker Armistead at Fort King under a white flag. The conference took place outside in a wooded area, food and drink were served, and everyone sat on the ground or on logs. Armistead had been forbidden by Washington to offer the chiefs land in Florida and instead tried to bribe them with $5,000 each to assemble their followers for emigration west. The chiefs asked for two weeks to consider the offer. The Seminole chiefs and their warriors remained around the fort for several days and freely partook of food, supplies, and liquor.

On the night of November 14, however, Thlocklo Tustenuggee and Halleck Tustenuggee and their warriors simply vanished into the wilderness. The chiefs had been enjoying the hospitality of the fort, but there had been a reason for their abrupt departure. Armistead, like so many army officers before and after him, had failed to understand the Native American mind. The general had not suspended field operations during the negotiations, and the Seminole chiefs viewed this act as more treachery by the white man and feared for their freedom. Armistead was incensed by this insult by the two chiefs and ordered that from then on all flags of truce would be ignored. During December, however, Echo Emathla, a Tallahassee chief, surrendered at Fort Clinch, but most of the band led by Thlocklo Tustenuggee refused to submit.[25]

Colonel William Harney had been champing at the bit to exact revenge on those Spanish Indians who had humiliated him the previous July on the Caloosahatchee River. In early December, General Armistead gave the colonel permission to organize an expedition and search for the hideout of Chakaika and his band. Harney, guided by a black man named John, led ninety men in canoes borrowed from Marines with the Mosquito Fleet and set out to locate this remote camp. The colonel and his troops from the Second Dragoons and Third Artillery departed Fort Dallas (present-day downtown Miami) and traveled down the Miami River into the Everglades. Harney had disregarded orders to the contrary from General Armistead and dressed his men like Seminoles. Apparently Harney believed that his costumed men would not be as easily recognized as soldiers as they made their way through the swamps.

Harney's flotilla soon encountered small parties of Seminole people paddling along in canoes, and his troopers were able to overtake a number of them. The colonel promptly hanged the men from the nearest tree and took the women and children captive. His guide, John, at one point lost his bearings and the soldiers had no choice but to sit and wait for him to get back on course. Meanwhile, Harney tried to make the captive women lead them to Chakaika's camp by threatening to hang their children. The women refused, but Harney never acted on his threat. Before long, John found his way again. It was just after sunrise when Harney's expedition approached the island camp of Chakaika and the Spanish Indians.

Dressed in Indian garb, the soldiers debarked on the island and stealthily approached the camp. Their unexpected appearance was a complete surprise to Chakaika and his band. Chakaika had been chopping wood when the attack started and realized he could not escape. Instead of running, he smiled and offered his hand. One of the soldiers was not in a friendly mood, however, and shot the warrior dead. A fierce but brief firefight ensued, and a number of Chakaika's comrades managed to slip away into the swamps by the time the smoke had cleared. Two captured warriors were hanged, and Harney ordered that Chakaika's dead body also be hanged beside them.[26]

Colonel Harney and his men pushed on but failed to locate the camps of Hospetarke and Arpeika, which had been rumored to be nearby. The detail returned to Fort Dallas after twelve days in the Everglades. Harney's command had killed four Indians and hanged another five while losing only one soldier killed. The Legislative Council of Florida was so impressed by Harney's success that they presented him with a commendation and a sword. The colonel was also rewarded with the command of the Second Dragoons.[27]

On December 28, exactly five years after the Dade Massacre, a war party of Seminoles—probably led by Coosa Tustenuggee and Halleck Tustenuggee—ambushed a thirteen-man army detail that was escorting an officer's wife to Fort Wacahoota. The woman, one officer, and three enlisted men were killed. The bodies were scalped and mutilated.[28]

By March 1841, General Armistead had petitioned Washington for enough money to bribe the chiefs into surrendering. His initial budget was $25,000, but he soon asked for $30,000 more after he had achieved some success. Coosa Tustenuggee, who had orchestrated the murders on December 28, was paid $5,000 for bringing in his band of sixty people. Several subchiefs received $200, and each warrior was given $30 and a new firearm. Certain previous commanders, Jesup in particular, could never have brought themselves to pay the murderer of an officer's wife under any circumstances.[29]

Coacoochee (Wild Cat) was now the most influential Seminole chief still at large. In March 1841, Micco, a former associate of King Philip, located Coacoochee and persuaded him to visit Fort Cummings (near present-day Cypress Gardens) for a parley with Colonel William Jenkins Worth. At about noon on March 3, the handsome young chief rode into the stockade with seven of his warriors and created quite a stir among the officers and the civilians present. Coacoochee, always the flamboyant showman, was dressed in the nodding plumes sock and buskin costume of Hamlet. One nearby warrior wore the royal purple and ermine of Richard III, another the simple garb of Horatio, and the rest of the men wore feathers, vests, and others shiny and colorful parts of medieval costumes. This was the wardrobe that had been plundered from the Shakespearean troupe these Seminoles had ambushed the previous May. The white onlookers were not amused by this flaunting of the spoils of war, especially when three actors had been killed in the attack. It must have been difficult for some army officers to honor the white flag of truce for these renegade Seminoles.

Coacoochee's little daughter heard her father's voice and dashed from her prison tent to his arms. She presented her father with presents—musket balls, pieces of cartridges, and packets of powder she had pilfered during her stay. Coacoochee was so moved at seeing his daughter that he burst into tears. He remained in camp for almost a week, taking advantage of the army's hospitality. At the end of these leisurely days, he promised to assemble his warriors and their families and peacefully emigrate.[30]

On March 9, Coacoochee departed the fort in the company of his daughter, with intentions of gathering his people for removal. He returned a week or so later and reported that his followers wanted to wait until after the Green Corn Dance to emigrate. He left his daughter in the care of Colonel Worth as a good-faith gesture. Worth had observed the earlier emotional reunion of Coacoochee and his daughter at the fort and felt certain the chief would honor his commitment. Coacoochee next met with General Armistead toward the end of March, and it was decided his band would assemble at Fort Pierce on the Atlantic Ocean. Hostilities would be suspended in his band's territory while they prepared to leave.

During April and May, Coacoochee frequently appeared at Fort Pierce, presenting a pass given to him by Armistead, and always receiving complimentary food and liquor. He was said to have behaved obnoxiously around the whites during his times at the fort. On one visit, he demanded a horse, which he was given, along with five and a half gallons of liquor. In another instance, he requested a large amount of rations and liquor for what he claimed was a council with Arpeika (Sam Jones), Holata Micco (Billy Bowlegs), and Hospetarke for the purpose of convincing them to emigrate.

This last demand raised suspicions about Coacoochee's true motives. Major Thomas Childs believed that the chief was stashing away supplies before disappearing into the Everglades for the summer. Childs was given permission to take Coacoochee and his band into custody without delay. William Tecumseh Sherman, then a second lieutenant, was assigned the task of bringing in the Seminole chief. Sherman grabbed Coacoochee, fourteen warriors, and three blacks, all of whom were escorted to Tampa Bay and on orders of Lieutenant Colonel William Gates immediately placed aboard a ship that sailed for New Orleans.[31]

By spring, General Walker Armistead was discouraged by his lack of progress and requested to be relieved of duty. On the general's watch, 450 Seminoles—about 120 of them warriors—had been sent west, and another 236 remained at Fort Brooke awaiting removal. Armistead estimated that there were no more than 300 warriors and their families left in Florida. The general's record was not at all poor compared to that of other commanders, but he had served two campaigns with General Thomas Jesup before taking command and was weary of the Florida duty. One of his final acts was to watch Coosa Tustenuggee and two hundred of his people sail from Tampa Bay to New Orleans.

General Armistead was replaced as commander of the Florida forces by Colonel William Worth, who had been in charge of the Eighth Infantry. The forty-eight-year-old Worth had been in the mercantile business when he applied for a commission during the War of 1812. He had been assigned as an aide to General Winfield Scott and become the general's protégé—indeed, Worth named his son Winfield Scott. Worth was seriously wounded by a blast of grapeshot in the thigh during that war and was hospitalized for more than a year. He was permanently disabled but allowed to remain in the military. From 1820 to 1828, he served as commandant at West Point and assumed command of the Eighth Infantry in 1838. Worth would now lead an estimated five thousand troops, who were deployed throughout the summer on what he termed "search-and-destroy" missions against those hostile Seminoles who continued their raids and depredations. Incidentally, John Sprague, the noted historian, would become Worth's aide-de-camp and later his son-in-law.[32]

Seminoles were still scattered throughout most of Florida, with many of the bands reduced to starvation. Perhaps worse than their physical condition was the fact that this summer of 1841 would be the first year ever that they would not hold the Green Corn Dance. There would be no annual ritual when fresh fires burned in every hearth to signify renewal, and minor crimes were forgiven and friendships restored, and childhood names were replaced by the emergence of manhood, and the black drink was consumed, and crops were blessed, and the tribe in general was cleansed. The army had not been able to subdue all of the Seminoles but had succeeded in striking a serious blow to Seminole society by making it impossible for them to perform this sacred ceremony.

Colonel Worth learned that Coacoochee had been shipped to New Orleans without his knowledge and angrily ordered that the chief be returned to Tampa Bay. The colonel intended to use Coacoochee to persuade the rest of the dissident Seminoles to surrender. Worth had a conference with Coacoochee, who was manacled in foot irons and handcuffs, aboard ship at Tampa Bay. Worth told the Seminole leader that he could not leave, but he could select a few messengers to send out to persuade the rest of his people to accept emigration. Coacoochee was warned by Worth that if those people refused to submit, "these warriors now seated before us, shall be hung to the yards of this vessel." Emissaries were dispatched to the various camps under Coacoochee's name, and small groups of people began straggling into Fort Brooke.[33]

On July 30, 1841, Osceola's closest white friend, John Graham, who had struck up a relationship with the Seminole warrior at Fort King in 1835, passed away. Graham had been promoted to captain of the Second Dragoons in October 1837, and for two months served as aide-de-camp to General Joseph Hernández. Graham had resigned his army commission on January 28, 1828, but remained in Florida to serve as adjutant general of the state and inspector general of Florida troops. He had succumbed to yellow fever at his Blackwood Plantation in Tallahassee, with his wife, the daughter of Florida governor Robert Raymond Reid, at his bedside. The family would later relate stories of how Graham had participated in a ceremony that had made him a blood brother of Osceola. This enduring friendship had demonstrated how Osceola could separate his feelings toward a specific white man from the white man in general.[34]

By October 11, a total of 211 Seminoles had surrendered as a result of Coacoochee's messages, including most of his own band. Other Seminole detainees were people led by Chief Hospetarke, who had himself been taken prisoner during a meeting with Colonel Worth. These Seminoles were placed aboard ship and transported to New Orleans and then their new home in the West.

In 1850, Coacoochee and John Cavallo would leave Arkansas Territory and journey to Mexico. There, they established a colony for Seminoles and blacks near San Fernando de Rosas. Coacoochee would die of smallpox six years later.[35]

Several days after Coacoochee and Hospetarke had set sail, Alligator returned to Florida at the request of Colonel Worth. It was believed that this chief—in the tradition of Coacoochee—could bring in the Tallahassee bands led by Nethlockemathla, Thlocklo Tustenuggee (Tiger Tail), as well as Halleck Tustenuggee. Alligator successfully induced the Tallahassee chiefs and two hundred of their people to come in, but trouble ensued when Halleck Tustenuggee attempted to surrender. Two of Alligator's emissaries were killed by hostiles, which scared Halleck back into hiding.[36]

It would be the following year, on April 19, 1842, that Colonel William Worth, with about four hundred soldiers, would personally lead an attack on Halleck Tustenuggee at Peliklakaha. The Seminole chief and his warriors had erected a log barricade in a hammock surrounded by water with a clear field of fire. The main force of soldiers tramped through mud and heavy vegetation to execute a frontal assault on this defensive position, while a detachment of dragoons attacked at the rear. This strategy eventually routed the warriors, who vanished into the hammock. The camp was burned and every piece of serviceable equipment confiscated. The army lost one killed and four wounded; the Seminoles had one killed and one captured.

Several days later, Halleck Tustenuggee and two of his wives and two children surrendered to the colonel at his camp at Warm Springs. Worth also managed to seize forty-three warriors, thirty-seven women, and thirty-four children, which he estimated was more than one-third of all the Seminoles that remained in Florida. This engagement against Halleck Tustenuggee's warriors at Peliklakaha was notable as the last real battle of the war.[37]

On August 14, 1842, Colonel William Worth was authorized to declare an end to the Great Seminole War.

In truth, this war never really ended; rather, it wound down from lack of interest by either side in pursuing it further at that time. According to official records, 3,824 Seminoles had been shipped off to the West by the end of

1843. Hiding deep in the Everglades, never to surrender, however, were about 300 Seminole men, women, and children, among them Alligator, Arpeika, and Holata Micco (Billy Bowlegs). These brave survivors would be the forefathers of the Seminole people who populate Florida today.

This Second Seminole War would be the longest, the most expensive, and the deadliest war ever fought by the United States against Native Americans. There was no analysis of the actual cost of this seven-year conflict at the time, but an estimate by the noted authority John Mahon stands at $30 million to $40 million. Total casualties are difficult to estimate as well. The number of army, navy and Marine regulars who served in Florida has been given as 10,169, in addition to around 30,000 militiamen and volunteers from Florida and the surrounding states. The U.S. Army officially recorded 1,466 deaths during the war, mostly from disease. The number actually killed in action, however, cannot be determined. Mahon believes that 328 regular army soldiers were killed in action, with almost half of those deaths occurring in the Dade Massacre, the Battle of Lake Okeechobee, and the Harney fight. In addition to regular army deaths, those of the militiamen, volunteers, and white civilians must be counted, which could easily be in the hundreds or higher.

The number of Seminoles killed or who died of starvation or disease, as might be expected, cannot be estimated.[38]

In 1836, Osceola had sent a message to General Duncan Clinch predicting that war against the Seminoles would last at least five years. This estimate was laughable to the general and authorities in Washington. No one believed that a ragtag Native American army led by Osceola could withstand the might of the government for even one year, much less five years. The army had underestimated Osceola, the Seminole warrior, and dearly paid the price for that mistake.[39]

Osceola had been the heart and soul of the Seminole revolution. When the chiefs wavered, he stood tall in word and deed to inspire the warriors and instill within them Seminole pride. He galvanized the entire tribe, red and black, into acting with one purpose in mind—to defend their Florida homeland. Osceola had not asked anything of his warriors or their families that he and his family would not endure with them. He had lived in their midst without complaint in the dismal swamps where daily existence was a challenge and supreme sacrifice was necessary for survival. He had demonstrated in battle that he was a superior tactician to every general the U.S. Army had assigned to defeat him, and he had even shed his own blood for the cause. He had trained his warriors to fight with discipline and ferocity that were no match for the soldiers who engaged them. Most of all, with the guidance of Osceola, the Seminole people, who had been obliged to depend on the United States for annuities and protection, had proved that they could stand on their own as an equal nation. Had the death of Osceola and the attrition rate not finally caught up to the tribe, there is no telling how long or how much more costly this war would have been.

For the Black Seminoles who had faced the cruel prospect of capture by the slave chasers, Osceola was the man who proclaimed that as long as he was alive no black would be returned to his or her master in the South. He could easily have tossed aside his loyalties to the blacks in favor of his Native American blood ties, and no one would have blamed him. He could have conceivably ended the war and the suffering of his people simply by abandoning the Black Seminoles and letting them fend for themselves. But the steadfast character of this man could not entertain such a betrayal. Osceola maintained his promise to his black brethren until the day he died.

Osceola was a self-made man, an individualist, who rose from obscurity to battlefield glory and finally to immortality. His spirit lives on in the hearts of freedom-loving people everywhere, and it is only fitting that his unique presence upon this earth has been memorialized. At least twenty towns, two lakes, two mountains, a state park, and a national forest in the United States, as well as countless private businesses, have adopted his name. For the surviving Florida Seminoles, as well as for every American, these landmarks serve as the proud legacy of the brilliant strategist and courageous warrior who led his people in the defense of their homelands and brought to the attention of the world their valiant struggle to attain justice and freedom.

Osceola, the Seminole war leader, truly is the incomparable symbol of Native American valor.

Appendixes

Appendix 1
Treaty of Fort Jackson

A rticles of agreement and capitulation, made and concluded this ninth day of August, one thousand eight hundred and fourteen, between major general Andrew Jackson, on behalf of the President of the United States of America, and the chiefs, deputies, and warriors of the Creek Nation.

WHEREAS an unprovoked, inhuman, and sanguinary war, waged by the hostile Creeks against the United States, hath been repelled, prosecuted and determined, successfully, on the part of the said States, in conformity with principles of national justice and honorable warfare—And whereas consideration is due to the rectitude of proceeding dictated by instructions relating to the re-establishment of peace: Be it remembered, that prior to the conquest of that part of the Creek nation hostile to the United States, numberless aggressions had been committed against the peace, the property, and the lives of citizens of the United States, and those of the Creek nation in amity with her, at the mouth of Duck river, Fort Mimms, and elsewhere, contrary to national faith, and the regard due to an article of the treaty concluded at New-York, in the year seventeen hundred ninety, between the two nations: That the United States, previously to the perpetration of such outrages, did, in order to ensure future amity and concord between the Creek nation and the said states, in conformity with the stipulations of former treaties, fulfill, with punctuality and good faith, her engagements to the said nation: that more than two-thirds of the whole number of chiefs and warriors of the Creek nation, disregarding the genuine spirit of existing treaties, suffered themselves to be instigated to violations of their national honor, and the respect due to a part of their own nation faithful to the United States and the principles of humanity, by impostures [impostors,] denominating themselves Prophets, and by the duplicity and misrepresentation of foreign emissaries, whose governments are at war, open or understood, with the United States. Wherefore,

1st—The United States demand an equivalent for all expenses incurred in prosecuting the war to its termination, by a cession of all the territory belonging to the Creek nation within the territories of the United States, lying west, south, and south-eastwardly, of a line to be run and described by persons duly authorized and appointed by the President of the United States:

> Beginning at a point on the eastern bank of the Coosa river, where the south boundary line of the Cherokee nation crosses the same; running from thence down the said Coosa river with its eastern bank according to its various meanders to a point one mile above the mouth of Cedar creek, at Fort Williams, thence east two miles, thence south two miles, thence west to the eastern bank of the said Coosa river, thence down the eastern bank thereof according to its various meanders to a point opposite the upper end of the great falls, (called by the natives Woetumka,) thence east from a true meridian line to a point due north of the mouth of Ofucshee, thence south by a like meridian line to the mouth of Ofucshee on the south side of the Tallapoosa river, thence up the same, according to its various meanders, to a point where a direct course will cross the same at the distance of ten miles from the mouth thereof, thence a direct line to the mouth of Summochico creek, which empties into the Chatahouchie river on the east side thereof below the Eufaulau town, thence east from a true meridian line to a point which shall intersect the line now dividing the lands claimed by the said Creek nation from those claimed and owned by the state of Georgia: Provided, nevertheless, that where any possession of any chief or warrior of the Creek nation, who shall have been friendly to the United States during the war and taken an active part therein, shall be within the territory ceded by these articles to the United States, every such person shall be entitled to a reservation of land within the said territory of one mile square, to include his improvements as near the centre thereof as may be, which shall inure to the said chief or warrior, and his descendants, so long as he or they shall continue to occupy the same, who shall be protected by and subject to the laws of the United States; but upon the voluntary abandonment thereof, by such possessor or his descendants, the right of occupancy or possession of said lands shall devolve to the United States, and be identified with the right of property ceded hereby.

2nd—The United States will guarantee to the Creek nation, the integrity of all their territory eastwardly and northwardly of the said line to be run and described as mentioned in the first article.

3d—The United States demand, that the Creek nation abandon all communication, and cease to hold any intercourse with any British or Spanish post, garrison, or town; and that they shall not admit among them, any agent or trader, who shall not derive authority to hold commercial, or other intercourse with them, by license from the President or authorized agent of the United States.

4th—The United States demand an acknowledgment of the right to establish military posts and trading houses, and to open roads within the territory, guaranteed to the Creek nation by the second article, and a right to the free navigation of all its waters.

5th—The United States demand, that a surrender be immediately made, of all the persons and property, taken from the citizens of the United States, the friendly part of the Creek nation, the Cherokee, Chickasaw, and Choctaw nations, to the respective owners; and the United States will cause to be immediately restored to the formerly hostile Creeks, all the property taken from them since their submission, either by the United States, or by any Indian nation in amity with the United States, together with all the prisoners taken from them during the war.

6th—The United States demand the caption [capture] and surrender of all the prophets and instigators of the war, whether foreigners or natives, who have not submitted to the arms of the United States, and become parties to these articles of capitulation, if ever they shall be found within the territory guaranteed to the Creek nation by the second article.

7th—The Creek nation being reduced to extreme want, and not at present having the means of subsistence, the United States, from motives of humanity, will continue to furnish gratuitously the necessaries of life, until the crops of corn can be considered competent to yield the nation a supply, and will establish trading houses in the nation, at the discretion of the President of the United States, and at such places as he shall direct, to enable the nation, by industry and economy, to procure clothing.

8th—A permanent peace shall ensue from the date of these presents forever, between the Creek nation and the United States, and between the Creek nation and the Cherokee, Chickasaw, and Choctaw nations.

9th—If in running east from the mouth of Summochico creek, it shall so happen that the settlement of the Kennards, fall within the lines of the territory hereby ceded, then, and in that case, the line shall be run east on a true meridian to Kitchofoonee creek, thence down the middle of said creek to its junction with Flint River, immediately below the Oakmulgee town, thence up the middle of Flint river to a point due east of that at which the above line struck the Kitchofoonee creek, thence east to the old line herein before mentioned, to wit: the line dividing the lands claimed by the Creek nation, from those claimed and owned by the state of Georgia. The parties to these presents, after due consideration, for themselves and their constituents, agree to ratify and confirm the preceding articles, and constitute them the basis of a permanent peace between the two nations; and they do hereby solemnly bind themselves, and all the parties concerned and interested, to a faithful performance of every stipulation contained therein.

In testimony whereof, they have hereunto, interchangeably, set their hands and affixed their seals, the day and date above written.

Signatories

Andrew Jackson, major general commanding Seventh Military District, [L. S.] [*locus sigilli,* "the place of the seal," i.e., where the signer makes his mark or signature]

Tustunnuggee Thlucco, speaker for the Upper Creeks, his x mark, [L. S.]

Micco Aupoegau, of Toukaubatchee, his x mark, [L. S.]

Tustunnuggee Hopoiee, speaker of the Lower Creeks, his x mark, [L. S.]

Micco Achulee, of Cowetau, his x mark, [L. S.]

William McIntosh, jr., major of Cowetau, his x mark, [L. S.]

Tuskee Eneah, of Cussetau, his x mark, [L. S.]

Faue Emautla, of Cussetau, his x mark, [L. S.]

Toukaubatchee Tustunnuggee of Hitchetee, his x mark, [L. S.]

Noble Kinnard, of Hitchetee, his x mark, [L. S.]

Hopoiee Hutkee, of Souwagoolo, his x mark, [L. S.]

Hopoiee Hutkee, for Hopoie Yoholo, of Souwogoolo, his x mark, [L. S.]

Folappo Haujo, of Eufaulau, on Chattohochee, his x mark, [L. S.]

Pachee Haujo, of Apalachoocla, his x mark, [L. S.]

Timpoeechee Bernard, Captain of Uchees, his x mark, [L. S.]

Uchee Micco, his x mark, [L. S.]

Yoholo Micco, of Kialijee, his x mark, [L. S.]

Socoskee Emautla, of Kialijee, his x mark, [L. S.]

Choocchau Haujo, of Woccocoi, his x mark, [L. S.]

Esholoctee, of Nauchee, his x mark, [L. S.]

Yoholo Micco, of Tallapoosa Eufaulau, his x mark, [L. S.]

Stinthellis Haujo, of Abecoochee, his x mark, [L. S.]

Ocfuskee Yoholo, of Toutacaugee, his x mark, [L. S.]

John O'Kelly, of Coosa, [L. S.]

Eneah Thlucco, of Immookfau, his x mark, [L. S.]

Espokokoke Haujo, of Wewoko, his x mark, [L. S.]

Eneah Thlucco Hopoiee, of Talesee, his x mark, [L. S.]

Efau Haujo, of Puccan Tallahassee, his x mark, [L. S.]

Talessee Fixico, of Ocheobofau, his x mark, [L. S.]

Nomatlee Emautla, or Captain Issacs, of Cousoudee, his x mark, [L. S.]

Tuskegee Emautla, or John Carr, of Tuskegee, his x mark, [L. S.]

Alexander Grayson, of Hillabee, his x mark, [L. S.]

Lowee, of Ocmulgee, his x mark, [L. S.]

Nocoosee Emautla, of Chuskee Tallafau, his x mark, [L. S.]

William McIntosh, for Hopoiee Haujo, of Ooseoochee, his x mark, [L. S.]

William McIntosh, for Chehahaw Tustunnuggee, of Chehahaw, his x mark, [L. S.]

William McIntosh, for Spokokee Tustunnuggee, of Otellewhoyonnee, his x mark, [L. S.]

Done at Fort Jackson, in presence of—
Charles Cassedy, acting secretary,
Benjamin Hawkins, agent for Indian affairs,
Return J. Meigs, A. C. nation,
Robert Butler, Adjutant General U.S. Army,
J. C. Warren, assistant agent for Indian affairs,
George Mayfield,
Alexander Curnels,
George Lovett,
Public interpreters.

Appendix 2

Treaty with the Florida Tribes of Indians, 1823
(Moultrie Creek)

⇥⟫❖⟪⇤

SEPT. 18, 1823. PROCLAMATION, JAN. 2, 1824.

ARTICLE 1.

THE undersigned chiefs and warriors, for themselves and their tribes, have appealed to the humanity; and thrown themselves on, and have promised to continue under, the protection of the United States, and of no other nation, power, or sovereign; and, in consideration of the promises and stipulations hereinafter made, do cede and relinquish all claim or title which they may have to the whole territory of Florida, with the exception of such district of country as shall herein be allotted to them.

ARTICLE 2.

The Florida tribes of Indians will hereafter be concentrated and confined to the following metes [measures] and boundaries: commencing five miles north of Okehumke, running in a direct line to a point five miles west of Setarky's settlement, on the waters of Amazura, (or Withlahuchie river,) leaving said settlement two miles south of the line; from thence, in a direct line, to the south end of the Big Hammock, to include Chickuchate; continuing, in the same direction, for five miles beyond the said Hammock—provided said point does not approach nearer than fifteen miles the sea coast of the Gulf of Mexico; if it does, the said line will terminate at that distance from the sea coast; thence, south, twelve miles; thence in a south 30° east direction, until the same shall strike within five miles of the main branch of Charlotte river; thence, in a due east direction, to within twenty miles of the Atlantic coast; thence, north, fifteen west, for fifty miles and from this last, to the beginning point.

ARTICLE 3.

The United States will take the Florida Indians under their care and patronage, and will afford them protection against all persons whatsoever; provided they conform to the laws of the United States, and refrain from making war, or giving any insult to any foreign nation, without having first obtained the permission and consent of the United States: And, in consideration of the appeal and cession made in the first article of this treaty, by the aforesaid chiefs and warriors, the United States promise to distribute among the tribes, as soon as concentrated, under the direction of their agent, implements of husbandry, and stock of cattle and hogs, to the amount of six thousand dollars, and an annual sum of five thousand dollars a year, for twenty successive years, to be distributed as the President of the United States shall direct, through the Secretary of War, or his Superintendents and Agent of Indian Affairs.

ARTICLE 4.

The United States promise to guaranty to the said tribes the peaceable possession of the district of country herein assigned them, reserving the right of opening through it such roads, as may, from time to time, be deemed necessary; and to restrain and prevent all white persons from hunting, settling, or otherwise intruding upon it. But any citizen of the United States, being lawfully authorized for that purpose, shall be permitted to pass and repass through the said district, and to navigate the waters thereof, without any hindrance, toll, or exaction, from said tribes.

ARTICLE 5.

For the purpose of facilitating the removal of the said tribes to the district of country allotted them, and, as a compensation for the losses sustained, or the inconveniences to which they may be exposed by said removal, the United States will furnish them with rations of corn, meat, and salt, for twelve months, commencing on the first day of February next; and they further agree to compensate those individuals who have been compelled to abandon improvements on lands, not embraced within the limits allotted, to the amount of four thousand five hundred dollars, to be distributed among the sufferers, in a ratio to each, proportional to the value of the improvements abandoned. The United States further agree to furnish a sum, not exceeding two thousand dollars, to be expended by their agent, to facilitate the transportation of the different tribes to the point of concentration designated.

ARTICLE 6.

An agent, sub-agent, and interpreter, shall be appointed, to reside within the Indian boundary aforesaid, to watch over the interests of said tribes; and the United States further stipulate, as an evidence of their humane policy towards said tribes, who have appealed to their liberality, to allow for the establishment of a school at the agency, one thousand dollars per year for twenty successive years; and one thousand dollars per year, for the same period, for the support of a gun and blacksmith, with the expenses incidental to his shop.

ARTICLE 7.

The chiefs and warriors aforesaid, for themselves and tribes, stipulate to be active and vigilant in the preventing the retreating to, or passing through, of the district of country assigned them, of any absconding slaves, or fugitives from justice; and further agree, to use all necessary exertions to apprehend and deliver the same to the agent, who shall receive orders to compensate them agreeably to the trouble and expenses incurred.

ARTICLE 8.

A commissioner, or commissioners, with a surveyor, shall be appointed, by the President of the United States, to run and mark, (blazing fore and aft the trees) the line as defined in the second article of this treaty, who shall be attended by a chief or warrior, to be designated by a council of their own tribes, and who shall receive, while so employed, a daily compensation of three dollars.

ARTICLE 9.

The undersigned chiefs and warriors, for themselves and tribes, having objected to their concentration within the limits described in the second article of this treaty, under the impression that the said limits did not contain a sufficient quantity of good land to subsist them, and for no other reason: it is, therefore, expressly understood, between the United States and the aforesaid chiefs and warriors, that, should the country embraced in the said limits, upon examination by the Indian agent and the commissioner, or commissioners, to be appointed under the 8th article of this treaty, be by them considered insufficient for the support of the said Indian tribes; then the north line, as defined in the 2d article of this treaty, shall be removed so far north as to embrace a sufficient quantity of good tillable land.

ARTICLE 10.

The undersigned chiefs and warriors, for themselves and tribes, have expressed to the commissioners their unlimited confidence in their agent, Col. Gad Humphreys, and their interpreter, Stephen Richards, and, as an evidence of their gratitude for their services and humane treatment, and brotherly attentions to their wants, request that one mile square, embracing the improvements of Enehe Mathla, at Tallahassee (said improvements to be considered as the centre) be conveyed, in fee simple, as a present to Col. Gad Humphreys.—

And they further request, that one mile square, at the Ochesee Bluffs, embracing Stephen Richard's field on said bluffs, be conveyed in fee simple, as a present to said Stephen Richards. The commissioners accord in sentiment with the undersigned chiefs and warriors, and recommend a compliance with their wishes to the President and Senate of the United States; but the disapproval, on the part of the said authorities, of this article, shall, in no wise, affect the other articles and stipulations concluded on in this treaty.

In testimony whereof, the commissioners, William P. Duval, James Gadsden, and Bernard Segui, and the undersigned chiefs and warriors, have hereunto subscribed their names and affixed their seals. Done at camp on Moultrie creek, in the territory of Florida, this eighteenth day of September, one thousand eight hundred and twenty-three, and of the independence of the United States the forty-eighth.

William P. Duval, [L. S.]
James Gadsden, [L. S.]
Bernard Segui, [L. S.]
Nea Mathla, his x mark, [L. S.]
Tokose Mathla, his x mark, [L. S.]
Ninnee Homata Tustenuky, his mark, [L. S.]
Miconope, his x mark, [L. S.]
Nocosee Ahola, his x mark, [L. S.]
John Blunt, his x mark, [L. S.]
Otlemata, his x mark, [L. S.]
Tuskeeneha, his x mark,[L. S.]
Tuski Hajo, his x mark, [L. S.]
Econchatimico, his x mark, [L. S.]
Emoteley, his x mark, [L. S.]
Mulatto King, his x mark, [L. S.]
Chocholohano, his x mark, [L. S.]
Ematlochee, his x mark, [L. S.]
Wokse Holata, his x mark, [L. S.]
Amathla Ho, his x mark, [L. S.]
Holatefiscico, his x mark, [L. S.]
Chefisco Hajo, his x mark, [L. S.]
Lathloa Mathla, his x mark, [L. S.]
Senufky, his x mark, [L. S.]
Alak Hajo, his x mark, [L. S.]
Fahelustee Hajo, his x mark, [L. S.]

Octahamico, his x mark, [L. S.]

Tuski Hajo, his x mark, [L. S.]

Okoskee Amathla, his x mark, [L. S.]

Ocheeny Tustenuky, his x mark [L. S.]

Phillip, his x mark, [L. S.]

Charley Amathla, his x mark, [L. S.]

John Hoponey, his x mark, [L. S.]

Rat Head, his x mark, [L. S.]

Holata Emathla, his x mark, [L. S.]

Foshatchimico, his x mark, [L. S.]

Signed, sealed, and delivered in the presence of—

George Murray, secretary to the commission,

G. Humphreys, Indian agent,

Stephen Richards, interpreter,

Isaac N. Cox,

J. Erving, captain, Fourth Artillery,

Harvey Brown, lieutenant, Fourth Artillery,

C. D'Espinville, lieutenant, Fourth Artillery,

Jno. B. Scott, lieutenant, Fourth Artillery,

William Travers,

Horatio S. Dexter.

ADDITIONAL ARTICLE. SEPT. 18, 1823

Whereas Neo Mathla, John Blunt, Tuski Hajo, Mulatto King, Emathlochee, and Econchatimico, six of the principal Chiefs of the Florida Indians, and parties to the treaty to which this article has been annexed, have warmly appealed to the Commissioners for permission to remain in the district of country now inhabited by them; and, in consideration of their friendly disposition, and past services to the United States, it is, therefore, stipulated, between the United States and the aforesaid Chiefs, that the following reservations shall be surveyed, and marked by the Commissioner, or Commissioners, to be appointed under the 8th article of this Treaty: For the use of Nea Mathla and his connections, two miles square, embracing the Tuphulga village, on the waters of Rocky Comfort Creek. For Blunt and Tuski Hajo, a reservation, commencing on the Apalachicola, one mile below Tuski Hajo's improvements, running up said river four miles; thence, west, two miles; thence southerly, to a point two miles due west of the beginning; thence east, to the beginning point. For Mulatto King and Emathlochee, a reservation, commencing on the Apalachicola, at a point to include Yellow Hairs improvements; thence, up said river, for four miles; thence, west, one mile; thence, southerly, to a point one mile west of the beginning; and thence, east, to the beginning point. For Econchatimico, a reservation, commencing on the Chatahoochie, one mile below Econchatimico's house; thence, up said river, for four miles; thence, one mile, west; thence, southerly, to a point one mile west of the beginning; thence, east, to the beginning point. The United States promise to guaranty the peaceable possession of the said reservations, as defined, to the aforesaid chiefs and their descendants only, so long as they shall continue to occupy, improve, or cultivate, the same; but in the event of the abandonment of all, or either of the reservations, by the chief or chiefs, to whom they have been allotted, the reservation, or reservations, so abandoned, shall revert to the United States, as included in the cession made in the first article of this treaty. It is further understood, that the names of the individuals remaining on the reservations aforesaid, shall be furnished, by the chiefs in whose favor the reservations have been made, to the Superintendent or agent of Indian Affairs, in the territory of Florida; and that no other individuals shall be received or permitted to remain within said reservations, without the previous consent of the Superintendent or Agent aforesaid; And, as the aforesaid Chiefs are authorized to select the individuals remaining with them, so they shall each be separately held responsible for the peaceable conduct of their towns, or the individuals residing on the reservations allotted them. It is further understood, between the parties, that this agreement is not intended to prohibit the voluntary removal, at any future period, of all or either of the aforesaid Chiefs and their connections, to the district of country south, allotted to the Florida Indians, by the second article of this Treaty, whenever either, or all may think proper to make such an election; the United States reserving the right of ordering, for any outrage or misconduct, the aforesaid Chiefs, or either of them, with their connections, within the district of country south, aforesaid. It is further stipulated, by the United States, that, of the six thousand dollars, appropriated for implements of husbandry, stock, &c. in the third article of this Treaty, eight hundred dollars shall be distributed, in the same manner, among the aforesaid chiefs and their towns; and it is understood, that, of the annual sum of five thousand dollars to be distributed by the President of the United States, they will receive their proportion. It is further stipulated, that, of the four thousand five hundred dollars, and two thousand dollars, provided for by the 5th article of this Treaty, for the payment for improvements and transportation, five hundred dollars shall be awarded to Neo Mathla, as a compensation for the improvements abandoned by him, as well as to meet the expenses he will unavoidably be exposed to, by his own removal, and that of his connections.

In testimony whereof, the commissioners, William P. Duval, James Gadsden, and Bernard Segui, and the undersigned chiefs and warriors have hereunto subscribed their names and affixed their seals. Done at camp, on Moultrie creek, in the territory of Florida, this eighteenth day of September, one thousand eight hundred and twenty-three, and of the independence of the United States the forty-eighth.

Wm. P. Duval, his x mark, [L. S.]
James Gadsden, [L. S.]
Bernard Segui, [L. S.]
Nea Mathla, his x mark, [L. S.]
John Blunt, his x mark, [L. S.]
Tuski Hajo, his x mark, [L. S.]
Mulatto King, his x mark, [L. S.]
Emathlochee, his x mark, [L. S.]
Econchatimico, his x mark, [L. S.]

Signed, sealed, delivered, in presence of—
George Murray, secretary to the commission
Ja. W. Ripley,
G. Humphreys, Indian agent,
Stephen Richards, interpreter.

The following statement shows the number of men retained by the Chiefs, who have reservations made them, at their respective villages.

Number of Men.
Blount . . 43
Cochran . . 45
Mulatto King . . 30
Emathlochee . . 28
Econchatimico . . 38
Neo Mathia . . 30
Total . . 214

Appendix 3

Treaty with the Seminole, 1832
(Payne's Landing)

＊⟫ ◈ ⟪＊

MAY 9, 1832. PROCLAMATION, APRIL 12, 1834.

The Seminole Indians, regarding with just respect, the solicitude manifested by the President of the United States or the improvement of their condition, by recommending a removal to a country more suitable to their habits and wants than the one they at present occupy in the Territory of Florida, are willing that their confidential chiefs, Jumper, Fuch-ta-lus-ta-Hadjo, Charley Emartla, Coi-had-jo, Holati Emathla Ya-hadjo; Sam Jones, accompanied by their agent Major Phagan, and their faithful interpreter Abraham, should be sent at the expense of the United States as early as convenient to examine the country assigned to the Creeks west of the Mississippi river, and should they be satisfied with the character of that country, and of the favorable disposition of the Creeks to reunite with the Seminoles as one people; the articles of the compact and agreement, herein stipulated at Payne's landing on one Ocklewaha river, this ninth day of May, one thousand eight hundred and thirty-two, between James Gadsden, for and in behalf of the Government of the United States, and the undersigned chiefs and head-men for and in behalf of the Seminole Indians, shall be binding on the respective parties.

ARTICLE 1.

The Seminole Indians relinquish to the United States, all claim to the lands they at present occupy in the Territory of Florida, and agree to emigrate to the country assigned to the Creeks, west of the Mississippi river; it being understood that an additional extent of territory, proportioned to their numbers, will be added to the Creek country, and that the

Seminoles will be received as a constituent part of the Creek nation and be re-admitted to all the privileges as members of the same.

ARTICLE 2.

For and in consideration of the relinquishment of claim in the first article of this agreement, and in full compensation for all the improvements, which may have been made on the lands thereby ceded; the United States stipulate to pay to the Seminole Indians, fifteen thousand, four hundred (15,400) dollars, to be divided among the chiefs and warriors of the several towns, in a ratio proportioned to their population, the respective proportions of each to be paid on their arrival in the country they consent to remove to; it being understood that their faithful interpreters Abraham and Cudjo shall receive two hundred dollars each of the above sum, in full remuneration for the improvements to be abandoned on the lands now cultivated by them.

ARTICLE 3.

The United States agree to distribute as they arrive at their new homes in the Creek Territory, west of the Mississippi river, a blanket and a homespun frock, to each of the warriors, women and children of the Seminole tribe of Indians.

ARTICLE 4.

The United States agree to extend the annuity for the support of a blacksmith, provided for in the sixth article of the treaty at Camp Moultrie for ten (10) years beyond the period therein stipulated, and in addition to the other annuities secured under that treaty: the United States agree to pay the sum of three thousand (3,000) dollars a year for fifteen (15) years, commencing after the removal of the whole tribe; these sums to be added to the Creek annuities, and the whole amount to be so divided, that the chiefs and warriors of the Seminole Indians may receive their equitable proportion of the same as members of the Creek confederation—

ARTICLE 5.

The United States will take the cattle belonging to the Seminoles at the valuation of some discreet person to be appointed by the President, and the same shall be paid for in money to the respective owners, after their arrival at their new homes; or other cattle such as may be desired will be furnished them, notice being given through their agent of their wishes upon this subject, before their removal, that time may be afforded to supply the demand.

ARTICLE 6.

The Seminoles being anxious to be relieved from repeated vexatious demands for slaves and other property, alleged to have been stolen and destroyed by them, so that they may remove unembarrassed to their new homes; the United States stipulate to have the same property investigated, and to liquidate such as may be satisfactorily established, provided the amount does not exceed seven thousand (7,000) dollars.—

ARTICLE 7.

The Seminole Indians will remove within three (3) years after the ratification of this agreement, and the expenses of their removal shall be defrayed by the United States, and such subsistence shall also be furnished them for a term not exceeding twelve (12) months, after their arrival at their new residence; as in the opinion of the President, their numbers and circumstances may require, the emigration to commence as early as practicable in the year eighteen hundred and thirty-three (1833), and with those Indians at present occupying the Big Swamp, and other parts of the country beyond the limits as defined in the second article of the treaty concluded at Camp Moultrie creek, so that the whole of that proportion of the Seminoles may be removed within the year aforesaid, and the remainder of the tribe, in about equal proportions, during the subsequent years of eighteen hundred and thirty-four and five, (1834 and 1835.)—

In testimony whereof, the commissioner, James Gadsden, and the undersigned chiefs and head men of the Seminole Indians. have hereunto subscribed their names and affixed their seals. Done at camp at Payne's landing, on the Ocklawaha river in the territory of Florida, on this ninth day of May, one thousand eight hundred and thirty-two, and of the independence of the United States of America the fifty-sixth.

James Gadsden, [L. S.]
Holati Emathla, his x mark, [L. S.]
Jumper, his x mark, [L. S.]
Fuch-ta-lus-ta-Hadjo, his x mark, [L. S.]
Charley Emartla, his x mark, [L. S.]
Coa Hadjo, his x mark, [L. S.]
Ar-pi-uck-i, or Sam Jones, his x mark, [L. S.]
Ya-ha Hadjo, his x mark, [L. S.]
Mico-Noha, his x mark, [L. S.]
Tokose-Emartla, or Jno. Hicks, his x mark, [L. S.]
Cat-sha-Tusta-nuck-i, his x mark, [L. S.]
Hola-at-a-Mico, his x mark, [L. S.]
Hitch-it-i-Mico, his x mark, [L. S.]
E-ne-hah, his x mark, [L. S.]
Ya-ha-emartla Chup-ko, his mark, [L. S.]
Moke-his-she-lar-ni, his x mark, [L. S.]

Witnesses:

Douglas Vass, Secretary to Commissioner,
John Phagan, Agent,
Stephen Richards, Interpreter,
Abraham, Interpreter, his x mark,
Cudjo, Interpreter, his x mark,
Erastus Rogers,
B. Joscan.

Appendix 4

Treaty of Fort Gibson, on the Arkansas River
with the Seminole on March 28, 1833
Proclamation, Apr. 12, 1834

≫※≪

WHEREAS, the Seminole Indians of Florida, entered into certain articles of agreement, with James Gadson, (Gadsden) Commissioner on behalf of the United States, at Payne's landing, on the 9th day of May, 1832: the first article of which treaty or agreement provides, as follows:

"The Seminoles Indians relinquish to the United States all claim to the land they at present occupy in the Territory of Florida, and agree to emigrate to the country assigned to the Creeks, west of the Mississippi river; it being understood that an additional extent of territory proportioned to their number will be added to the Creek country, and that the Seminoles will be received as a constituent part of the Creek nation, and be re-admitted to all the privileges as members of the same."

And whereas, the said agreement also stipulates and provides, that a delegation of Seminoles should be sent at the expense of the United States to examine the country to be allotted them among the Creeks, and should this delegation be satisfied with the character of the country and of the favorable disposition of the Creeks to unite with them as one people, then the aforementioned treaty would be considered binding and obligatory upon the parties.

And whereas a treaty was made between the United States and the Creek Indians west of the Mississippi, at Fort Gibson, on the 14th day of February 1833, by which a country was provided for the Seminoles in pursuance of the existing arrangements between the United States and that tribe.

And whereas, the special delegation, appointed by the Seminoles on the 9th day of May 1832, have since examined the land designated for them by the undersigned Commissioners, on behalf of the United States, and have expressed themselves satisfied with the same, in and by their letter dated, March 1833, addressed to the undersigned Commissioners.

Now, therefore, the Commissioners aforesaid, by virtue of the power and authority vested in them by the treaty made with Creek Indians on the 14th day of February 1833, as above stated, hereby designate and assign to the Seminole tribe of Indians, for their separate future residence, forever, a tract of country lying between the Canadian river and the north fork thereof, and extending west to where a line running north and south between the main Canadian and north branch, will strike the forks of Little river, provided said west line does not extend more than twenty-five miles west from the mouth of said Little river.

And the undersigned Seminole chiefs, delegated as aforesaid, on behalf of their nation hereby declare themselves well satisfied with the location provided for them by the Commissioners, and agree that their nation shall commence the removal to their new home, as soon as the Government will make arrangements for their emigration, satisfactory to the Seminole nation.

And whereas, the said Seminoles have expressed high confidence in the friendship and ability of their present agent, Major Phagen, and desire that he may be permitted to remove them to their new homes west of the Mississippi; the Commissioners have considered their request, and cheerfully recommend Major Phagan as a suitable person to be employed to remove the Seminoles as aforesaid, and trust his appointment will be made, not only to gratify the wishes of the Indians but as conducive to the public welfare.

In testimony whereof, the commissioners on behalf of the United States, and the delegates of the Seminole nation, have hereunto signed their names, this 28th day of March, A.D. 1833, at Fort Gibson.

Montfort Stokes,
Henry L. Ellsworth,
John F. Schermerhorn.

Seminole Delegates:

John Hick, representing Sam Jones, his x mark.

Holata Emathla, his x mark.

Jumper, his x mark.

Col Hadgo, his x mark.

Charley Emartta, his x mark.

Ya-ha-hadge, his x mark.

Ne-ha-tho-clo, representing Fuch-ta-lus-ta-Hadjo, his x mark,

On behalf of the Seminole nation.

❧ *Notes* ❦

❧✦❦

CHAPTER 1: THE CREEK REFUGEES

1. The best and most complete book about the Creeks—the culture, traditions, values, and early history in detail—is Debo, *The Road to Disappearance*.
2. Boyd, "Asi-Yahola or Osceola," 255.
3. Woodward, *Reminiscences*, 9; "Osceola," Florida Memory Project, Florida State Library and Archives, 2007; Monroe, "The Seminole Women of Florida," 27; Cohen, *Notices of Florida*, 234.
4. Coe, *Red Patriots*, 28.
5. Coe, "The Parentage and Birthplace of Osceola," 234, 238.
6. Cohen, *Notices of Florida*, 238; Mahon, *Second Seminole War*, 10, 91.
7. Sprague, *Florida War*, 37. Sprague, who was an army officer who served in the Second Seminole War, had an excellent eye for detail. His keen observations make this an indispensable source.
8. Swanton, "Social Organization and Social Usages," 171.
9. Ibid., 466–70; Debo, *Road to Disappearance*, 15.
10. Swanton, "Social Organization and Social Usages," 171, 371, 380–84, 403; Bartram, *Travels*, 386f., 394f.; Debo, *Road to Disappearance*, 19.
11. Adair, *History of the American Indians*, 406–09, 430; Bartram, *Travels*, 191, 509–11; Hawkins, *A Sketch of the Creek Country*, 35.
12. Bartram, *Travels*, 191f.; Hawkins, *A Sketch of the Creek Country*, 35.
13. Bartram, *Travels*, 38; Adair, *History of the American Indians*, 402–05.

14. Capron, "Medicine Bundles," 182–83.
15. Mahon, *Second Seminole War*, 15.
16. Coe, *Red Patriots*, 29.
17. Sugden, *The Shooting Star*, 104; Martin, *Sacred Revolt*, 118; Bradbury, *Travels*; Debo, *Road to Disappearance*, 77–78.
18. Braund, *Deerskins and Duffels*, 7–8; Green, *The Politics of Indian Removal*, 7; Wright, *Creeks and Seminoles*, 171.
19. Green, *The Politics of Indian Removal*, 36–37; Braund, *Deerskins and Duffels*, 184; Grant and Davis, "The Wedding of Col. Benjamin Hawkins," 308.
20. Braund, *Deerskins and Duffels*, 184; Martin, *Sacred Revolt*, 79–81.
21. Braund, *Deerskins and Duffels*, 4–5, 183–85; Green, *The Politics of Indian Removal*, 36–37.
22. Braund, "The Creek Indians, Blacks, and Slavery," 622; Martin, *Sacred Revolt*, 82; Green, *The Politics of Indian Removal*, 11–12, 39–41.
23. Florette, *The Southern Indians and Benjamin Hawkins*, 269; Dowd, *A Spirited Resistance*, 156; also see Woodward to F. A. Rutherford, 2 April 1858, in Woodward, *Reminiscences*, 37.
24. Braund's *Deerskins and Duffels* contains a complete account of how the deerskin trade affected Creek traditions and values; Wright, *Creeks and Seminoles*, 171.
25. Owsley, *Struggle for the Gulf Borderlands*, 11; Florette, *The Southern Indians and Benjamin Hawkins*, 269; Dowd, *A Spirited Resistance*, 156.
26. Woodward, *Reminiscences*, 44.
27. Hatch, *Encyclopedia of the Alamo and the Texas Revolution*, 72.
28. Woodward, *Reminiscences*, 44.
29. Numerous excellent books chronicle the Creek War of 1813–14. The best volumes include (in alphabetical order) Buchanan, *Jackson's Way*; Coles, *The War of 1812*; Halbert and Ball, *The Creek War of 1813 and 1814*; Langguth, *Union 1812*; O'Brien, *In Bitterness and in Tears*; Owsley, *Struggle for the Gulf Borderlands*; Remini, *The Battle of New Orleans*; and Wright, *Creeks and Seminoles*.

CHAPTER 2: BLACK DRINK SINGER

1. Remini, *Andrew Jackson and His Indian Wars*, 88–93; Owsley, *Struggle for the Gulf Borderlands*, 87–89.
2. Reid and Eaton, *The Life of Andrew Jackson*, 190–91.
3. Smith, "Presidents in Retirement," 17.
4. As is the case with every president, there is a voluminous bibliography for Jackson. Many sources are listed in the bibliography of this book.
5. Capron, "Medicine Bundles," 172ff.

6. Coe, *Red Patriots,* 25–30.

7. Covington, "Migration of the Seminoles," 354.

8. Griffin, "Some Comments on the Seminoles," 45; Krogman, "The Racial Composition of the Seminole Indians," 419; Covington, "Migration of the Seminoles," 351; Craig and Peebles, "Ethnohistorical Change," 91–92.

9. Swanton, *Indian Tribes of North America,* 139; Fairbanks, *Ethnohistorical Report,* 91–92.

10. Craig and Peebles, "Ethnohistorical Change," 92; Mulroy, "Ethnogenesis and Ethnohistory," 292, 295; Porter, "Negroes and the Seminole War, 1817–1818," 252.

11. Brevard, *A History of Florida,* 42–43.

12. Porter, *The Negro on the American Frontier,* 184; Giddings, *The Exiles of Florida,* 37–38; Wright, *Creeks and Seminoles,* 190–91.

13. Andrew Jackson to Zuniga, April 23, 1816, in Jackson, *Correspondence,* 2:266.

14. Parton, *Life of Andrew Jackson,* 1:219.

15. Boyd, "Events at Prospect Bluff," 76; Coker and Watson, *Indian Traders,* 306.

16. Patrick, *Florida Fiasco,* 301; Porter, *The Black Seminoles,* 16–18; Giddings, *The Exiles of Florida,* 46.

17. Parton, *Life of Andrew Jackson,* 2:399, 407; Giddings, *The Exiles of Florida,* 42–44.

18. Patrick, *Aristocrat in Uniform,* 33.

19. Parton, *Life of Andrew Jackson,* 2:428.

20. Gaines to Jackson, Nov. 21, 1817, *American State Papers, Military Affairs,* 1:686 (hereafter cited as *ASPMA*).

21. Parton, *Life of Andrew Jackson,* 2:430; Giddings, *The Exiles of Florida,* 48.

22. Jackson, *Correspondence,* 4:165.

23. Jackson to Calhoun, April 8, 1818, Jackson, *Correspondence,* 2:358–59; Peters, *The Florida Wars,* 47.

24. Jackson to Calhoun, April 26, 1818, Jackson, *Correspondence,* 2:363; Woodward, *Reminiscences,* 5; Covington, "Migration of the Seminoles," 356.

25. Hatch, *Black Kettle,* 47–48.

26. Swanton, "Religious Beliefs and Medical Practices"; Swanton, "The Green Corn Dance"; Adair, *History of the American Indians,* 430.

27. Capron, "Medicine Bundles."

28. Caleb Swan, *Archives of Aboriginal Knowledge,* in Schoolcraft, *The Indian Tribes of the United States,* 2:266.

29. Capron, "Medicine Bundles."

30. Quoted in Schoolcraft, *The Indian Tribes of the United States,* 2:266–67.

31. Boyd, "Asi-Yahola or Osceola," 250–51; Coe, *Red Patriots,* 27.

CHAPTER 3: TREACHERY AT MOULTRIE CREEK

1. MacCauley, *The Seminole Indians of Florida*, 481–82.
2. Castelnau, "Essay on Middle Florida," 249.
3. Parton, *Life of Andrew Jackson*, 2:550, 570.
4. Weigley, *History of the United States Army*, 140; Thompson, *Jacksonian Democracy*, 1.
5. Vignoles, *Observations Upon the Floridas*, 129, 134.
6. Abel, "History of Events," 328–29; *Territorial Papers of the United States*, 22:29 (hereafter cited as *Florida Territorial Papers*).
7. *Florida Territorial Papers*, 22:294.
8. Boyd, "Horatio S. Dexter," 66–67.
9. Mahon, *Second Seminole War*, 59.
10. "Treaty of Amity, Settlement, and Limits Between the United States and His Catholic Majesty," February 22, 1819, *American State Papers, Foreign Relations*, 4:623–25 (hereafter cited as *ASPFR*).
11. Wright, *Creeks and Seminoles*, 94–96.
12. Porter, *The Black Seminoles*, 27.
13. Message of the President, December 3, 1822, S. Doc. No. 1, 7.
14. Committee on Indian Affairs to HR, February 21, 1823, *ASPIA*, 2:408–10.
15. *Florida Territorial Papers*, 22:644, 649, 652, 695.
16. Knauss, "William Pope DuVal," 95–139; Mahon, *Second Seminole War*, 35.
17. Boyd, "Horatio S. Dexter," 69.
18. *Florida Territorial Papers*, 22:495, 557, 578.
19. Ibid., 22:42n, 659–60; Gadsden to SW, June 11, 1823, *ASPIA*, 22:433–34.
20. *St. Augustine Florida Herald*, September 6, 1823; Boyd, "Horatio S. Dexter," 86; *Florida Territorial Papers*, 22:681.
21. Kappler, *Indian Affairs*, 2:203–05.
22. *Florida Territorial Papers*, 22:832; Wright, *Creeks and Seminoles*, 220.
23. Glenn, "A Diary of Joshua Nichols Glenn," 148–49.
24. Minutes of Council, *ASPIA*, 2:437–38.
25. Mahon, "Treaty of Moultrie Creek," 367; Minutes of Council, *ASPIA*, 2:438–39.
26. Porter, *Black Seminoles*, 28.
27. Minutes of Council, *ASPIA*, 2:439; Treaty of Moultrie Creek, Kappler, *Indian Affairs*, 2:203–05; Mahon, "Treaty of Moultrie Creek," 368–70.
28. Patrick, *Aristocrat in Uniform*, 68.
29. Minutes of Council, *ASPIA*, 2:439; Kappler, *Indian Affairs*, 2:203–05; Mahon, "Treaty of Moultrie Creek," 369.
30. Brevard, *A History of Florida*, 1:89; Washington Irving, "Conspiracy of Neamathla," 1855.

31. *Florida Territorial Papers,* 23:385, 603–05, 635–37.

32. Sprague, *Florida War,* 19, 65–67.

CHAPTER 4: PAYNE'S LANDING BETRAYAL

1. Wickman, *Osecola's Legacy,* 24–27.

2. McKenney and Hall, *Indian Tribes of North America,* 2:368.

3. Cohen, *Notices of Florida,* 62.

4. Sprague, *Florida War,* 101.

5. *Florida Territorial Papers,* 22:918.

6. Martin, *Florida During the Territory Days,* 66; Brevard, *A History of Florida,* 89.

7. *Florida Territorial Papers,* 23:335.

8. *ASPIA,* 2:665.

9. *Florida Territorial Papers,* 23:445.

10. Cubberly, "Fort King"; Motte, *Journey into Wilderness,* 276.

11. Sprague, *Florida War,* 101; Cohen, *Notices of Florida,* 237.

12. Swanton, "Social Organization and Social Usages," 368–84.

13. Giddings, *The Exiles of Florida,* 98.

14. *Florida Territorial Papers,* 23:801, 816–18.

15. Ibid., 385, 409, 603–05, 635–37; Boyd, "Horatio S. Dexter," 87.

16. Sprague, *Florida War,* 37.

17. Cohen, *Notices of Florida,* 236.

18. Sprague, *Florida War,* 37–38.

19. Ibid., 60–62; *Florida Territorial Papers,* 24:94, 97, 164–66, 232–34.

20. Sprague, *Florida War,* 60; *Florida Territorial Papers,* 24:209–10, 197–98, 212–14.

21. *Florida Territorial Papers,* 24:381.

22. Indian Removal Act, May 28, 1830, *United States Statutes at Large,* 21st Cong., 1st Sess., Chapter 148, 411–12.

23. *Florida Territorial Papers,* 24:632, 667, 678–80.

24. Cohen, *Notices of Florida,* 235.

25. *ASPMA,* 6:473.

26. Ibid., 6:472; H.R. Doc. No. 271, 7–11.

27. Treaty of Payne's Landing, Kappler, *Indian Affairs,* 2:344–45.

28. Hitchcock, *Fifty Years in Camp and Field,* 78–80.

29. Porter, "The Negro Abraham," 38.

30. Treaty of Payne's Landing, Kappler, *Indian Affairs,* 2:344.

31. Hitchcock, *Fifty Years in Camp and Field,* 80–81.

32. *ASPMA,* 6:492.

33. *Florida Territorial Papers*, 24:381.

34. Abel, "History of Events," 393n; "Abstract of Council," October 25, 1834, S. Doc. No. 152, 25–26.

35. *Florida Territorial Papers*, 24:728, 740.

36. Peters, *The Florida Wars*, 91.

37. "Proceedings of a Council Held with a Delegation of Florida Indians at Fort Gibson," Sen. Records 23B-C1, Record group 46, National Archives; Treaty of Fort Gibson, Kappler, *Indian Affairs*, 2:394–95.

38. Hitchcock, *Fifty Years in Camp and Field*, 80–82.

39. *Florida Territorial Papers*, 24:873, 916–18, 633–37.

40. Ex. Doc., 24th Cong., 1st Sess., 104.

41. Boyd, "Asi-Yahola or Osceola," 252, 261; Sprague, *Florida War*, 90; Potter, *War in Florida*, 53–55.

42. *Florida Territorial Papers*, 25:129.

43. Cohen, *Notices of Florida*, 51, 55; Mahon, *Second Seminole War*, 96; Giddings, *The Exiles of Florida*, 98; Brevard, *A History of Florida*, 1:167; Sprague, *Florida War*, 96, 101, 105.

CHAPTER 5: OSCEOLA DECLARES WAR

1. *New Bern* (NC) *Spectator*, February 26, 1836; *Army and Navy Chronicle* 2, no. 13 (March 31, 1836): 199.

2. Welch, *A Narrative of the Early Days*, 47; Storrow, "Osceola," 430; Sprague, *Florida War*, 80.

3. Bemrose, *Reminiscences*, 25.

4. Boyd, "Asi-Yahola or Osceola," 273–74; McReynolds, *The Seminoles*, 146n.

5. Giddings, *The Exiles of Florida*, 98; Porter, "The Episode of Osceola's Wife."

6. Sprague, *Florida War*, 86.

7. Thompson to Gibson, June 3, 1835, Office of Indian Affairs: Seminole—Emigration, S. Doc. No. 152, 43 (hereafter cited as *OIA*).

8. McKenney and Hall, *Indian Tribes of North America*, 2:376.

9. *ASPMA*, 6:437.

10. Cohen, *Notices of Florida*, 237.

11. Debo, *Road to Disappearance*, 17–18.

12. Giddings, *The Exiles of Florida*, 98–99; Porter, "The Episode of Osceola's Wife," 92ff.

13. Wickman, *Osceola's Legacy*, 15, 85.

14. Sprague, *Florida War*, 81; Porter, *The Black Seminoles*, 33.

15. Gen. Call to President Jackson, March 22, 1835, *OIA*.

16. Thompson to Harris, May 22, 1835, *OIA*.

17. Harris to Thompson, May 22, 1835, *OIA*.

18. McReynolds, *The Seminoles*, 152.

19. Ibid., 147–48.

20. Nabokov, *Native American Testimony*, 125.

21. *ASPMA*, 6:67–68.

22. Ibid.

23. Bemrose, *Reminiscences*, 31.

24. Boyd, *Florida Aflame*, 85–86; Potter, *War in Florida*, 96–97; McKenney and Hall, *Indian Tribes of North America*, 2:380–81.

25. Thompson to Gibson, November 30, 1835, *OIA*.

26. *Florida Territorial Papers*, 25:200, 209, 213–14; Boyd, *Florida Aflame*, 85–86; Sprague, *Florida War*, 88n.

27. *Florida Territorial Papers*, 25:205, 216–17.

28. Peters, *The Florida Wars*, 100.

29. Coe, *Red Patriots*, 56.

30. *Florida Territorial Papers*, 25:216–17; Boyd, *Florida Aflame*, 56–57; Potter, *War in Florida*, 100–01.

31. *Florida Territorial Papers*, 25:200; Sprague, *Florida War*, 89–90; *ASPMA*, 6:561; *Niles' Weekly Register*, January 30, 1836, 368.

32. Roberts, "The Dade Massacre"; Sprague, *Florida War*, 90–91; Potter, *War in Florida*, 102–09; Cohen, *Notices of Florida*, 69–78; Bemrose, *Reminiscences*, 62–69.

33. H.R. Doc. No. 271, 250–51; Barr, *A Correct and Authentic Narrative*, 10–11; Mahon, *Second Seminole War*, 106; *Niles' Weekly Register*, April 2, 1836, 87.

34. Cubberly, "Dade Massacre," S. Doc. No. 33, 6, 5; McCall, *Letters from the Frontiers*, 305–07.

35. Sprague, *Florida War*, 89–91; Cohen, *Notices of Florida*, 69–76; *ASPMA*, 7:425.

CHAPTER 6: BATTLE OF THE WITHLACOOCHEE

1. H.R. Doc. No. 2, 24th Cong., 1st Sess., 52–58.

2. Perhaps the most interesting and informative biography of Secretary of War Lewis Cass is Andrew C. McLaughlin's *Lewis Cass*.

3. H.R. Doc. No. 2, 52–58; *Niles' Weekly Register*, January 9, 1836, 313.

4. H.R. Doc. No. 2, 5.

5. Ibid., 296.

6. Bemrose, *Reminiscences*, 20, 34, 54, 59, 75.

7. Ibid., 31–34.

8. Ibid. 36; H.R. Doc. 271, 245–50.

9. Ibid., 32, 35–36, 80.

10. S. Doc. No. 152, 24, 1–5; General Duncan Clinch to Adjutant General, U.S. Army, January 4, 1836, Adjutant General, Letters Received, National Archives (hereafter cited as *AGLR*).

11. *Military and Naval Magazine of the United States,* 1:98–99.

12. H.R. Doc. No. 2, 24th Cong., 1st Sess., 229; *Army Regulations,* 160.

13. H.R. Doc. No. 2, 245–50; S. Doc. No. 152, 1–5.

14. Boyd, *Florida Aflame,* 73.

15. Potter, *War in Florida,* 112–16; Clinch to Adjutant General, U.S. Army, January 4, 1836, *AGLR.*

16. Potter, *War in Florida,* 112–16; *Army and Navy Chronicle,* 3:323–25.

17. *Military and Naval Magazine,* 6:166.

18. H.R. Doc. No. 2, 229.

19. Bemrose, *Reminiscences,* 52–53.

20. Coe, *Red Patriots,* 30.

21. Bemrose, *Reminiscences,* 25.

22. Welch, *A Narrative of the Early Days,* 34.

23. Coe, *Red Patriots,* 32–33, 48–50; Potter, *War in Florida,* 112–16.

24. Sprague, *Florida War,* 92–93.

25. Coe, *Red Patriots,* 51.

26. Sprague, *Florida War,* 92–93.

27. Porter, *The Black Seminoles,* 46.

28. Clinch to Adjutant General, U.S. Army, January 4, 1836, *AGLR.*

29. Ibid.

30. Ibid., 32–33, 48–50.

31. Gen. Call to Editor, *Tallahassee Floridian,* July 20, 1837, in *Niles' Weekly Register,* 52:315–18, 395–96; Gen. Call to Macomb, *St. Augustine Florida Herald,* August 3 and 25, 1837.

32. Bemrose, *Reminiscences,* 52.

33. Coe, *Red Patriots,* 67–68.

34. Sprague, *Florida War,* 94.

35. Porter, *The Black Seminoles,* 27.

36. Cohen, *Notices of Florida,* 125–26.

CHAPTER 7: GENERALS IN CONFUSION

1. *St. Augustine Herald,* January 13, 1836; *Niles' Weekly Register,* February 6, 1836.

2. Ibid.

3. *Florida Territorial Papers,* 25:224–26.

4. Porter, *The Black Seminoles,* 46.

5. Bemrose, *Reminiscences,* 60.

6. *Congressional Globe,* III, 76, Acts of Jan. 14 and Jan. 29, 18__,5 USSL 1; Mahon, *Second Seminole War,* 138.

7. S. Doc. No, 152, 4, 15; S. Doc. No. 224, 279–80, 215–17, 231, 235–44.

8. For more about Scott, see Eisenhower, *Agent of Destiny*; Johnson, *Winfield Scott*; Peskin, *Winfield Scott and the Profession of Arms*; Scott, *Memoirs.*

9. Potter, *War in Florida,* 133, 136, 143; McCall, *Letters from the Frontiers,* 299–333; Hitchcock, *Fifty Years in Camp and Field,* 88–91.

10. Hitchcock, *Fifty Years in Camp and Field,* 88–89; S. Doc. No. 224, 376, 518–31.

11. McCall, *Letters from the Frontiers,* 299–333; Potter, *War in Florida,* 140.

12. Sprague, *Florida War,* 113.

13. Potter, *War in Florida,* 143.

14. Mahon, *Second Seminole War,* 147; Potter, *War in Florida,* 144.

15. Potter, *War in Florida,* 144; S. Doc. No. 224, 381–90.

16. McCall, *Letters from the Frontiers,* 299–303; Potter, *War in Florida,* 144–46.

17. Hitchcock, *Fifty Years in Camp and Field,* 93.

18. Ibid., 95.

19. For a day-by-day account of the siege, biographies of every Alamo defender, and other relevant information, see Hatch, *Encyclopedia of the Alamo.*

20. Potter, *War in Florida,* 146; Hitchcock, *Fifty Years in Camp and Field,* 93–94.

21. Cohen, *Notices of Florida,* 100–01; Potter, *War in Florida,* 156–59.

22. Excellent accounts of the siege of Camp Izard can be found in Sprague, *Florida War,* 107–13; Cohen, *Notices of Florida,* 96–105; Giddings, *The Exiles of Florida,* 120–24; Potter, *War in Florida,* 140–56; McCall, *Letters from the Frontiers,* 299–33.

23. Bemrose, *Reminiscences,* 79.

24. S. Doc. No. 224, 231, 132–34.

25. Bemrose, *Reminiscences,* 91; Potter, *War in Florida,* 172–73.

26. Potter, *War in Florida,* 172–73; Cohen, *Notices of Florida,* 166–67.

27. Cohen, *Notices of Florida,* 174; Potter, *War in Florida,* 173–74.

28. Potter, *War in Florida,* 167.

29. Ibid., 170; Lindsay to Scott, April 10, 1836, *AGLR.*

30. Bemrose, *Reminiscences,* 88.

31. Potter, *War in Florida,* 170; Lindsay to Scott, April 10, 1836, *AGLR.*

32. Potter, *War in Florida,* 176; Cohen, *Notices of Florida,* 189.

33. *ASPMA,* 7:385.

CHAPTER 8: OSCEOLA DEFENDS HIS TERRITORY

1. Cohen, *Notices of Florida,* 192.

2. S. Doc. No. 224, 327–30, 337, 347–50, 355–58; Cohen, *Notices of Florida,* 195–96.

3. Bemrose, *Reminiscences,* 91–92; S. Doc. No, 278, 38–41; Cohen, *Notices of Florida,* 198.

4. S. Doc. No. 224, 554–55, 604, 627; *St. Augustine Florida Herald,* May 12, 1836.

5. Cohen, *Notices of Florida,* 198–200; Knotts, "History of the Blockhouse"; S. Doc. No. 278, 38–41, 47–48.

6. Cohen, *Notices of Florida,* 194–95; S. Doc. No. 224, 347–50.

7. Cohen, *Notices of Florida,* 198–200; Knotts, "History of the Blockhouse"; S. Doc. No. 278, 38–41, 47–48.

8. Cohen, *Notices of Florida,* 196–98.

9. S. Doc. No. 224, 363–64; Elliott, *Winfield Scott,* 309.

10. *St. Augustine Florida Herald,* May 19, 1836.

11. H.R. Doc. No. 267, 21; S. Doc. No. 224, 372–73.

12. H.R. Doc. No. 267, 21.

13. Doherty, *Richard Keith Call,* 4–25, 28, 34, 42.

14. Williams, *The Territory of Florida,* 247.

15. Sprague, *Florida War,* 158–59; Childs, "Major Childs, U. S. A.," 2:302–03; Giddings, *The Exiles of Florida,* 131–32.

16. Wickman, *Osceola's Legacy,* 90; Boyd, "Asi-Yaholo or Osceola," 298–99; Sprague, *Florida War,* 92–93.

17. Doherty, *Richard Keith Call,* 103.

18. Guild, *Old Times in Tennessee,* 130; Hollingsworth, "Tennessee Volunteers," 351–56, 363–64.

19. Hollingsworth, "Tennessee Volunteers," 349–57; Williams, *The Territory of Florida,* 256.

20. Hollingsworth, "Tennessee Volunteers," 365.

21. Williams, *The Territory of Florida,* 257.

22. Guild, *Old Times in Tennessee,* 133; *ASPMA,* 6:993–97; Williams, *The Territory of Florida,* 257.

23. Hollingsworth, "Tennessee Volunteers," 61–62; Guild, *Old Times in Tennessee,* 132–33; S. Doc. No. 278.

24. Hollingsworth, "Tennessee Volunteers," 64–67; Williams, *The Territory of Florida,* 257.

25. Sprague, *Florida War,* 162; Giddings, *The Exiles of Florida,* 129–31.

26. Hollingsworth, "Tennessee Volunteers," 68–70.

27. Williams, *The Territory of Florida,* 260–61; Sprague, *Florida War,* 162; S. Doc. No. 278, 92.

28. Sprague, *Florida War,* 162; Williams, *The Territory of Florida,* 261; S. Doc. No. 278, 92–98.

29. S. Doc. No. 278, 92–98; Sprague, *Florida War,* 163–65; Williams, *The Territory of Florida,* 263; Mahon, *Second Seminole War,* 185; Giddings, *The Exiles of Florida,* 113; Hollingsworth, "Tennessee Volunteers," 177–78.

30. *Florida Territorial Papers,* 25:339–341, 344–59.

CHAPTER 9: JESUP'S NEW STRATEGY

1. Sprague, *Florida War,* 167; Childs, "Major Childs, U. S. A.," 371.

2. H.R. Doc. No. 183, 1–2, 8; Hollingsworth, "Tennessee Volunteers," 236.

3. H.R. Doc. No. 183, 8.

4. For more about Jesup, see Kieffer, *Maligned General.*

5. *Florida Territorial Papers,* 25:341–42.

6. *ASPMA,* 7:993.

7. *Army and Navy Chronicle,* January 5, 1837, 12.

8. *ASPMA,* 7:820–22.

9. Hollingsworth, "Tennessee Volunteers," 243–53.

10. Sprague, *Florida War,* 167; Boyd, "Asi-Yahola or Osceola," 289.

11. Childs, "Major Childs, U. S. A.," 371–72; Sprague, *Florida War,* 170–71.

12. Sprague, *Florida War,* 171–77; Childs, "Major Childs, U. S. A.," 373; *ASPMA,* 7:829–30; H.R. Doc. No. 78, 66, 70.

13. *ASPMA,* 7:832.

14. *Army and Navy Chronicle* 4, no. 24 (1837): 378.

15. *ASPMA,* 7:828; Childs, "Major Childs, U. S. A.," 374.

16. Sprague, *Florida War,* 173.

17. H.R. Doc. No. 78, 66; Williams, *The Territory of Florida,* 269; Giddings, *The Exiles of Florida,* 136–37.

18. Giddings, *The Exiles of Florida,* 136–37.

19. *ASPMA,* 7:827, 830–32.

20. Ibid., 833, 865–66; Childs, "Major Childs, U. S. A.," 170.

21. H.R. Doc. No. 78, 76–77; Childs, "Major Childs, U. S. A.," 281; *Niles' Weekly Register,* 52: 50.

22. *Florida Territorial Papers,* 25:380–81.

23. H.R. Doc. No. 225, 7; *St. Augustine Florida Herald,* April 27, 1837.

24. *Florida Territorial Papers,* 25:386.

25. Giddings, *The Exiles of Florida,* 148; Coe, *Red Patriots,* 78.

26. Forry, "Letters," 134.

27. *ASPMA*, 7:871; Francke, *Fort Mellon*, 24, 28.

28. *St. Augustine Florida Herald*, July 1837.

29. Coe, *Red Patriots*, 78.

CHAPTER 10: FINAL BETRAYAL

1. Page to Harris, June 1, 1837, *OIA*.

2. Forry, "Letters," 134.

3. Page to Harris, June 1, 1837, *OIA*.

4. Sprague, *Florida War*, 180; Boyd, "Asi-Yahola or Osceola," 293–94; H.R. Doc. No. 78, 157–58.

5. Forry, "Letters," 133.

6. Jesup to Harris, June 5 and 6, 1837, *OIA*.

7. McKay, *Pioneer Florida*, 2:497.

8. H.R. Doc. No. 78, 5.

9. Jesup to AG, Aug. 2, July 10, 1837, *AGLR*.

10. Jesup to Poinsett, June 10 and 16, 1837, *OIA*.

11. Jesup to Freeman, Sept. 9, 1837, *OIA*.

12. Motte, *Journey into Wilderness*, 116; Giddings, *The Exiles of Florida*, 158–63.

13. Mahon, *Second Seminole War*, 211.

14. Jesup to Poinsett, Sep. 22, 1837, *OIA*.

15. Foreman, *Indian Removal*, 349.

16. Forry, "Letters," 133; Coe, *Red Patriots*, 103.

17. Jesup to Casey, July 18, 1837, J145, *AGLR*.

18. Boyd, *Florida Aflame*, 61.

19. Motte, *Journey into Wilderness*, 121.

20. Ibid., 116–20; Forry, "Letters," 215; H.R. Doc. No. 78, 108–12.

21. Motte, *Journey into Wilderness*, 123.

22. Ibid., 116–34.

23. Forry, "Letters," 88.

24. *Army and Navy Chronicle*, 26 October 1837, 269–70.

25. *ASPMA*, 7:848; Giddings, *The Exiles of Florida*, 164–67.

26. Forry, "Letters," 88.

27. Ibid.

28. Sprague, *Florida War*, 217; H.R. Doc. No. 327, 5–6.

29. Sprague, *Florida War*, 218.

30. Ibid.

31. Jarvis, "An Army Surgeon's Notes," 278.

32. Sprague, *Florida War,* 217–18; H.R. Doc. No. 327, 410–11; Boyd, "Asi-Yahola or Osceola," 54–55; Motte, *Journey into Wilderness,* 138–39; Forry, "Letters," 90.

CHAPTER 11: GONE TO BE WITH THE SPIRITS

1. Motte, *Journey into Wilderness,* 141.
2. Ibid.
3. Sprague, *Florida War,* 337.
4. Ibid.
5. Forry, "Letters, 95.
6. *Niles' National Register,* November 4, 1837.
7. "The White Flag," Osceola issue, *Florida Historical Quarterly,* 225–31; Boyd, "Asi-Yahola or Osceola," 295–97; Motte, *Journey into Wilderness,* 140.
8. Dr. Robert Lebby to Dr. Johnson, 21 June 1844, in Ellis, *Nathaniel Lebby,* 317.
9. H.R. Doc. No. 78, supp., 42, 123.
10. Foreman, *Indian Removal,* 426; *Army and Navy Chronicle,* 21 December 1837, 395.
11. Porter, "Seminole Flight from Fort Marion," 112–33; Sprague, *Florida War,* 325–27.
12. *Army and Navy Chronicle,* 21 December, 1837, 394; Storrow, "Osceola," 443; Jarvis, "An Army Surgeon's Notes," 278.
13. Francke, *Fort Mellon,* 122.
14. Foreman, *Indian Removal,* 428–36; *ASPMA,* 7:886–91.
15. Sprague, *Florida War,* 191–92.
16. S. Doc. No. 227, 5–6; Sprague, *Florida War,* 213–14.
17. Hartley, *Osceola,* 243–44.
18. Wickman, *Osceola's Legacy,* 116–17.
19. Storrow, "Osceola," 443.
20. Winthrop Williams to Mrs. Susan M. S. Crouch, 6 January 1838, in Rogers, "A Description of Osceola."
21. Truettner, *The Natural Man Observed,* 36; Bearss, *Osceola at Fort Moultrie,* 16.
22. Storrow, "Osceola," 444–45.
23. Wickman, *Osceola's Legacy,* 56–63.
24. Storrow, "Osceola," 443.
25. Ellis, *Nathaniel Lebby,* 317.
26. Catlin, *North American Indians.*
27. Ibid.
28. Storrow, "Osceola," 443.
29. Wickman, *Osceola's Legacy,* 97–98.
30. Bearss, *Osceola at Fort Moultrie,* 22–23.

31. Wickman, *Osceola's Legacy,* 99–100.
32. Catlin, *North American Indians,* 251.

CHAPTER 12: OSCEOLA'S WAR

1. *Niles' National Register,* February 3, 1838.
2. Coe, *Red Patriots,* 117–18.
3. Ward, "The Disappearance of the Head of Osceola," 198.
4. Wickman, *Osceola's Legacy,* 106–14, 144–53.
5. Ibid., 154–84.
6. Milanich, "Osceola's Head," 51–52.
7. Buker, *Swamp Sailors,* 56–63; Motte, *Journey into Wilderness,* 182–84.
8. Motte, *Journey into Wilderness,* 193–96; Jarvis, "An Army Surgeon's Notes," 1–3; H.R. Doc. No. 219, 1–4.
9. Jarvis, "An Army Surgeon's Notes," 52; Motte, *Journey into Wilderness,* 209–10, 213–17.
10. *Army and Navy Chronicle* 6, no. 3 (1838): 42; Coe, *Red Patriots,* 119; Sprague, *Florida War,* 324.
11. Giddings, *The Exiles of Florida,* 185.
12. Coe, *Red Patriots,* 180–81; Foreman, *Indian Removal,* 362.
13. Motte, *Journey into Wilderness,* 217–18; Sprague, *Florida War,* 199–202.
14. *Army and Navy Chronicle* 6, no. 19 (1838): 297.
15. General Orders No. 7, Headquarters, Department of the Army, April 10, 1838.
16. H. R, Doc. No. 225, [p] 97.
17. General Orders No. 7.
18. *Army and Navy Chronicle* 7, no. 3 (1838): 45.
19. Mahon, *Second Seminole War,* 255–57; Sprague, "Macomb's Mission to the Seminoles," 145, 175, 178–81, 184–85.
20. Sprague, *Florida War,* 233–36, 316–19; McKay, *Pioneer Florida,* 2:509–14.
21. Covington, "Cuban Bloodhounds"; Giddings, *The Exiles of Florida,* 272; *Niles' Weekly Register,* 58:51, 279.
22. Hitchcock, *Fifty Years in Camp and Field,* 123, 132–33.
23. *Niles' Weekly Register,* 58:243, 260.
24. Sprague, *Florida Wars,* 502–04.
25. *Florida Territorial Papers,* 224–25; Hitchcock, *Fifty Years in Camp and Field,* 123.
26. Coe, *Red Patriots,* 156; Sturtevant, "Chakaika and the 'Spanish Indians,'" 51–53.
27. Sturtevant, "Chakaika and the 'Spanish Indians,'" 54.
28. Sprague, *Florida War,* 249–52.
29. Ibid., 253–56.

30. Ibid., 258–60; Hitchcock, *Fifty Years in Camp and Field*, 125–27.

31. Sprague, *Florida War*, 260, 262–63, 277.

32. For more about Worth, see Wallace, *General William Jenkins Worth*.

33. Sprague, *Florida War*, 288.

34. Wickman, *Osceola's Legacy*, 41.

35. Porter, *Black Seminoles*, 128–34.

36. Foreman, *Indian Removal*, 378–80.

37. Sprague, *Florida War*, 456–60.

38. Mahon, *Second Seminole War*, 321–27.

39. *Army and Navy Chronicle* 2, no. 7 (1836): 99.

❧ *Bibliography* ❧

❧ ◈ ❧

NEWSPAPERS
Charleston Courier
Charleston Mercury
New Bern (NC) *Spectator*
New York Times
Niles' Weekly Register, 76 vols.
St. Augustine Florida Herald
Tallahassee Floridian

COLLECTIONS
Alabama Department of Archives and History, Montgomery
Georgia Department of Archives and History, Atlanta
Library of Congress
National Archives
New York Public Library

GOVERNMENT PUBLICATIONS
Acts of the Legislative Council of the Territory of Florida 1822–1845. Tallahassee: S. S.
    Sibley, 1844.
*American State Papers: Documents, Legislative and Executive, of the Congress of the
    United States.* 38 vols. Washington, D.C.: Gales and Seaton, 1832–61.

American State Papers, Foreign Relations (ASPFR). 6 vols. 1789–1828.

American State Papers, Indian Affairs (ASPIA). 7 vols. 1832–34.

American State Papers, Military Affairs (ASPMA). 2 vols. 1832–34.

Army and Navy Chronicle. 13 vols. Ed. and published by Benjamin Homans, Washington, D.C., 1835–42.

Army Regulations, 1835. National Archives.

Military and Naval Magazine of the United States. 6 vols. Ed. and published by Benjamin Homans, Washington, D.C., March 1833–February 1836.

Office of Indian Affairs: Seminole—Emigration. Washington, D.C.: National Archives, 1832–48.

Territorial Papers of the United States. Washington, D.C.: GPO, 1934, Florida.

CONGRESSIONAL DOCUMENTS

Senate

S. Doc. No. 1, 17th Cong., 1st Sess. (1821).

S. Doc. No. 152, 24th Cong., 1st Sess. (1835).

S. Doc. No. 224, 24th Cong., 2nd Sess. (1836).

S. Doc. No. 227, 25th Cong., 2nd Sess. (1837).

S. Doc. No. 278, 26th Cong., 1st Sess. (1839).

S. Doc. No. 33, 67th Cong., 1st Sess. (1921).

House of Representatives

H.R. Doc. No. 2, 24th Cong., 1st Sess. (1835).

H.R. Doc. No. 183, 24th Cong., 1st Sess. (1835).

H.R. Doc. No. 267, 24th Cong., 1st Sess. (1835).

H.R. Doc. No. 271, 24th Cong., 1st Sess. (1835).

H.R. Doc. No. 140, 24th Cong., 2nd Sess. (1836).

H.R. Doc. No. 78, 25th Cong., 2nd Sess. (1837).

H.R. Doc. No. 78, 25th Cong., 2nd Sess, supp. (1837).

H.R. Doc. No. 133, 25th Cong., 2nd Sess. (1837).

H.R. Doc. No. 219, 25th Cong., 2nd Sess. (1837).

H.R. Doc. No. 327, 25th Cong., 2nd Sess. (1837).

H.R. Doc. No. 225, 25th Cong., 3rd Sess. (1838).

BOOKS AND JOURNAL ARTICLES

Abel, Annie Heloise. "History of Events Resulting in Indian Consolidation West of the Mississippi." American Historical Association, Annual Report (1906): 233–450.

Adair, James. *History of the American Indians*. Tuscaloosa: University of Alabama Press, 2005 [1930].

American Anti-Slavery Almanac. Boston: Webster and Southard, 1839.

Anderson, David G., and Kenneth E. Sassaman, eds. *The Paleoindian and Early Archaic Southeast*. Tuscaloosa: University of Alabama Press, 1996.

Barr, James. *A Correct and Authentic Narrative of the Indian War in Florida with a Description of Major Dade's Massacre*. New York: J. Narine, 1836.

Bartram, William. *Travels Through North and South Carolina, Georgia, East and West Florida, the Cherokee Country, the Extensive Territories of the Muscogulges or Creek Confederacy, and the Country of the Chactaws*. New Haven: Yale University Press, 1958 [1791].

———. *William Bartram on the Southeastern Indians*. Ed. Gregory A. Waselkov and Kathryn E. Holland Braund. Lincoln: University of Nebraska Press, 1995.

Bassett, John Spencer. *The Life of Andrew Jackson*. 2 vols. in 1. Hamden, Conn.: Archon Books, 1967 [1911].

Bearss, Edwin C. *Osceola at Fort Moultrie, Sullivan's Island, South Carolina, Fort Sumter National Monument*. Washington, D.C.: Division of History, Office of Archaeology and Historic Preservation, 1968.

Bemrose, John. *Reminiscences of the Second Seminole War*. Ed. John K. Mahon. Gainesville: University Press of Florida, 1966.

Bittle, George C. "The Florida Militia's Role in the Battle of Withlacoochee." *Florida Historical Quarterly* 44, no. 4 (April 1964): 303-11.

Boyd, Mark F. "Asi-Yahola or Osceola." *Florida Historical Quarterly* 33 (January–April 1955): 245-57.

———. "Events at Prospect Bluff on the Apalachicola River, 1808–1818: An Introduction to Twelve Letters of Edmund Doyle, Trader." *Florida Historical Quarterly* 16 (October 1937): 55-96.

———. *Florida Aflame: Background and Onset of the Seminole War, 1835*. Tallahassee: Florida Board of Parks and Historic Memorials, 1951.

———. "Horatio S. Dexter and Events Leading to the Treaty of Moultrie Creek with the Seminole Indians." *Florida Anthropologist* 11, no. 3 (September 1958): 65-95.

———. "The Seminole War: Its Background and Onset." *Florida Historical Quarterly* 30, no.1 (July 1951): 3-115.

Bradbury, John. *Travels in the Interior of America, in the Years 1809, 1810, and 1811*. Lincoln: University of Nebraska Press, 1986 [1817].

Braund, Kathryn E. Holland. "The Creek Indians, Blacks, and Slavery." *Journal of Southern History* 57 (November 1991): 601-36.

———. *Deerskins and Duffels: Creek Indian Trade with Anglo-America, 1685-1815*. Lincoln: University of Nebraska Press, 1993.

Brevard, Caroline Mays. *A History of Florida, from the Treaty of 1763 to Our Own Times.* 2 vols. Ed. James Alexander Robertson. Deland: Florida State Historical Society, 1924–25.

———. "Richard Keith Call." *Florida Historical Quarterly* 1 (1908): 3–12, 8–20.

Brinton, Daniel G. *Notes on the Floridian Peninsula: Its Literary History, Indian Tribes and Antiquities.* Philadelphia: Joseph Sabin, 1859.

Brown, Canter Jr. "The Florida Crisis of 1826–1827 and the Second Seminole War." *Florida Historical Quarterly* 73, no. 4 (April 1995): 419–42.

———. "Race Relations in Territorial Florida, 1821–1845." *Florida Historical Quarterly* 73, no. 3 (January 1995): 287–307.

Brown, Wilbur S. *The Amphibious Campaign for West Florida and Louisiana, 1814–1815.* Tuscaloosa, Ala.: University of Alabama Press, 1969.

Brown, William Garrott. *Andrew Jackson.* Boston: Houghton Mifflin, 1900.

Buchanan, John. *Jackson's Way: Andrew Jackson and the People of the Western Waters.* New York: John Wiley, 2001.

Buker, George E. *Swamp Sailors: Riverine Warfare in the Everglades, 1835–1842.* Gainesville: University Press of Florida, 1975.

Capron, Louis. "The Medicine Bundles of the Florida Seminole and the Green Corn Dance." Smithsonian Institution, Bureau of American Ethnology, *Bulletin 151,* Anthropological Paper No. 35, Washington, D.C.: GPO, 1953.

Carey, Arthur Merwyn. *American Firearms Makers: When, Where, and What They Made, from the Colonial Period to the End of the Nineteenth Century.* New York: Crowell, 1953.

Castelnau, Francis Comte de. "Essay on Middle Florida, 1837–1838." Trans. Arthur R. Seymour. *Florida Historical Quarterly* 26 (January 1948): 199–255.

Catlin, George. *North American Indians, Being Letters and Notes on Their Manners, Customs, and Conditions, Written During Eight Years' Travel Amongst the Wildest Tribes of Indians in North America, 1832–1839.* 2 vols. Edinburgh: J. Grant, 1926 [1866].

Chidsey, Donald Barr. *Andrew Jackson, Hero.* Nashville: T. Nelson, 1976.

Childs, Major Thomas. "Major Childs, U. S. A.: Extracts from His Correspondence with His Family, from the Original Manuscripts." *Historical Magazine,* 3rd ser., 2: 299–304, 371–74, 3rd ser., 3: 169–71, 280–84.

Coe, Charles H. "The Parentage and Birthplace of Osceola." *Florida Historical Quarterly* 17, no. 4 (April 1939): 304–11.

———. *Red Patriots: The Story of the Seminoles.* Gainesville, University Press of Florida, 1974 [1898].

Coffin, Joshua. *An Account of Some of the Principal Slave Insurrections, and Others,*

Which Have Occurred, or Been Attempted, in the United States and Elsewhere, During the Last Two Centuries. Baltimore: Black Classic Press, 2004 [1860].

Cohen, Myer M. *Notices of Florida and the Campaigns.* Gainesville: University Press of Florida, 1964 [1836].

Coit, Margaret L. *Andrew Jackson.* Boston: Houghton Mifflin, 1965.

Coker, William S., and Thomas D. Watson. *Indian Traders of the Southeastern Spanish Borderlands.* Gainesville: University Press of Florida, 1986.

Colburn, David R., and Jane L. Landers, eds. *The African American Heritage of Florida.* Gainesville: University Press of Florida, 1995.

Coles, Harry L. *The War of 1812.* Chicago: University of Chicago Press, 1965.

Cotterill, R. S. *The Southern Indians: The Story of the Civilized Tribes Before Removal.* Norman: University of Oklahoma Press, 1954.

Coulter, Robert. "Seminole Land Rights in Florida and the Award of the Indian Claims Commission." *American Journal of the Institute for the Development of Indian Law* 4, no. 8 (August 1978): 2–27.

Covington, James W. "Cuban Bloodhounds and the Seminoles." *Florida Historical Quarterly* 33, no. 2 (October 1954): 111–19.

———. "Migration of the Seminoles into Florida, 1700–1820." *Florida Historical Quarterly* 46, no. 4 (April 1968): 340–57.

———. *The Seminoles of Florida.* Gainesville: University Press of Florida, 1993.

Craig, Alan K., and Christopher Peebles, "Ethnohistorical Change Among the Seminoles, 1740–1840." *Geoscience and Man* 5 (June 10, 1974): 90–95.

Craven, Avery O., ed. "Letters of Andrew Jackson." *Huntington Library Bulletin* 3 (February 1933): 109–34.

Cubberly, Frederick. "Fort King." *Florida Historical Quarterly* 5 (January 1927): 139–52.

Curtis, James C. *Andrew Jackson and the Search for Vindication.* Boston: Little, Brown, 1976.

Davis, Burke. *Old Hickory: A Life of Andrew Jackson.* New York: Dial Press, 1977.

Davis, T. Frederick. "The Seminole Council, October 23–25, 1834." *Florida Historical Quarterly* 7 (April 1929): 330–56.

———. "United States Troops in Spanish East Florida, 1812–1813." *Florida Historical Quarterly* 9 (July 1930): 3–23, 96–116, 135–55, 259–78.

Debo, Angie. *The Road to Disappearance: A History of the Creek Nation.* Norman: University of Oklahoma Press, 1941.

Densmore, Frances. *Seminole Music.* Washington, D.C.: GPO, 1956.

DePratter, Chester B. *Late Prehistoric and Early Historic Chiefdoms in the Southeastern United States.* New York: Garland, 1991.

DeVane, Albert. *DeVane's Early Florida History*. Sebring, Fla.: Sebring Historical Society, 1978.

Doherty, Herbert J. *Richard Keith Call, Southern Unionist*. Gainesville: University Press of Florida, 1961.

———. "Richard K. Call vs. the Federal Government on the Seminole War." *Florida Historical Quarterly* 31, no. 3 (January 1953): 163–80.

Doster, James F. *The Creek Indians and Their Florida Lands, 1740–1823*. 2 vols. New York: Garland, 1974.

Dowd, Gregory Evans. *A Spirited Resistance: The North American Indian Struggle for Unity, 1745–1815*. Baltimore: Johns Hopkins University Press, 1992.

Downs, Dorothy. "British Influences on Creek and Seminole Men's Clothing, 1733–1858." *Florida Anthropologist* 33, no. 2 (June 1980): 46–65.

Eisenhower, John S. D. *Agent of Destiny: The Life and Times of General Winfield Scott*. New York: Free Press, 1997.

Elliott, Charles Winslow. *Winfield Scott: The Soldier and the Man*. New York: Arno Press, 1979 [1937].

Ellis, E. Detreville. *Nathaniel Lebby, Patriot, and Some of His Descendants*. Privately printed, 1967.

Ellis, Edward Sylvester. *Osceola, Chief of the Seminoles*. New York: Dutton, 1899.

Ely, James W. Jr. "Andrew Jackson as Tennessee State Court Judge, 1798–1804." *Tennessee Historical Quarterly* 40 (Summer 1981): 144–57.

———. "The Legal Practice of Andrew Jackson." *Tennessee Historical Quarterly* 38 (Winter 1979): 421–35.

Ely, James W. Jr., and Theodore Brown Jr., eds. *Legal Papers of Andrew Jackson*. Knoxville: University of Tennessee Press, 1987.

Fairbanks, Charles H. *Ethnohistorical Report on the Florida Indians*. New York: Garland Publishing Company, 1974.

Feller, Daniel. "Andrew Jackson versus the Senate." In *Congress and the Emergence of Sectionalism: From the Missouri Compromise to the Age of Jackson,* edited by Paul Finkelman and Donald R. Kennon. Athens: Ohio University Press, 2008.

Field, Ron. *The Seminole Wars, 1818–58*. New York: Osprey Publishing, 2009.

Florette, Henri. *The Southern Indians and Benjamin Hawkins, 1796–1816*. Norman: University of Oklahoma Press, 1986.

Forbes, James Grant. *Sketches, Historical and Topographical, of the Floridas, More Particularly of East Florida*. Ed. James W. Covington. Gainesville: University Press of Florida, 1964 [1821].

Foreman, Grant. *Indian Removal: The Emigration of the Five Civilized Tribes of Indians*. Norman: University of Oklahoma Press, 1972.

Forry, Samuel. "Letters of Samuel Forry, Surgeon U. S. Army, 1837–1838." *Florida Historical Society Quarterly* 6 (1928): 133–48; 7:88–105.

Francis, Samuel W. *Memoir of the Life and Character of Prof. Valentine Mott, Facile Princeps*. New York: W. J. Widdleton, 1865.

Francke, Arthur E. Jr. *Fort Mellon: 1837–42: A Microcosm of the Second Seminole War*. Miami: Banyan, 1977.

Franklin, John Hope. *Runaway Slaves: Rebels on the Plantation*. New York: Oxford University Press, 1999.

Garbarino, Merwyn S. *Big Cypress: A Changing Seminole Community*. Prospect Heights, Ill.: Waveland Press, 1986.

———. *The Seminole*. New York: Chelsea House, 1989.

Gatschet, Albert S. *A Migration Legend of the Creek Indians, with a Linguistic, Historic and Ethnographic Introduction*. New York: AMS Press, 1969 [1884–88].

Giddings, Joshua R. *The Exiles of Florida; or, The Crimes Committed by Our Government Against the Maroons Who Fled from South Carolina and Other Slave States, Seeking Protection Under Spanish Law*. Gainesville: University Press of Florida, 1964 [1858].

Gifford, John C. *Billy Bowlegs and the Seminole War*. Coconut Grove, Fla.: Triangle Company, 1925.

Glenn, Joshua Nichols. "A Diary of Joshua Nichols Glenn: St. Augustine in 1823." *Florida Historical Quarterly* 24, no. 2 (October 1945): 121–61.

Godfrey, Mary. *An Authentic Narrative of the Seminole War*. New York: Garland, 1977 [1836].

Goggin, John M. "Osceola: Portraits, Features, and Dress." *Florida Historical Quarterly* 33 (January–April 1955): 161–92.

Goodpasture, Albert Virgil. *Andrew Jackson, Tennessee and the Union*. Nashville: Brandon Printing, 1895.

Gordon, Colonel H. R. [Edward Sylvester Ellis]. *Osceola: Chief of the Seminoles*. New York: Dutton, 1899.

Grant, C. L., and Gerald H. Davis. "The Wedding of Col. Benjamin Hawkins." *North Carolina Historical Review* 54 (July 1977): 304–12.

Green, Michael D. *The Politics of Indian Removal: Creek Government and Society in Crisis*. Lincoln: University of Nebraska Press, 1982.

Greenlee, Robert F. "Folktales of the Florida Seminole." *Journal of American Folklore* 58, no. 228 (1945): 138–43.

Griffin, John W., ed. "Some Comments on the Seminoles in 1818." *Florida Anthropologist* 10 (1957): 41–56.

Griffith, Benjamin W. *McIntosh and Weatherford: Creek Indian Leaders*. Tuscaloosa: University of Alabama Press, 1988.

Guild, Josephus Conn. *Old Times in Tennessee*. Knoxville: Tenase, 1971 [1878].

Halbert, Henry S., and T. H. Ball. *The Creek War of 1813 and 1814*. Tuscaloosa, Ala.: University of Alabama Press, 1969 [1895].

Hammond, E. A., ed. "Bemrose's Medical Case Notes from the Second Seminole War." *Florida Historical Quarterly* 47, no. 4 (April 1969): 401–13.

Hartley, William and Ellen. *Osceola: The Unconquered Indian*. New York: Dutton, 1973.

Hassig, Ross. "Internal Conflict in the Creek War of 1813–1814." *Ethnohistory* 21, no. 3 (Summer 1974): 251–71.

Hatch, Thom. *Black Kettle: The Cheyenne Chief Who Sought Peace but Found War*. New York: John Wiley, 2004.

———. *The Blue, the Gray, and the Red: Indian Campaigns of the Civil War*. Mechanicsburg, Pa.: Stackpole Books, 2003.

———. *The Encyclopedia of the Alamo and the Texas Revolution*. Jefferson, N.C.: McFarland & Company, 1999.

Haverstock, Mary Sayre. *Indian Gallery: The Story of George Catlin*. New York: Four Winds Press, 1973.

Hawkins, Benjamin. *Letters, Journals, and Writings of Benjamin Hawkins*. Ed. C. L. Grant. 2 vols. Savannah: Beehive Press, 1980.

———. *A Sketch of the Creek Country in the Years 1798 and 1799*. In *The Collected Works of Benjamin Hawkins, 1796–1810*, edited by Thomas Foster. Tuscaloosa: University of Alabama Press, 2003.

Heidler, David S., and Jeanne T. Heidler. *Old Hickory's War: Andrew Jackson and the Quest for Empire*. Mechanicsburg, Pa.: Stackpole Books, 1996.

Hitchcock, Ethan Allen. *Fifty Years in Camp and Field: Diary of Major-General Ethan Allen Hitchcock, U. S. A*. Ed. W. A. Croffut. New York: Putnam, 1909.

Hollingsworth, Henry. "Tennessee Volunteers in the Seminole Campaign of 1836: The Diary of Henry Hollingsworth." Ed. Stanley F. Horn. *Tennessee Historical Quarterly* 1 (September 1942): 269–74, 344–66.

Horsman, Reginald. *The Origins of Indian Removal, 1815–1824*. East Lansing: Michigan State University Press, 1970.

Hudson, Charles M., ed. *Black Drink: A Native American Tea*. Athens: University of Georgia Press, 1979.

Jackson, Andrew. *Correspondence of Andrew Jackson*. Ed. John Spencer Bassett. 7 vols. in 6. New York: Kraus Reprint, 1969 [1926–35].

———. *The Papers of Andrew Jackson*. 8 vols. to date. Knoxville: University of Tennessee Press, 1980–.

James, Marquis. *The Life of Andrew Jackson, Complete in One Volume*. Indianapolis: Bobbs-Merrill, 1938.

Jarvis, Nathan S. "An Army Surgeon's Notes of Frontier Service, 1833–48." *Journal of the Military Service Institution of the United States* 39 (July 1906): 3–9; (September–October 1906): 275–86.

Johnson, Timothy D. *Winfield Scott: The Quest for Military Glory.* Lawrence: University of Kansas Press, 1998.

Kappler, Charles J., ed. *Indian Affairs: Laws and Treaties.* 5 vols. Washington, D.C.: GPO, 1904–41.

Katz, William Loren. *Black Indians: A Hidden Heritage.* New York: Atheneum, 1986.

Kieffer, Chester L. *Maligned General: The Biography of Thomas Sidney Jesup.* San Rafael, Calif.: Presidio Press, 1979.

Klos, George. "Blacks and the Seminole Removal Debate, 1821–1835." *Florida Historical Quarterly* 68, no. 1 (July 1989): 55–78.

Knauss, James Owen. "William Pope DuVal, Pioneer and State Builder." *Florida Historical Quarterly* 11 (January 1933): 95–139.

Knetsch, Joe. *Florida's Seminole Wars: 1817–1858.* Charleston: Arcadia Publishing, 2003.

Knotts, Tom. "History of the Blockhouse on the Withlacoochee." *Florida Historical Quarterly* 49, no. 3 (January 1971): 245–54.

Krogman, Wilton M. "The Racial Composition of the Seminole Indians of Florida and Oklahoma." *Journal of Negro History* 19 (October 1934): 408–20.

Lancaster, Jane F. *Removal Aftershock: The Seminoles' Struggles to Survive in the West, 1836–1866.* Knoxville: University of Tennessee Press, 1994.

Landers, Jane. *Black Society in Spanish Florida.* Urbana: University of Illinois Press, 1999.

Langguth, A. J. *Union 1812: The Americans Who Fought the Second War of Independence.* New York: Simon & Schuster, 2006.

Laumer, Frank. *Dade's Last Command.* Gainesville: University Press of Florida, 1995.

Littlefield, Daniel F. Jr. *Africans and Creeks: From the Colonial Period to the Civil War.* Westport, Conn.: Greenwood Press, 1979.

MacCauley, Clay. *The Seminole Indians of Florida.* Smithsonian Institution, Bureau of American Ethnology, Fifth Annual Report, 1883–1884. Washington, D.C.: GPO, 1887.

Mahon, John K. *History of the Second Seminole War, 1835–1842.* Rev. ed. Gainesville: University Press of Florida, 1992.

———. "The Treaty of Moultrie Creek, 1823." *Florida Historical Quarterly* 40, no. 4 (April 1962): 350–72.

———. "Two Seminole Treaties: Payne's Landing, 1832, and Ft. Gibson, 1833." *Florida Historical Quarterly* 41, no. 1 (July 1962): 1–21.

Martin, Joel W. *Sacred Revolt: The Muscogees' Struggle for a New World.* Boston: Beacon Press, 1991.

Martin, Sidney Walter. *Florida During the Territory Days.* Athens: University of Georgia Press, 1944.

McCall, George A. *Letters from the Frontiers: Written During a Period of Thirty Years' Service in the Army of the United States.* Gainesville: University Press of Florida, 1974 [1868].

McKay, D. B., ed. *Pioneer Florida.* 3 vols. Tampa: Southern Publishing Company, 1959.

McKenney, Thomas L. *Memoirs, Official and Personal.* 2nd ed. Lincoln: University of Nebraska Press, 1973 [1846].

McKenney, Thomas L., and James Hall. *The Indian Tribes of North America, with Biographical Sketches and Anecdotes of the Principal Chiefs.* 3 vols. Edinburgh: John Grant, 1933–34.

McLaughlin, Andrew C. *Lewis Cass.* New York: AMS Press, 1972 [1891].

McNeer, May Yonge. *War Chief of the Seminoles.* New York: Random House, 1954.

McReynolds, Edwin C. *The Seminoles.* Norman: University of Oklahoma Press, 1957.

Meacham, Jon. *American Lion: Andrew Jackson in the White House.* New York: Random House, 2008.

Meltzer, Milton. *Hunted Like a Wolf: The Story of the Seminole War.* Sarasota, Fla.: Pineapple Press, 2004.

Milanich, Jerald T. *Florida Indians and the Invasion from Europe.* Gainesville: University Press of Florida, 1995.

———. "Osceola's Head." *Archaeology* 57 (January/February 2004): 48–53.

Milanich, Jerald T., and Susan Milbrath, eds. *First Encounters: Spanish Explorations in the Caribbean and the United States, 1492–1570.* Gainesville: University Press of Florida, 1989.

Milligan, John D. "Slave Rebelliousness and the Florida Maroon." *Prologue* 6 (Spring 1974): 4–18.

Missall, John, and Mary Lou Missal. *Seminole Wars: America's Longest Indian Conflict.* Gainesville: University Press of Florida, 2004.

Monroe, Mary Barr. "The Seminole Women of Florida." *Tequesta* 41 (1981): 27.

Moore-Willson, Minnie. *The Seminoles of Florida.* New York: Moffat, Yard and Company, 1910, 1911 [1896].

Moser, Harold D., Sharon Macpherson, John Reinbold, and Daniel Feller, eds. *The Papers of Andrew Jackson 1770–1845: A Microfilm Supplement.* Wilmington, Del.: Scholarly Resources, 1987. 39 reels and guide.

Motte, Jacob Rhett. *Journey into Wilderness: An Army Surgeon's Account of Life in Camp and Field During the Creek and Seminole Wars, 1836–1838*. Gainesville: University Press of Florida, 1963.

Mulroy, Kevin. "Ethnogenesis and Ethnohistory of the Seminole Maroons." *Journal of World History* 4, no. 2 (Fall 1993): 287–305.

———. *Freedom on the Border: The Seminole Maroons in Florida, the Indian Territory, Coahuila, and Texas*. Lubbock: Texas Tech University Press, 1993.

Nabokov, Peter, ed., *Native American Testimony: A Chronicle of Indian-White Relations from Prophecy to the Present, 1492–1992*. New York: Viking, 1991.

O'Brien, Sean Michael. *In Bitterness and in Tears: Andrew Jackson's Destruction of the Creeks and Seminoles*. Westport, Conn.: Praeger, 2003.

Opala, Joseph. "Seminole-African Relations on the Florida Frontier." *Papers in Anthropology* 22, no. 1 (1981): 11–51.

Osceola issue. *Florida Historical Quarterly* 33, nos. 3 and 4 (January–April 1955).

Owsley, Frank Lawrence Jr. *Struggle for the Gulf Borderlands: The Creek War and the Battle of New Orleans*. Gainesville: University Press of Florida, 1981.

Parton, James. *Life of Andrew Jackson*. 3 vols. New York: Mason Brothers, 1859–61.

Patrick, Rembert W. *Aristocrat in Uniform: General Duncan L. Clinch*. Gainesville: University Press of Florida, 1963.

———. *Florida Fiasco: Rampant Rebels on the George-Florida Border, 1810–1815*. Athens: University of Georgia Press, 1954.

Pearson, Fred Lamar Jr. *Spanish-Indian Relations in Florida: A Study of Two Vistas, 1657–1678*. New York: Garland, 1990.

Peskin, Allan. *Winfield Scott and the Profession of Arms*. Kent, Ohio: Kent State University Press, 2003.

Peters, Virginia Bergman. *The Florida Wars*. Hamden, Conn.: Archon Books, 1979.

Porter, Kenneth W. *The Black Seminoles: History of a Freedom-Seeking People*. Gainesville: University Press of Florida, 1966.

———. "The Episode of Osceola's Wife: Fact or Fiction?" *Florida Historical Quarterly* 26, no. 1 (July 1947): 92–98.

———. "Florida Slaves and Free Negroes in the Seminole War, 1835–1842." *Journal of Negro History* 28, no. 4 (October 1943): 390–421.

———. "John Caesar, Seminole Negro Partisan." *Journal of Negro History* 31 (April 1946): 190–207.

———. "Louis Pacheco: The Man and the Myth." *Journal of Negro History* 28, no. 1 (January 1943): 65–72.

———. "The Negro Abraham." *Florida Historical Quarterly* 25, no. 1 (July 1946): 1–43.

———. "Negroes and the East Florida Annexation Plot, 1811–1813." *Journal of Negro History* 30 (January 1945): 9–29.

———. "Negroes and the Seminole War, 1817–1818." *Journal of Negro History* 36, no. 3 (July 1951): 249–80.

———. "Negroes and the Seminole War, 1835–1842." *Journal of Southern History* 30 (1964): 427–50.

———. "Negro Guides and Interpreters in the Early Stages of the Seminole War, December 28, 1835–March 6, 1837." *Journal of Negro History* 35 (April 1950): 174–82.

———. *The Negro on the American Frontier.* New York: Arno Press, 1971.

———. "Osceola and the Negroes." *Florida Historical Quarterly* 33 (January–April 1955): 235–39.

———. "Seminole Flight from Fort Marion." *Florida Historical Quarterly* 22 (January 1944): 113–33.

Potter, Woodburne. *The War in Florida.* Ann Arbor: University Microfilms, 1966 [1836].

Pound, Merritt B. *Benjamin Hawkins: Indian Agent.* Athens: University of Georgia Press, 1951.

Price, Richard, ed. *Maroon Societies: Rebel Slave Communities in the Americas.* 3rd ed. Baltimore: Johns Hopkins University Press, 1996.

Prucha, Francis Paul. "Andrew Jackson's Indian Policy: A Reassessment." *Journal of American History* 56, no. 3 (December 1969): 527–39.

Read, William A. *Florida Place-Names of Indian Origin and Seminole Personal Names.* Tuscaloosa: University of Alabama Press, 2004 [1934].

Reid, John, and John Henry Eaton. *The Life of Andrew Jackson.* Ed. Frank L. Owsley Jr. Tuscaloosa, Ala.: University of Alabama Press, 1974 [1817].

Remini, Robert V. *Andrew Jackson.* New York: Twayne Publishers, 1966.

———. *Andrew Jackson and the Course of American Democracy, 1833–1845.* New York: Harper, 1984.

———. *Andrew Jackson and the Course of American Empire, 1767–1821.* New York: Harper, 1977.

———. *Andrew Jackson and the Course of American Freedom, 1822–1832.* New York: Harper, 1981.

———. *Andrew Jackson and His Indian Wars.* New York: Viking, 2001.

———. *The Battle of New Orleans: Andrew Jackson and America's First Military Victory.* New York: Viking Penguin, 1999.

———. *The Life of Andrew Jackson.* New York: Penguin Books, 1990.

Remini, Robert V., and Robert O. Rupp, comps. *Andrew Jackson: A Bibliography.* Westport, Conn.: Meckler, 1991.

Rivers, Larry Eugene. *Slavery in Florida: Territorial Days to Emancipation.* Gainesville: University Press of Florida, 2000.

Roberts, Albert H. "The Dade Massacre." *Florida Historical Quarterly* 5, no. 3 (January 1927): 123–38.

Rogers, George C. "A Description of Osceola." *South Carolina Historical Magazine* 65 (April 1964): 85–86.

Rogin, Michael Paul. *Fathers and Children: Andrew Jackson and the Subjugation of the American Indian.* New York: Knopf, 1975.

Rosen, Deborah A. "Wartime Prisoners and the Rule of Law: Andrew Jackson's Military Tribunals During the First Seminole War." *Journal of the Early Republic* 28, no. 4 (Winter 2008): 559–95.

Ryan, William. *Osceola: His Capture and Seminole Legends.* Flagler Beach, Fla.: Old Kings Road Press, 2010.

Schlesinger, Arthur M. Jr. *The Age of Jackson.* Boston: Little, Brown, 1945.

Schoolcraft, Henry Rowe. *The Indian Tribes of the United States: Their History, Antiquities, Customs, Religion, Arts, Language, Traditions, Oral Legends, and Myths.* Ed. Francis S. Drake. 2 vols. Philadelphia: Lippincott., 1884.

Schwartzman, Grace M., and Susan K. Barnard. "A Trail of Broken Promises: Georgians and Muscogee/Creek Treaties, 1796–1826." *Georgia Historical Quarterly* 75, no. 4 (Winter 1991): 697–718.

Scott, Winfield. *Memoirs of Lieut.-General Scott, LL.D.* Freeport, N.Y.: Books for Libraries Press, 1970 [1864].

Shaw, Ronald E., ed. *Andrew Jackson, 1767–1845: Chronology, Documents, Bibliographical Aids.* Dobbs Ferry, N.Y.: Oceana Publications, 1969.

Simmons, William H. *Notices of East Florida, with an Account of the Seminole Nation of Indians.* Gainesville: University Press of Florida, 1973 [1822].

Smith, Beverly Jr. "Presidents in Retirement." *Saturday Evening Post,* May 6, 1961, 17.

Smith, W. W. *Sketch of the Seminole War and Sketches During a Campaign, by a Lieutenant of the Left Wing.* Charleston: Dan J. Dowling, 1836.

Somit, Albert. "Andrew Jackson: Legend and Reality." *Tennessee Historical Quarterly* 7 (December 1948): 291–313.

———. "Andrew Jackson as Political Theorist." *Tennessee Historical Quarterly* 8 (June 1949): 99–126.

Southall, Eugene P. "Negroes in Florida Prior to the Civil War." *Journal of Negro History* 19 (January 1934): 78–86.

Southerland, Henry DeLeon Jr., and Jerry Elijah Brown. *The Federal Road Through Georgia, the Creek Nation, and Alabama, 1806–1836.* Tuscaloosa: University of Alabama Press, 1989.

Sprague, John T. "Macomb's Mission to the Seminoles: John T. Sprague's Journal Kept

During April and May, 1839." Ed. Frank F. White Jr. *Florida Historical Quarterly* 35, no. 2 (October 1956): 130–93.

——. *The Origin, Progress, and Conclusion of the Florida War.* Gainesville: University Press of Florida, 1964 [1948].

Storrow, Thomas W. "Osceola, the Seminole War-Chief." *Knickerbocker Magazine* 24 (November 1844): 427–48.

Sturtevant, William C. "Chakaika and the 'Spanish Indians.'" *Tequesta* 13 (1953): 35–73.

——. "Creek into Seminole." In *North American Indians in Historical Perspective,* edited by Eleanor Burke Leacock and Nancy Oestreich Laurie. New York: Random House, 1971.

——. "Notes on Modern Seminole Traditions of Osceola." *Florida Historical Quarterly* 33 (January–April 1955): 206–17.

Sugden, John. *The Shooting Star.* New York: Times Books, 1997.

Sumner, William Graham. *Andrew Jackson.* New York: Chelsea House, 1980 [1899].

Swanton, John R. *Early History of the Creek Indians and Their Neighbors.* Gainesville: University Press of Florida, 1998 [1922].

——. "The Green Corn Dance." *Chronicles of Oklahoma* 10, no. 2 (June 1932): 170–95.

——. *Indian Tribes of North America.* Washington, D.C.: Smithsonian Institution Press, 1969.

——. "Religious Beliefs and Medical Practices of the Creek Indians." *Forty-second Annual Report,* Bureau of American Ethnology. Washington, D.C.: GPO: 1928, 546–614.

——. "Social Organization and Social Usages of the Indians of the Creek Confederacy." *Forty-second Annual Report,* Bureau of American Ethnology. Washington, D.C.: GPO, 1928, 171, 371, 380–84, 403.

Thomas, Hugh. *The Slave Trade: The Story of the Atlantic Slave Trade, 1440–1870.* New York: Simon & Schuster, 1997.

Thompson, Arthur William. *Jacksonian Democracy on the Florida Frontier.* Gainesville: University Press of Florida, 1961.

Truettner, William H. *The Natural Man Observed: A Study of Catlin's Indian Gallery.* Washington, D.C.: Smithsonian Institution Press, 1979.

Twyman, Bruce Edward. *The Black Seminole Legacy and Northern American Politics, 1693–1845.* Washington, D.C.: Howard University Press, 1999.

Vignoles, Charles Blacker. *Observations Upon the Floridas.* Gainesville: University Press of Florida, 1977 [1823].

Viola, Herman J. *Thomas L. McKenney: Architect of America's Early Indian Policy, 1816–1830.* Chicago: Sage Books, 1974.

Walker, Arda S. "Andrew Jackson: Frontier Democrat." *East Tennessee Historical Society's Publications* 18 (1946): 59–86.

———. "The Educational Training and Views of Andrew Jackson." *East Tennessee Historical Society's Publications* 16 (1944): 22–29.

———. "The Religious Views of Andrew Jackson." *East Tennessee Historical Society's Publications* 17 (1945): 61–70.

Wallace, Edward S. *General William Jenkins Worth, Monterey's Forgotten Hero.* Dallas: Southern Methodist University Press, 1953.

Walton-Raji, Angela Y. *Black Indian Genealogy Research: African American Ancestors Among the Five Civilized Tribes.* Bowie, Md.: Heritage Books, 1993.

Ward, May McNeer. "The Disappearance of the Head of Osceola." *Florida Historical Quarterly* 33 (January–April 1955): 193–201.

Waselkov, Gregory A., and Brian M. Wood. "The Creek War of 1813–1814: Effects on Creek Society and Settlement Pattern." *Journal of Alabama Archaeology* 32, no. 1 (June 1986): 1–24.

Watson, Thomas Edward. *The Life and Times of Andrew Jackson.* Thomson, Ga.: Jeffersonian Publishing, 1912.

Weigley, Russell F. *History of the United States Army.* Bloomington: Indiana University Press, 1984.

Weisman, Brent Richards. *Like Beads on a String: A Culture History of the Seminole Indians in Northern Peninsular Florida.* Tuscaloosa: University of Alabama Press, 1989.

———. *Unconquered People: Florida's Seminole and Miccosukee Indians.* Gainesville: University Press of Florida, 1999.

Welch, Andrew. *A Narrative of the Early Days and Remembrances of Oceola Nikkanochee, Prince of Econchatti, a Young Seminole Indian; Son of Econochatti-Mico, King of the Red Hills, in Florida; with a Brief History of His Nation, and His Renowned Uncle, Oceola, and His Parents, Written by His Guardian. 1841.* Gainesville: University Press of Florida. 1977 [1841].

Wickman, Patricia R. *Osceola's Legacy.* Rev. ed. Tuscaloosa: University of Alabama Press, 2006.

———. *The Tree That Bends: Discourse, Power, and the Survival of the Maskókî People.* Tuscaloosa: University of Alabama Press, 1999.

Williams, Edwin L. Jr. "Negro Slavery in Florida." *Florida Historical Quarterly* 28, no. 2 (October 1949): 95–102.

Williams, John Lee. *The Territory of Florida: or, Sketches of the Topography, Civil and Natural History, of the Country, the Climate, and the Indian Tribes from the First Discovery to the Present Time.* Gainesville: University Press of Florida, 1962 [1837].

Wish, Harvey. "American Slave Insurrections Before 1861." *Journal of Negro History* 22, no. 3 (July 1937): 299–320.

Wood, Peter H., Gregory A. Waselkov, and M. Thomas Hatley. *Powhatan's Mantle: Indians in the Colonial Southeast.* Rev. and expanded ed. Lincoln: University of Nebraska Press, 2006.

Woodward, Thomas S. *Woodward's Reminiscences of the Creek or Muscogee Indians, Contained in Letters to Friends in Georgia and Alabama.* Tuscaloosa: Alabama Book Store, 1939 [1859].

Wright, J. Leitch Jr. *Creeks and Seminoles: The Destruction and Regeneration of the Muscogulge People.* Lincoln: University of Nebraska Press, 1986.

———. "A Note on the Seminole War as Seen by the Indians, Negroes, and Their British Advisors." *Journal of Southern History* 34 (1968): 565–75.

———. *The Only Land They Knew: The Tragic Story of the American Indians in the Old South.* New York: Free Press, 1981.

Wyatt-Brown, Bertram. "Andrew Jackson's Honor." *Journal of the Early Republic* 17, no. 1 (Spring 1997): 1–36.

» Index «

»✦«